*Black College Nines*
*The History of HBCU Baseball*
*and Integrators of Historically White College Baseball Programs*

# BLACK COLLEGE NINES

The History of HBCU Baseball and Integrators of
Historically White College Baseball Programs

## Jay Sokol

in collaboration with
### John Winters, PhD
Associate Professor of Health, Physical Education and Recreation
Langston University

Forward by Rickie Weeks, Jr.

Cover design by Jay Sokol

On the cover: circa 1905 Atlanta University baseball team (colorized by Jay Sokol)

Courtesy of Atlanta University Center Robert W. Woodruff Library

ISBN: 979-8-218-08972-6

First Edition: October 2022

To my wife, Kathy
whose patience made this effort possible!

# Table of Contents

# Foreword

*"It's a story that's extremely important for the making of the history of American Baseball."*

\- Roger Cador

Former Southern University Baseball Coach

Baseball and life at my HBCU, Southern University, was an amazing experience. When I left Altamonte Springs, Florida, and arrived in Baton Rouge, Louisiana as a college "rookie", little did I appreciate the profound impact it would have on my future.

Athletics, culture and history intertwined once a year when our coach, Roger Cador, arranged for the team and our rival, Grambling State University, to wear "throwback" uniforms of various teams from the long-gone Negro Leagues.

I was familiar with the Negro Leagues and "Jim Crow" issues that existed in segregated black baseball. My grandfather, Victor, played professionally for a short stint in the 1940s with the Newark Eagles, and we would talk about those days. However, many of my Southern University teammates knew little of our elders who had to compete in the shadows of men who were, more often than not, no more talented than themselves. The throwback games gave us the sense of walking in their shoes.

When it came to HBCU baseball, my teammates and I knew of fellow Southern Jaguar great Lou Brock and his team's 1959 NAIA baseball national championship, but not much beyond that.

Coach Cador, an American Baseball Coaches Association Hall of Famer, was once asked why HBCU baseball history matters. He responded by saying it's a story that is extremely important for the making of the history of American baseball. He went on to say that it's crucial to remember the sociopolitical conditions in which many HBCU baseball programs developed in the late 19th century and early 20th century.

This book introduces the beginnings of black college intercollegiate baseball competition, which, to my surprise, involved my own Southern University in 1887. It touches on many HBCU programs and their ballplayers in the early 20th century and progresses through the 2019 season, ending with the historical relationship between HBCU baseball and the Negro Leagues.

Coach Cador was right on target with his response when asked why HBCU baseball history matters. This book is the first detailed account of black college baseball's heritage and makes me so proud to have been part of its legacy.

Rickie Weeks, Jr.

# Introduction

"*Despite the depth and breadth of baseball literature, there is no comprehensive record of the role of Historically Black Colleges and Universities (HBCU) in promoting baseball.*"

- Daryl Russell Grigsby,
author of *Celebrating Ourselves: African-Americans and the Promise of Baseball*

My journey into the history of Historically Black College and University (HBCU) baseball first began in late 2008 as a sidebar to a research project that began earlier that summer. However, I became a fan of HBCU baseball years before when I first read about the accomplishments of Grambling College's Ralph Garr in the "Faces in the Crowd" section of *Sports Illustrated* in June 1967.

During that summer of 2008, I was well into my 10th season volunteering as general manager of a summer collegiate wooden bat baseball team based in Delaware, Ohio, which is also the home of Ohio Wesleyan University. Ohio Wesleyan is the school where Branch Rickey played and coached both baseball and football in the early-1900s. One student-athlete Rickey coached was a gentleman little known to the world of baseball. Still, the conditions in which he competed were often cited as an inspiration to Branch Rickey's efforts to desegregate Organized Baseball years later.

For his inspirational role in the integration of baseball, I arranged a presentation honoring his achievements, and the Mayor of Delaware proclaimed May 28, 2008, Charles Lee Thomas Day in Delaware, Ohio. Later in this book, you'll learn the significance of his relationship with Branch Rickey and professional baseball's integration.

That May date in 2008 was not the end of my research, but the beginning of a deeper dive into the life of Charles Thomas. My research matched the previously unknown C. Thomas, referenced in Phil Dixon's *American Baseball Chronicles: Great Teams, the 1905 Philadelphia Giants*, to being Ohio Wesleyan's Charles Lee Thomas. The other significant discovery identified Dr. Thomas as one of the earliest African-American baseball stars at a historically white college (also sometimes referred to as a predominately white institution or PWI).

Late in 2008, that research became a website blog about early African-American integrators of PWI baseball programs and HBCU baseball pioneers. Ultimately, that website transformed into what it is today... *www.blackcollegenines.com*, a full-fledged site of current black college baseball happenings while preserving the legacy of HBCU baseball's past.

Taking up the charge of luminaries such as Daryl Russell Grigsby, Roger Cador and Dr. Richard Lapchick, founder and director of the Institute for Diversity and Ethics in Sport, this HBCU baseball research is now chronologically detailed on the following pages. It also includes many early integrators of historically white college baseball programs. Though they did not attend HBCUs, more than a few became coaches, professors, administrators, and presidents at black colleges. Many also became community civil rights activists. And, like their baseball-playing brethren at HBCUs, these PWI pioneering ballplayers, such as Charles Thomas, also played Negro Leagues Baseball... which, according to the Center for Negro League Baseball Research, encompasses both major and minor leagues equivalent to those in Organized Baseball, African-American barnstorming teams, independent and local town teams, as well as industrial league teams.

# Acknowledgements

While this book highlights the significant history of black college baseball, the real story is about all those who have played and represented their HBCU institutions. Many, from now-defunct black colleges and defunct college baseball programs, to those who made a living in Major League Baseball, sought nothing more than to play the game they loved while advancing their education. While not every college baseball program received documentation on the following pages, nor every individual accomplishment noted, they are all vital pieces of HBCU baseball history.

Kudos to the journalists who recorded the events of early black college baseball as they unfolded and to those few authors who documented its history. Two scribes who gave it more of the attention it deserved were Edwin Bancroft Henderson, whose body of work included *The Negro in Sports* and Ocania Chalk, who wrote *Black College Sport*. I marvel at what they were able to research and document without the resources available today.

Other researchers extraordinaire and writers of baseball history, including Negro League history, whose works I have read and cited for this project include John Thorn, Harold Seymour, Larry Lester, James Brunson and Phil Dixon.

I am particularly grateful for the assistance given by Dr. John Winters who contributed a fair amount of his time, when not instructing young college minds, assisting me with the research of integrators of historically white college baseball programs and the compilation of the records section of this book.

I also want to thank Alex Painter, Douglas Malan and Ryan Whirty, fellow researchers and more professional writers than me (or is it more than I), who gave me encouragement along the way, as well as Michael Coker, Bo Carter, Harold Michael Harvey, Ruffin Bell, Roger Cador and

Dr. Mike Gustafson, who all share my love for the great sport of college baseball.

# CHAPTER 1

# In the Beginning

## (through 1859)

In one form or another, a game akin to present-day baseball has been played in the United States dating back to the mid-eighteenth century. Some versions only remotely resembled the game played today. Other later versions incorporated structure and rules that either remain relatively similar to their original design or have been morphed over time into our game of modern baseball.

Through the years, there have been countless theories about the origin of baseball. Unlike the sport of basketball, there is no one defining period in which the game was born. Volumes have been written, but the history of baseball is not the enigma it once was. Today, the consensus among students of its history concludes that baseball is an evolution of many similarly inspired games. Scholars of the game no longer spend much time pondering its origin, but, conversely, a great deal of time researching, uncovering, and sharing more and more about the history of baseball and baseball-like games.

There was a time, however, when the birth of baseball was debated with zealous passion. It began to heat up in the third quarter of the nineteenth century, not long after baseball became a professional sport. It was taken to an extreme in 1905 when the Mills Commission, a group of seven prominent men in the sporting world, assembled to put the issue to rest once and for all. Was baseball strictly an American creation or a game adapted from an older game such as one played in England? That was the point of contention facing the commission.

The individual most commonly identified in baseball lore as the inventor of the game in 1839 and the one the Mills Commission officially endorsed as its founding father, Abner Doubleday, never claimed to be the inventor. In fact, Doubleday's only recorded reference to baseball came in the form of a requisition for baseball equipment for the troops he commanded in Texas shortly after the Civil War ended.[1] Doubleday went to his grave in 1893, not knowing his name would be associated with founding the game.[2] Nonetheless, based on flimsy, unsubstantiated evidence, Civil War hero Abner Doubleday was tabbed founder, erroneously proving that the game of baseball was created on American soil. Nowadays, all but the most casual baseball fans acknowledge that Abner Doubleday had nothing to do with inventing the game of baseball. However, Doubleday does have a "first" attached to his name for directing the first retaliatory shot from Fort Sumter in Charleston, South Carolina, essentially starting the Civil War.

Whether baseball has its roots in ancient games played on other continents using elements comparable to bats and balls, in English games such as Rounders, or in one of our own versions like Town Ball or Old Cat, the game that most closely resembled the style of baseball now played, first appeared on the scene in the mid-nineteenth century.

Before the Civil War, baseball was confined primarily to the eastern section of the country, where evidence of rudimentary bat and ball playing is claimed to date back more than a century before the War Between the States.

From the east, the game extended further south and west by the time the Civil War unfolded. During the war, baseball served as a diversion from the rigors of battle. Though the growth of baseball slowed during this time, when the conflict was settled, interest in the game picked up right where it left off four years prior.[3]

*In 1862, Union troops muster in front, while other soldiers play a game of baseball behind them inside Georgia's Fort Pulaski.*

While a few versions were being played as baseball's popularity grew, by the mid-nineteenth century, the game played by Knickerbocker Rules of New York area teams was gaining favor and ultimately won out over the one played by Massachusetts Rules. The New York game was more closely aligned with modern baseball than the Massachusetts game. The batter (then known as a "striker") was situated at home plate in the New York version. However, the rules of the Massachusetts version placed the striker halfway between home plate and first base on a parallel line 35' from the pitcher, who threw overhand. In the New York game, pitchers threw underhand and from a further distance to the striker.

Within the rules of the New York style of play, an opponent could record an out by tagging the base runner or touching the base before the runner reached it. In the more "manly" Massachusetts Game, the runner had to be hit by the opponent's thrown baseball. This was known as "soaking" the runner. Balls hit in the air had to be caught on the fly under the rules of the Massachusetts Game, while New York's Knickerbocker Rules added the option of recording the out by catching the baseball on the first bounce.

Foul lines and base paths played a massive part in differentiating the two styles, and those rules translated to far more runs being scored in the Massachusetts Game. The New York style game had foul and fair territory and base running was confined to base paths. In the Massachusetts style game, a ball batted fair could be placed anywhere on the grounds (even behind the catcher). With no baseline restrictions, a base runner could get to the next base (an approximate 4' wooden post) anyway he could find to avoid getting soaked. With no territorial constraints and even though only one out retired a team's side for the inning, games played employing Massachusetts Rules tended to take far longer to play and resulted in more runs scored.

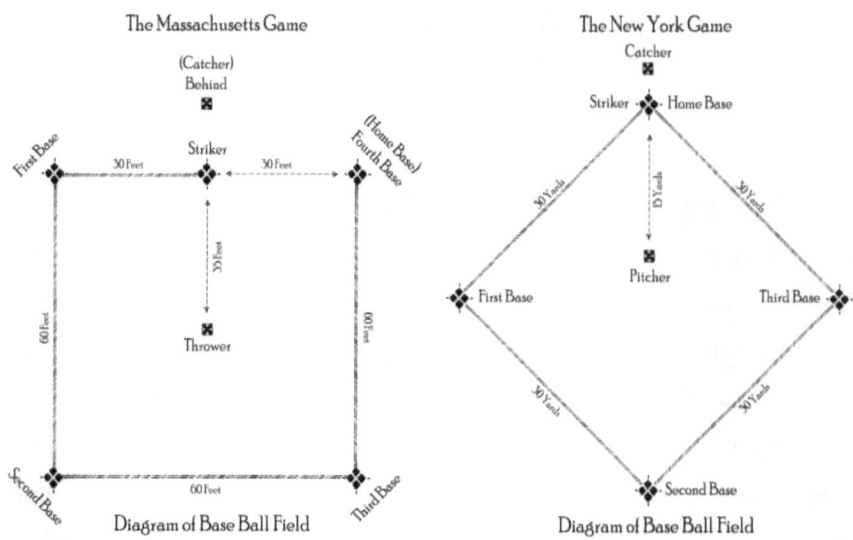

Though baseball became a segregated event, playing the game was not restricted by race, gender, or status. In the second half of the nineteenth century, it seemed that everyone was baseball crazy. The game was already being called America's "national pastime" in 1856 by the *New York Mercury*.[4] It was said that even Abraham Lincoln enjoyed a game of ball. An unsubstantiated story in the San Francisco *Daily Evening Bulletin* of June 16, 1860 indicated that Lincoln had to be interrupted during a game of town ball in order to receive the news of his 1861 Republican nomination for the presidency of the United States.[5] While the validity of that story has often been challenged, it's been documented in several accounts that Abraham Lincoln was at least a spectator of, if not a participant in ballgames.[6]

The black man's introduction to the game of baseball often came via plantation life as an enslaved person. As early as 1773, newspaper articles gave an indication of ball-playing among African Americans, at times in the form of public notices restricting such activities. According to one notice in the March 11, 1797 edition of The *North-Carolina Minerva and Fayetteville Adviser*, any Negro seen playing "at ball" on the Sabbath shall be flogged with up to 15 lashes and jailed if resistance ensues.[7] Frederick Douglass, the esteemed African-American social reformer of his day, penned in his book of 1845, *Narrative of the Life of Frederick Douglass, an American Slave*, that during the days between Christmas and New Year's Day, his masters' slaves were required to do minimal labor and mostly spent time engaging in merriment, such as playing ball.[8]

Besides those enslaved in the south and African Americans who possibly discovered baseball while serving military duty during the Civil War, the game was also played elsewhere by free men of color. Such a man was Octavius Catto of Philadelphia, Pennsylvania.

*Octavius Catto*

Generally, free Negroes, or similarly used terminology, referred to a class of individuals who enjoyed some of the same rights as free whites... though their freedom mainly was in name only.[9] Like other free males who lived in the north before the Civil War, Octavius Catto grew up in an environment of the more genteel English game of cricket and then eventually gravitated to baseball. Catto became an instructor and principal of the boys' department at the Institute for Colored Youth, founded in 1837 as the country's first African-American institution of higher learning and where he had been educated. While working at the institute, which ultimately became Cheyney University, Octavius Catto helped establish the all-black Pythians Base Ball Club of Philadelphia.

Following the 1867 season, the Pythians, led by Catto, sought admittance in the Pennsylvania state chapter of the National Amateur Association of Base Ball Players, but later withdrew its application when it became clear that the all-white organization would not accept the club. Later that year, in December, the Pythians made one last attempt to gain membership, this time applying directly to the national association. However, the club's effort, which would have made it the first African-American organization to be granted membership, was again thwarted.[10] In 1869, the Pythians again tested baseball's interracial barriers by challenging Philadelphia's oldest ball club, the Olympics, to a match. On September 3rd, the two teams squared off; thus, for the first time on record, black and white teams played a game of baseball against one another. Though Catto and his Pythians lost the contest 44-23, the match was a significant event leading to more interracial competition in other cities.[11]

Besides being a respected educator and sportsman, Octavius Catto was a political activist and social reformer within the African-American community of Philadelphia and beyond. Unfortunately, because of his commitment to issues of the day, Catto's life was cut short in 1871 at the age of 32. Ironically, as a result of his leadership in the African-American suffrage movement to gain voting privileges for blacks in Pennsylvania (established by the ratification of the 15th Amendment to the Constitution in 1870), on Election Day, October 10, 1871, Octavius Catto was gunned down while attempting to take advantage of the recently passed voting rights he fought to acquire.[12]

*The all-black Mutuals Base Ball Club of Washington D.C. and its president, Charles Douglass (right), made the great orator of his time, Frederick Douglass (left), an honorary member of its organization in 1870.*

Frederick Douglass was another who made baseball part of his life. His son Charles played on two all-black Washington, D. C. teams, first with the Mutuals Base Ball Club and later with the Alerts. When the opportunity presented itself, Frederick Douglass would attend games, and when he couldn't be there in person, his son Charles would write Frederick with details of his baseball activities. On September 5, 1870, the Mutual Base Ball Club, led by team president Charles Douglass, awarded his father Frederick an honorary membership onto the Mutual Base Ball Club.

During this era of baseball mania, ball-playing was also gaining popularity on college campuses. The emphasis on extracurricular activities was shifting from those of the mind, such as debate clubs, oratorical contests and literary societies, to those of a physical nature. Baseball was the leading activity of choice by the student bodies at many schools.

*James Claflin*

Until 1859, such baseball contests typically pitted class against class or students versus faculty. Baseball was strictly recreational. However, when students at Massachusetts' Amherst College challenged nearby rival Williams College to a game of baseball on July 1st of that year, it marked the nation's first intercollegiate baseball game. The competition, which included the challenge of a chess match, was advertised as a contest of muscle and mind. Playing the game using Massachusetts Rules, the final score, in favor of Amherst College, was 73-32.[13] The catcher and captain of the Amherst nine was James Fitzgerald Claflin, the only participant to compete in both the baseball game and chess match. His "back-strike" for a home run (the Massachusetts Game technique of hitting behind the catcher, thus taking advantage of a field without boundaries) constituted several firsts in intercollegiate baseball annals. It represented college baseball's first at bat, first hit, first home run, and first run scored (then referred to as a "tally). Following graduation, James Claflin began a distinguished career in education, which included a stint in 1874 as the lead administrator of historically black Tougaloo College in Mississippi, serving in the capacity of interim principal/president.[14]

The first recognized intercollegiate contest played using New York Rules of baseball took place in New York on November 3, 1859 between the Fordham Rose Hill Club of Saint John's College (now Fordham University) and the now-defunct College of Saint Francis Xavier. In that match, Rose Hill took the measure of Saint Francis Xavier by a score of 33-11.[15]

Interest in intercollegiate ball playing first took hold at schools in the east and spread from there. As schools found the means to support intercollegiate teams, college baseball grew fairly rapidly. In the beginning, many intercollegiate baseball programs were funded and run by student associations, but eventually were taken over by school administrators.

---

[1] Millen, Patricia E. *From Pastime to Passion: Baseball and the Civil War, 55-56*. Westminister, MD: Heritage Books, 2001.

[2] Ryczek, William J. *Baseball's First Inning: A History of the National Pastime Through the Civil War.* 16. Jefferson, NC: McFarland, 2009.

[3] Allardice, Bruce. "The Spread of Base Ball, 1859-1870." Protoball. Last modified September 2013. http://protoball.org/The_Spread_of_Base_Ball.

[4] Tygiel, Jules. *Past Time: Baseball as History*, 6. New York: Oxford University Press, USA, 2000.

[5] *Daily Evening Bulletin* (San Francisco). "How Lincoln Received the Nomination." June 16, 1860.

[6] Zoss, Joel, John Bowman, and John S. Bowman. *Diamonds in the Rough: The Untold History of Baseball*, 84-85. Lincoln: University of Nebraska Press, 2004.

[7] *The North Carolina Minerva and Fayetteville Advertiser (Fayetteville, NC). March 11, 1797, 3. https://www.newspapers.com/.*

[8] Douglass, Frederick. *Narrative of the Life of Frederick Douglass, an American Slave*, 74. Boston: The Anti-Slavery Office, 1849, Google Play(e-book).

[9] Biddle, Daniel R., and Murray Dubin. *Tasting Freedom: Octavius Catto and the Battle for Equality in Civil War America*, 2. Philadelphia: Temple University Press, 2010

[10] Ibid., 365-368

[11] Ibid., 364-376

[12] Ibid., 421-430.

[13] Schrag, Peter. "The First Intercollegiate Game." In *Official NCAA Baseball Guide*, 32-33. New York: The National Collegiate Athletic Bureau, 1958.

[14] Bounds, Tony. "James Fitzgerald Claflin." E-mail message to author. February 26, 2019.

[15] Curry, Jack. "For 150 Years, Fordham Baseball's Tradition of Winning." *The New York Times*, April 5, 2009. https://www.nytimes.com/2009/04/06/sports/baseball/06fordham.html.

# CHAPTER 2

# Early Black College Baseball

## (1887-1930)

While intercollegiate baseball was first played at schools in the east, the hotbed of college baseball at all-black schools first sprang up in the south. The earliest documented game between two black colleges was possibly the one played in early April 1887 between two New Orleans, Louisiana based institutions, those being Straight University and Southern University. In that contest, Straight University (which merged with New Orleans University in 1934 to form Dillard University) took the measure of Southern by a score of 24-9. Then, a few weeks later, on April 23rd, the "Bergers" of Straight University (presumably named for Professor of Theology M. L. Berger) again defeated Southern University, this time by the score of 29-10. The most recognizable name in those contests was that of Southern's pitcher, Bismarck R. Pinchback. Pinchback was the son of the country's first African-American governor, Pinckney Benton Stewart Pinchback, who served as interim governor of Louisiana for two months in late 1872 through early 1873. Governor Pinchback, an influential Republican, also had a significant role in the founding of Southern University in 1880. Dr. Bismarck Pinchback, who completed his medical training at Howard University, played a prominent role in the life-long nurturing and mentoring of his nephew, Jean Toomer.

Toomer was the American poet and novelist often identified as one of the founders of the Harlem Renaissance (considered an early twentieth-century rebirth of the African-American cultural arts).

On the other side of the baseball diamond, Straight University's club included two others who, besides Bismark Pinchback, would become medical doctors of note. The second baseman, Dickerson Alphonse Smith, became the first African-American doctor in Shreveport, Louisiana. Team president James W. Ames, like Pinchback, graduated medical school from Howard University and later led a group of fellow Detroit doctors in founding what was one of the few hospitals readily providing care to African-Americans. Ames also served in the Michigan House of Representatives.

*Dr. Bismark Pinchback (left) and Dr. James W. Ames (right) participated in the first documented series of games involving two HBCU schools in 1887.*

Besides in New Orleans, which later counted Leland College and New Orleans University as competition for Southern University and Straight University, another hotbed of early HBCU baseball activity was in Atlanta, Georgia. The first two ball-playing schools there were Atlanta University and Clark University. The second set of documented black college games were probably those played between the two schools in 1888. After their game on April 21st, the *Atlanta Constitution* reported that "this game concludes the championship of 1887-1888 in favor of Atlanta University, the latter having won two out of a series of three games."[1]

By 1896, two additional Atlanta-based colleges, Morris Brown University and Atlanta Baptist Seminary (renamed Atlanta Baptist College in 1897 and then Morehouse College in 1913) had added baseball. That year the four schools formed the nation's first black intercollegiate baseball league. Each team played six games, two against each of the other schools, and a silk pennant was awarded to the league's champion. It was reported that every team's level of play was uplifted by the competition, first won by Atlanta University in 1896, and each school showed a level of support not seen before. Eventually, the A. G. Spalding Company, the nation's leader in manufacturing sporting goods, began providing a trophy to the annual league champion.

In 1897, Atlanta's intercollegiate baseball league pennant was shared by Atlanta University, Clark University, and Morris Brown. The following year, Clark University claimed the pennant outright. And in 1899, a three-way tie was resolved with Morris Brown winning a playoff for the championship.[2]

The Atlanta-based intercollegiate baseball league was the first organized black college sports league of any kind. But just as important might have been the lead several members took in attempting to unify and patrol eligibility requirements among its competing schools. The lack of rules and the non-compliance of existing rules plagued schools across the country, be they historically black or white. These abuses were, in part, the impetus for founding the National Collegiate Athletic Association (originally known as the Intercollegiate Athletic Association of the United States) in 1906. Until the National Association of Intercollegiate Athletics (NAIA) began admitting HBCU schools in 1953 and the NCAA in 1956, rules for black college athletic programs were traditionally established and governed by conferences such as the Colored Intercollegiate Athletic Association (now known as the Central Intercollegiate Athletic Association) and the Southern Intercollegiate Athletic Conference.

Notable members of those pioneering Atlanta college teams included Samuel Walker Houston, James Weldon Johnson, Henry A. Hunt, Robert W. Gadsden, and George A. Towns, all from Atlanta University. Others included James Madison Nabrit, Alfred D. Jones, and Zachary T. Hubert of Atlanta Baptist, as well as Charles L. Harper and E. K. Nichols of Morris Brown College and C. I. Taylor of Clark University.

Samuel Walker Houston and his battery mate, pitcher John William Young, played together on Atlanta University's team of 1888. Young became an instructor of Latin and Mathematics and the first African-American professor at Atlanta University before furthering his education at Harvard College.[3] He was also a respected local social activist. Unfortunately, the athletically gifted and well-liked Young developed peritonitis and died in 1891 while still at Harvard.

Samuel Walker Houston was the namesake of his father Joshua's prominent slave-owner, Sam Houston, the former Texas freedom fighter and governor of the state. After leaving Atlanta University, Houston became one of the most involved and respected African Americans in Texas, where he established probably the first county training school for black children in the state.[4]

A teammate of Samuel Houston at Atlanta University in the early 1890s was James Weldon Johnson. A pitcher of note, Johnson was one of the first African-American schoolboys to master a curveball, which was taught to him as a youth by a member of the Original Cuban Giants, the first salaried professional black baseball team in America.[5]

James Weldon Johnson was an author, educator, lawyer, diplomat, songwriter, and civil rights activist. He is best remembered for his leadership within the National Association for the Advancement of Colored People (NAACP), heading the organization as its executive secretary. Johnson also received acclaim for his novels and poems. His *Lift Ev'ry Voice and Sing* was set to music by brother Rosamond, and later the inspirational tune came to be known unofficially as the Negro National Anthem.[6]

Atlanta University graduates Henry A. Hunt, Robert Gadsden, and George A. Towns became highly regarded educators. Hunt became principal at what would become Fort Valley State College and served on Franklin Delano Roosevelt's "black cabinet", an informal group of public policy advisors.[7] Robert Gadsden was a leading black educator, school principal, and respected civic leader in Savannah, Georgia, while George Towns was a noted poet, playwright, and longtime professor at his alma mater. As the representative of Atlanta University, Towns assisted in the formation of the Southern Intercollegiate Athletic Conference in 1913. As well, George Towns was a charter member and officer in the Atlanta chapter of the NAACP and organized branches in other Georgia cities.[8]

James Madison Nabrit, an organizer of that first Negro intercollegiate baseball league in Atlanta, was regarded as probably the best player on his

15

Atlanta Baptist College nine, but chose a career path as a Baptist minister. Besides his duties as a clergyman, duties that elevated him to Director of the Georgia Baptist Convention and Secretary of the National Baptist Convention, Dr. Nabrit was also a professor of Greek and Latin. He might be most remembered for the educational standards he set for his family as one son, James Jr., who at one time was the baseball coach at what is now the University of Arkansas at Pine Bluff, became president of Howard University, and another son, Samuel, became president of Texas Southern University.[9]

Like many others who played ball in the nineteenth century Atlanta area college baseball league, James Nabrit's Atlanta Baptist College teammate, Zachary T. Hubert also went into the field of education. His teaching at what is now Florida A & M University preceded a career as president at both Jackson College (now Jackson State University) and Langston College.

After graduating from Atlanta Baptist, Alfred D. Jones went to medical school at Howard University and then returned to Atlanta to become his alma mater's medical director and baseball coach. In addition to having a private medical practice, Jones was the sports editor and columnist for the *Atlanta Independent*, the city's leading black newspaper of the day.

Morris Brown College's contribution to this group of distinguished alumni includes Charles Lincoln Harper and Reverend Edward Kingston Nichols. Harper was the longtime principal of Atlanta's Booker T. Washington High School, which by the time of his retirement was believed to be the largest African-American high school in the United States.[10] Additionally, Charles Harper was a civil rights leader and one-time president of the Atlanta Chapter of the NAACP. Edward Nichols, who was captain of his Morris Brown baseball team, continued his education at Yale University and received his Doctor of Divinity degree from Morris Brown in 1918. During his career, Nichols led, and was highly regarded by, congregations in Georgia, Massachusetts, Connecticut, and Pennsylvania.

Of the Atlanta-based black college pioneers, the one who made the most of his baseball training was Charles Isham "C.I." Taylor.

After he returned from service to his country as a member of the famed all-black Buffalo Soldiers unit during the Spanish-American War of 1898, C.I. Taylor entered Atlanta's Clark University.[11] While there, the *Indianapolis Freeman* reported, on April 21, 1900, that Taylor was the best third baseman in the Atlanta [Negro] Intercollegiate League.[12]

Following college, C.I. Taylor continued his baseball career as a player, coach, and team owner. He is best known for assembling and developing his Indianapolis ABC teams of the mid-1910s to early-1920s that rivaled the powerhouse Chicago American Giants and its famous coach, Major League Baseball Hall of Famer Rube Foster. Taylor died prematurely in 1922 and is remembered as one of the finest Negro League coaches of his time.

While the names and accomplishments of many of these nineteenth-century athletes have long been forgotten, the mention of them during their lifetimes brought immediate recognition by African-American communities far and wide. And while the story of that Atlanta-based intercollegiate baseball league is no longer familiar to most, its importance to the growth and popularity of HBCU baseball prior to the Great Depression should not be minimized.

Atlanta area institutions weren't the only black schools to play baseball before the arrival of the twentieth century. Students at some schools, playing under the banner of their college name, but not officially recognized, organized teams even before the Atlanta area schools began competing. Typically they faced other organizations on campus or local and nearby town-organized teams.

From 1877 to 1923, Hampton Institute sponsored a program accepting Native-American Indian students. During this time, Hampton had teams made up exclusively of American Indian students and teams composed of both African Americans and American Indians. Even earlier, at the Institute of Colored Youth (now Cheyney University), baseball was being played. While there is no record of Cheyney formally sponsoring an intercollegiate team, being the oldest African-American school for higher education in the country, it is not surprising that baseball was being played on campus before it was played at most other black colleges.

Howard University did not formally start its baseball program until 1894, but area newspapers recount matches between the Howard University club and other local teams dating back to the early 1880s. Wilberforce University in Ohio also fielded teams in the early 1880s and competed against teams located in its own Greene County and nearby Clinton County. Later, Wilberforce scheduled matches with area schools, Cedarville College, Wilmington College, and Antioch College of Yellow Springs.

Morgan College of Baltimore, Maryland (now known as Morgan State University) and Tuskegee Institute were two other schools that began baseball programs before the turn of the century.

Besides being one of the pioneering schools in black college baseball, Tuskegee was one of its early powers. Its first team manager, James B. Washington, was the half-brother of the school's founder, the renowned Booker T. Washington. One of Tuskegee's earliest stars was William Clarence Matthews, who, in the day of loosely regulated eligibility rules, continued his postgraduate education at Harvard and integrated its team in 1902. A second nineteenth-century star at Tuskegee, and most likely a teammate of Matthews in the late 1890s, was Jubie Bragg who later

*Coach Jubie Bragg (in suit on right) and his 1906 Florida State Normal and Industrial College for Negroes (now Florida A&M) baseball team*

helped found the athletic program at Florida A & M and became that school's first official baseball and football coach.

Credit for participating in the earliest collegiate contests of any sport between a black college and a predominantly white school most likely goes to Howard University and Wilberforce University. Howard faced both Trinity College (of Connecticut) and the Kendall School (now Gallaudet University in

Washington D.C.) in 1894.[13] On those Howard teams were prepster James F. Gregory, who integrated Amherst College baseball in 1896, Frank Avant, who became the first black physician to practice in the state of North Carolina[14] and Dwight Oliver Wendell Holmes, who served as president of Morgan College from 1937 to 1948.

It isn't clear whether Wilberforce officially supported a school team in the 1880s when they faced their opponents Cedarville, Wilmington, and Antioch. However, by 1896, Wilberforce was still competing against those schools and, for years to come, would be the only black college to regularly schedule games against predominantly white colleges. In fact, Wilberforce University was possibly the first HBCU to affiliate with white colleges, forming an athletic conference of Ohio-based schools in 1928.[15]

*Ohio's Wilberforce University regularly faced all-white college baseball teams since there were few HBCUs nearby to schedule. Pictured in this photo, but not identified by name, is most likely future baseball Hall of Famer, Sol White (top row, second from right).*

Members of those early Wilberforce nines included Alphonso T. Arnett, son of influential clergyman and political leader Bishop Benjamin Arnett, Theo Bryant, and William Wallace. A team photo from 1897, including the likeness of Sol White, and a newspaper story indicating White was an athletic instructor at Wilberforce during that time, gives rise to speculation that the future Major League Baseball Hall of Fame inductee was associated with the team. Though schooled at Wilberforce, by this time, White probably would have been the coach or served as the team's business manager, albeit he could have also played. Sol White was a longtime player and manager in the Negro Leagues and is remembered for recording and publishing the first exhaustive history of black baseball in 1907, simply entitled *History of Colored Baseball*.

The early twentieth century was a time of rapid growth in intercollegiate baseball competition among African-American institutions. Biddle University (now Johnson C. Smith University) baseball gained popularity in 1900 after attempting to literally settle the score of an earlier football match with Livingstone College. The two bitter rivals battled on the gridiron that January; the contest being called a draw with no score. A baseball game between the two schools was then proposed, with the winning team getting credit for the football victory as well. While an account of that game was not kept, the baseball rivalry between the two schools was born and became one of the most publicized and well-attended contests between black colleges in the 1920s.[16]

*1904 Fisk University Baseball Club*
*Coached by former Oberlin University standout, Merton Robinson*

Nashville, Tennessee's Fisk University and Roger Williams University joined the ranks of baseball-playing institutions prior to the twentieth century and competed against each other as early as 1894. Then, along with fellow Nashville area school Walden University, formed a baseball league in 1909.[17] A fourth member was Pearl High School, which claimed the first league pennant. During the infancy of college baseball, it was not uncommon for college teams to face area high schools. While the association did not rise to the competitive level of the aforementioned Atlanta based intercollegiate league, the Nashville colleges continued to compete for several years, with Tennessee A&I State College (now Tennessee State University) eventually replacing Pearl High School. By the late 1920s, Roger Williams University, the 1911 league champion, merged with another school (later becoming LeMoyne-Owen College), and the 1924 champion, Walden University, closed due to financial difficulties.

***

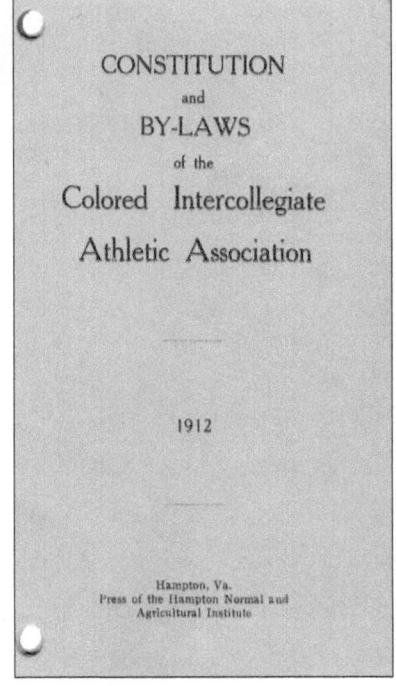

*Original CIAA Constitution*

A significant landmark for black college athletics occurred on February 2, 1912, when representatives from Hampton Institute, Howard University, Lincoln (PA) University, Shaw University, and Virginia Union University took initial steps toward forming the Colored Intercollegiate Athletic Association.

Following the lead of the CIAA, one year later, in 1913, the Southern Intercollegiate Athletic Conference was formed. Initially known as the Southeastern Intercollegiate Athletic Conference, the original membership included Alabama State University, Atlanta University, Clark College, Fisk University, Jackson College,

Morehouse College, Morris Brown College, Talladega College, and Tuskegee Institute. The SIAC began declaring baseball champions in 1915, with Morris Brown claiming the first two pennants.

In the years before conference baseball champions were selected, powerhouse teams could be found at Howard University in the east and Tuskegee Institute in the south.

Within the pages of the *New York Age* of May 16, 1912, Howard University declared itself baseball champion of the country. On a two-week trip through the south, the Howard nine defeated ten of the eleven most prominent schools in the region to earn this self-proclaimed title.[18] Members of the team included Lorenzo Dow Turner, Frank Forbes, and Hudson Oliver.

*In the early 1910s, Howard University fielded strong teams featuring players like "Huddy" Oliver (front row center) and Lorenzo Dow Turner (with baseball in his hand).*

Dr. Lorenzo Dow Turner became an acclaimed professor of English and Linguistics. He dedicated much of his professional career to the study of the Creole and Gullah dialects (found in the low country region of Georgia, North Carolina, South Carolina, and Florida) and their relationships to African languages. His pioneering work was an important catalyst in the creation of the African-American studies movement in colleges during the 1960s.[19]

Frank Forbes was a true renaissance man of sport. Following his graduation from Howard University, where he played football, basketball and baseball, Forbes began a lifelong career in sports as an athlete, administrator, and official. He competed professionally with various Negro League teams including the Lincoln Giants, Bacharach Giants, and as a manager with the New York Cubans. On the hardcourt, Forbes was a founding member of the New York Renaissance ("Rens"), one of the most dominant all-black teams of the 1920s and 1930s. Besides umpiring baseball and refereeing basketball, Forbes was a boxing official and judged matches featuring both Joe Louis and Mohammed Ali. Frank Forbes also worked in the baseball front offices of both the Negro League's New York Cubans and the National League's New York Giants. Once leaving the Giants' organization, Forbes became a sporting event promoter.[20]

Another leader of the Howard University varsity nine was Hudson "Huddy" Oliver, who captained the team in 1911. An all-around athlete in college, Oliver was best known for his basketball expertise. Before turning full-time to the medical profession for which he trained at Howard, Hudson Oliver was considered one of the best African-American basketball players of the early twentieth century. During his career, Oliver played on four Colored Basketball World Championship teams.[21]

While Howard University was ruling the east, Tuskegee Institute was doing likewise in the south. The Golden Tigers completed the 1912 season amassing a sparkling 17-1 record, with the single loss coming at the hands of Atlanta's Clark University.[22] The following year, Tuskegee nearly duplicated its previous season output compiling a 16-2 record.[23] Ace of the pitching staff was Hayes Garfield Sloan who, according to accounts, won 17 games without a loss for Tuskegee during those two years.[24] One of the school's stars was its slugging first baseman, Charles Howard, the same Charles Howard who integrated Drake University baseball a few years later. Tuskegee's baseball program was ably coached by Thomas Jarvis Taylor, an early integrator of college baseball at Wesleyan University in Connecticut. Booker T. Washington's half-brother James served as Tuskegee's business manager.

Possibly the first all-star team of black college ballplayers (an All-Southern team) was introduced in the pages of *Spalding's 1913 Interscholastic*

*Association of Middle Atlantic States Official Handbook* and included Watson of Tuskegee (catcher), Sloan of Tuskegee (pitcher), Black of Clark University (pitcher), Barnes of Morris Brown (pitcher), Howard of Tuskegee (first base), Sullins of Tuskegee (second base), Lewis of Atlanta Baptist (shortstop), Moore of Talladega (third base), Gilmore of Tuskegee (left field), Washington of Tuskegee (center field) and Brock of Atlanta Baptist (right field).[25]

Other successful teams in the 1910s included the strong teams of Shaw University in North Carolina, Arkansas Baptist College, and Morehouse College. In 1911, Shaw University anointed itself champions among all Negro colleges after returning from a southern trip winning 10 of 11 ballgames.[26] The star pitcher for Shaw was Jeff "Big Chief" Lytle, who in one game versus Lincoln University (PA) on April 12[th,] struck out 11 batters and on April 21st struck out 13 Howard University batters. Lytle went on to be Shaw University's baseball coach and years later led the Bears to CIAA crowns in 1964 and 1965.

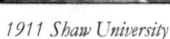

*1911 Shaw University*

*Tuskegee Institute ca. 1915*
*(James Washington in suit)*

Morehouse College's strong team of 1913 featured two recruits off the football team, John Davis Lewis and George D. Brock, and was coached by the integrator of the South Dakota State program, Cleve Abbott. As a result of their strong seasons, both Lewis and Brock were named to Spalding's All-Southern baseball team. Brock went on to become a college professor and baseball coach at West Virginia State and a leading advocate of health education for the benefit of African-American youth.[27]

Arkansas Baptist recorded an unbeaten season in 1913 winning 17 straight games. The most recognizable names on that team were Wabishaw "Doc" Wiley and Floyd "Jelly" Gardner. Gardner played 14 seasons in the Negro Leagues, 10 of which were with the Chicago American Giants. Before a professional career that meshed both baseball with the Cuban Giants and dentistry, Doc Wiley continued his education at Howard University, where he teamed with Frank "Doc" Sykes to form one of the strongest batteries in black college baseball.

*Frank "Doc" Sykes*
*Painting by Graig Kreindler*
*from the collection of Jay*
*Caldwell*

Frank Sykes had pitched in 1911 and 1912 with the Atlanta Baptist club, but transferred to Howard University the following year and became the second Sykes brother to play for the Washington, D.C. based school. Brother Leo starred at Howard on its dominant teams just prior to Frank's arrival. Like Doc Wiley, Frank Sykes played professionally (primarily with the Baltimore Black Sox and Hillsdale Daisies) and later became a dentist. Sykes took an active role in civil rights affairs, and his testimony during the nationally publicized trial of Alabama's "Scottsboro Boys" in the early 1930s exposed unfair jury representation in the south.

*New Orleans University team ca. 1915 (pictured on the left). David Malarcher in his*
*Chicago American Giants uniform (pictured on the right).*
*Malarcher painting by Graig Kreindler from the collection of Jay Caldwell*

Deep in the south, New Orleans University baseball teams dominated from 1913 through 1916. It was reported that during a three-year stretch, the Tigers of NOU were never defeated.[28] New Orleans University was led by a duo of future Negro League stars in David Malarcher and Bobby Williams.

"Gentleman Dave" Malarcher, as he was called because of his cultured, gentle, soft-spoken demeanor, enjoyed a thirteen-year career as an infielder and then became an even more successful manager.[29] Bobby Williams played fifteen seasons of professional baseball and for several years teamed with Malarcher in the infield of the Chicago American Giants.

In 1914, the *Indianapolis Freeman* newspaper featured a recap of a noteworthy Wilberforce University home game versus Ohio State University played on April 10th. While Wilberforce lost 2-1, there was a masterful pitching display by Wilberforce's Lawrence Simpson and George Trautman of Ohio State. Simpson played for the famous Negro team, the West Baden Sprudels, and went on to play with other well know Negro League teams. OSU's Trautman became the president of the National Association of Professional Baseball Leagues, from 1946 to 1963, which oversaw the entire minor league baseball system. Another future Negro Leaguer at Wilberforce in 1914 was Ted Kimbro, who played with Lawrence Simpson for the Sprudels.

The following year, Isaac Sappe Lane migrated from Georgia State Industrial College (now known as Savannah State University) and starred on Wilberforce teams in 1915 and 1916. Before returning to the school as its head coach in 1927, Lane played professionally with the Dayton Marcos, Columbus Buckeyes, and Detroit Stars. Once the Wilberforce University baseball program was terminated, Isaac Lane found a home virtually across the street at Central State (the two-year teacher and industrial training program of Wilberforce University until it received independent status in 1947) where he remained until the mid-1960s.

Two years after the creation of the Southern Intercollegiate Athletic Conference, the conference began sponsoring league championships in baseball. The winner of the first two pennants of 1915 and 1916 belonged to Morris Brown College. The Giants, as they were known before officially adopting the Wolverine as its mascot in the 1920s, included Talley Addison, Tom "Cyclone" Williams, John Reese, and William Fountain Jr., who became the seventh president of Morris Brown College in 1928. Cyclone Williams, who Negro League Baseball mogul Rube Foster once called a "perfect mound artist", began a well-traveled baseball career after leaving Morris Brown, playing a decade in the Negro Leagues with such teams as the Chicago American Giants and Brooklyn Royal Giants.[30] Likewise, John Reese played with several teams including the American Giants and Saint Louis Stars.

*Morris Brown College (ca. 1915) won the first two SIAC conference titles.*

Another baseball participant in 1916 was Walter White, who later became the executive secretary of the NAACP succeeding fellow Atlanta University graduate, James Weldon Johnson.[31] Early in his career with the NAACP, because of his light skin, blue eyes and wavy blond hair, Walter White was able to infiltrate scenes of white mob violence and race riots while investigating, exposing and campaigning against the horrific acts of lynching (the socially accepted practice in many pockets of the country at that time). Continuing his fight for human rights, White became the organization's director, serving in that capacity from 1931 to 1955. Often amid danger, it was reported that White was once rescued from an angry crowd in New York City by John Reese, an old baseball foe from Morris Brown College.[32]

In April 1916, two powerhouses from their respective geographic regions squared off when Howard University traveled to Atlanta on its southern tour to face Morris Brown College. The *Atlanta Constitution* noted in its April 7th edition that the matchup would determine the national championship. The contest was so well attended that, according to news reports, little-used ground rules had to be established to accommodate the overflow crowd. Howard's ace, Frank Sykes, was pitted against Cyclone Williams of Morris Brown, with Sykes proving to be the stronger pitcher that day. Yielding only three hits the entire game and aided by the hitting of Wabishaw Wiley, Howard University took the measure of its southern counterpart by the score of 4-1. [33] Interestingly, the contest was umpired by Atlanta's Dick "Cannonball" Redding, regarded as perhaps the hardest throwing pitcher in the history of Negro Leagues Baseball.

Morehouse College won three of the next four SIAC titles, with Alabama's Talladega College interrupting the streak in 1919. Atlanta area colleges remained dominant with Atlanta University claiming the titles in 1921 and 1922 followed by a run of four additional titles from 1923 to 1926 by the Morehouse College Tigers. This gave schools based in Atlanta 11 of the first 12 SIAC baseball championships.

The Talladega College championship ball club of 1919 was led by four-sport star, George H. Lockhart, who reportedly lost only two games during his college pitching career. The coach of the Tornadoes was Jubie Bragg. After leaving Talladega, Lockhart pitched several seasons in the Negro Leagues with both the Bacharach Giants and the Chicago American Giants. After retiring as a player, George Lockhart became the baseball coach at Alabama State and remained there for 42 years.

Members of the championship Morehouse teams of the early-to-mid 1920s included Arthur Idlett, Vinicius "Nish" Williams, Melvin Sykes, Charles

Clark, Franklin Forbes, C. J. Dunn, and Guy Rodgers

*The Morehouse team of 1923 featured Charles Clark, Charles Dunn and Nish Williams (pictured in back row, second, third and fourth from the left).*

Catcher Nish Williams, the stepfather of Morehouse and New York Mets great Donn Clendenon, enjoyed a long career as a player and then as a coach with several teams in the Negro Leagues. Williams concluded his baseball career coaching at Morehouse College.

Like Nish Williams, pitcher Charles Clark played professionally with the Homestead Grays and other Pittsburgh area teams. Franklin Forbes was a two-sport star at Morehouse playing both baseball and football. After graduating, Forbes became a longtime coach and administrator at Morehouse, and commissioner of the Southern Intercollegiate Athletic Conference. Melvin Sykes was the youngest brother of Leo and Frank Sykes and played for both the Hillsdale Daisies and the Chicago American Giants before turning to a career in medicine. Arthur Idlett played professionally with the Atlanta Black Crackers and then became a school principal.

Charles Johnson Dunn was the captain of the powerhouse 1923 Morehouse team and starred on the basketball team. After leaving school,

Dunn became a basketball coach and then the longtime athletic director at Alabama State University. He was honored in 1973 with induction into the National Association of Collegiate Directors of Athletics Hall of Fame, and the basketball arena at Alabama State bears his name along with one other.

Another key member of the Morehouse ball club was Guy Rodgers, who played a solid shortstop, then tried his hand at professional baseball with the Atlanta Black Crackers. Rodgers is remembered as the namesake of son Guy Rodgers Jr., who was an All-American basketball player at Temple University, pro basketball all-star, and 2014 inductee into the Naismith Basketball Hall of Fame.

Closing out the decade of the 1920s in the SIAC, Alabama State won titles in 1927 and 1928, while Clark College won its only league crown in 1929. Former conference standouts George Lockhart from Talladega and Charles Johnson Dunn from Morehouse coached the Alabama State Hornets to championships, while future Negro League pitching ace, William "Shug" Cornelius starred for the Clark College Panthers. Another performer of note for the Panthers was Ric Roberts, who became one of the country's leading African-American sportswriters while working for the *Atlanta Daily World* and *Pittsburgh Courier*.

***

The Colored Intercollegiate Athletic Association, formed a year before the Southern Intercollegiate Athletic Conference, did not crown a baseball champion until 1921. However, it appears that teams unofficially claimed titles before then. By 1921, the conference had an established governing body and had added one additional school, Virginia Normal and Industrial Institute (now Virginia State University), which secured the first title by going undefeated in league play.

During the next twelve years, Virginia Normal continued to dominate conference play, winning nine additional pennants before the CIAA temporarily suspended its sponsorship of baseball in 1934. Virginia Normal's arch-rival, Virginia Union University, earned titles in 1922 and 1925, while

Lincoln University of Pennsylvania claimed the baseball crown in 1930.

*1926 Virginia Normal and Industrial Institute*

In those early years, both Virginia-based schools were known more for their excellent overall team play than for having individual stars. Led by Coach T. L. Puryear, the Virginia Normal "Hilltoppers" won titles with "Slim" Armstead, James Nicholas, Eric Epps, Ernest Joe Scott, and "Jumping Joe" Wiggins. Both Scott and Wiggins would later play professionally in the Negro Leagues. The Virginia Union teams, coached by Harold D. Martin (integrator of Norwich University baseball) and T. W. Harvey, were led by future pros James Shields, William Merritt, and Holsey "Scrip" Lee. Captain of the 1922 championship Virginia Union Panthers was Addison A. Branch, a defensive marvel who later served a stint as the president of Tougaloo College.

\*\*\*

The third major HBCU organization to come into prominence was the Southwestern Athletic Conference (originally known as the Southern Athletic Conference until 1928), which was founded in 1920. Following the SWAC, the Midwestern Athletic Association (MWAA) was founded in 1926. The South Central Atlantic Conference was formed in 1923, but its status as a baseball league never reached the level of prominence found in the other four athletic conferences.

The six founding Texas-based colleges of the Southwestern Athletic Conference included Prairie View Normal and Industrial College (later becoming Prairie View A&M University), Wiley College, Samuel Huston College (now Huston-Tillotson University), Bishop College (which no longer exists), Paul Quinn College and Texas College. In 1923, Wiley College won what is believed to be the first conference baseball crown, winning eight of nine league contests. According to the *Philadelphia Tribune*, Prairie View Normal and Industrial College claimed the 1925 pennant, followed by a repeat in 1926. The next season ushered in a three-year run by the Texas College Steers (1927-1929), while Wiley College won the championship in

*Pat Patterson (l) and Henry Milton (r) were a dynamic duo in high school at East Chicago Washington in Indiana, in college at Wiley College and as pros with the Kansas City Monarchs.*

1930 and then repeated the following year. The last title claimed, before a temporary suspension of baseball as a conference sport, was awarded to Texas College in 1932.[34]

Prairie View A&M claims Hilton Smith, a Kansas City Monarchs pitching ace and 2001 inductee into the National Baseball Hall of Fame, to have been an active member of its teams in 1928 and 1929 and fellow Hall of Famer, Willie Wells (HOF class of 1997), supposedly toiled in the infield at Samuel Huston College in 1931. The great Wiley College teams included future Negro League stars Henry Milton, Grady Orange, Andrew "Pat" Patterson, James Shackleford, LeRoy Taylor, and William Ware. Shackleford became a lawyer in Cleveland, Ohio, and was president of the fledgling United States League for the two years (1945-1946) that the upstart Negro professional baseball league existed.

At the conclusion of the 1923 season, an all-star baseball team was selected from Southern Athletic Conference member schools and, though unofficial, seems to be the very first such group honored by the conference. Named to the team were Ware (first base), Shackleford (third base), Orange (shortstop), Parker (right field), Pardee (catcher) and Lucas (pitcher), all from Wiley College, Dykes (second base) and Sedbury (center field), both from Paul Quinn College, Alexander (left field) from Samuel Huston College and both Baker (pitcher) and Bell (pitcher) of Texas College.

\*\*\*

The last of the big four conferences was the Midwestern Athletic Association. The founding institutions included Kentucky State College (now Kentucky State University), West Virginia State College (now West Virginia State University), Wilberforce University and Louisville Municipal College, which closed in 1951.

As a conference, baseball did not take hold until shortly after World War II. Football was king in the MWAA and, like schools in other HBCU conferences, did not support baseball for nearly a decade, beginning in the mid-1930s.

One of the few exceptions was Wilberforce University. Because of its considerable distance from other HBCU schools, Wilberforce had been regularly playing predominantly white institutions since its infancy. It was not only able to field teams, but also schedule full seasons when few other HBCUs could. Wilberforce faced several Ohio-based programs, such as Cedarville College, Antioch College, Wilmington College, the University of Dayton, and Capital University.

One of Wilberforce University's most recognized names was multi-sport star Harry "Wu Fang" Ward. Ward excelled in football (a *Pittsburgh Courier* All-American), basketball, baseball, and track. Big and strong with home run power, Ward was once referred to as "the Babe Ruth of college baseball."[35] After a stint playing basketball professionally with the Homestead Grays and baseball with the Cincinnati Tigers, Harry Ward became an umpire and worked the 1945 East-West Negro League All-Star Game featuring Jackie Robinson of the Kansas City Monarchs and Roy Campanella of the Baltimore

33

Elite Giants.

A teammate of Harry Ward at Wilberforce was the well-traveled infielder Halley Harding. It has been reported that football took him to four different schools (including HBCUs Fisk University and Wiley College) over a seven-year period. After a professional athletic career playing segregated baseball with the Indianapolis ABCs, Detroit Stars and Kansas City Monarchs, Harding became a sports columnist and editor.[36] While employed at the *Los Angeles Tribune*, Halley Harding became a leader in, and ultimately most remembered for his involvement in the re-integration of professional football after it was announced that the National

*Harry "Wu Fang" Ward*
*Wilberforce University*

Football League champion Cleveland Rams would move west for the 1946 season. Ironically, with the assistance of Harding, the NFL re-integrated in 1946 when the Los Angeles Rams signed Kenny Washington, who was also the integrator of UCLA baseball.

Shortly after Wu Fang Ward and Halley Harding left the Wilberforce campus, in 1931 James "Buster" Clarkson arrived to take Ward's place as the star of the Wilberforce Big Green baseball team and Clarkson's star continued to shine well after his days in college. His professional career included stops with the Newark Eagles, Pittsburgh Crawfords, and Philadelphia Stars, as well as with teams in Canada, Mexico, and Puerto Rico. After a long career outside of Organized Baseball, the moniker used during baseball's segregated era referencing the white Major League, Clarkson finally signed his first Minor League contract in 1950 with the Boston Braves organization. Then, on April 30, 1952, at age 37, Buster Clarkson was called up to the parent club, which gave him the distinction of being the very first Major Leaguer with an HBCU baseball playing experience.

\*\*\*

Though the South Central Athletic Conference was founded before the Midwestern Athletic Association, its collective member schools were not considered as strong athletically as the aforementioned big four conferences, though baseball was possibly its most competitive sport. The founding institutions included Alcorn Agricultural and Mechanical College (now Alcorn State University), Jackson College (now Jackson State University), Rust College, and Tougaloo College. Founding member schools that have since shuttered operations included Mississippi-based colleges Campbell College, Haven Institute, Mississippi Industrial College, Mount Beulah College, and Okolona Industrial School. For a time, beginning in 1925, the conference experimented by adding several high schools, including The Piney Woods School.

*Pictured on the left with his Alcorn teammates is future Major League Hall of Famer Bill Foster (far right and next to Aubery Owens, another future Negro Leaguer) and above while coaching at Alcorn A&M.*

The SCAC's first baseball championship was awarded to Alcorn A&M in 1927 and the White Sox, as they were then known, won the next two crowns as well. No champion was declared in 1930 and when the 1931 team garnered its fourth straight title, the roster included William Foster and Malvin "Putt" Powell. Foster, the half-brother of the pioneering Negro baseball immortal Rube Foster, was already pitching in the Negro Leagues, but for the lax rules of the day, used time while in school as "spring training" for his professional career.

William Foster became one of the most dominant left-handed pitchers in Negro League Baseball and, in 1996, was voted into the National Baseball Hall of Fame. After retirement, Foster became the longtime coach of Alcorn A&M and also held the administrative position of Dean of Men.

Putt Powell gave Alcorn a strong 1-2 punch on the mound with William Foster and was also an asset at bat and in the outfield. Like Foster, Powell played in the Negro Leagues, and for a time, the two were teammates on strong Chicago American Giants teams.

*Bill Foster*
*Cuban Baseball Club of 1927*
*Painting by Graig Kreindler*
*from the collection of Jay*
*Caldwell*

While the South Central Athletic Conference did not rise to the level of the SWAC, SIAC, and CIAA, on the baseball diamond, the conference, unlike the other three, was able to support a full schedule of games and a league championship well into the 1930s.

One team that challenged Alcorn A&M for SCAC titles was The Piney Woods School based in Mississippi. The school was technically not a college, but a boarding school established for the education and training of rural African Americans. Interestingly, the baseball team went by the name of the "Giant Collegians." Being a boarding school, Piney Woods had to recruit students far beyond its home base. To promote its name and the school's accomplishments, as well as raise funds for the school, the Giant Collegians barnstormed the country playing professional and semi-pro African American teams, as well as black college teams. In the mid-to-late 1930s, the club was coached by onetime Negro leaguer Owen Smaulding, an early integrator of the baseball program at the University of Idaho in 1923.

One documented contest featured Alcorn A&M and famed pitcher William Foster versus the Piney Woods School on May 5, 1933 in which the

*A typical broadside of the barnstorming Piney Woods Giant Collegians*

Giant Collegians bested Foster's White Sox 4-3.[37] While it is safe to say that many of the Giant Collegian recruits were not the traditional students found at the boarding school and were recruited mainly to play ball and promote the school, in its heyday, Piney Woods could compete against and beat most of the best teams around.

\*\*\*

From the early days of Negro Leagues, black college baseball served somewhat as its feeder system, just as the Minor Leagues did for the Major League in Organized Baseball. Among the lesser-known baseball programs to turn out professionals was Edward Waters College, which produced Dean Everett, Charles "Schute" Merritt, and John "Buck" O'Neil. Everett and Merritt had only brief stays playing professionally. However, Buck O'Neil had an illustrious career as a first baseman and manager in the Negro American League, primarily with the famed Kansas City Monarchs. When Major League Baseball integrated in the late 1940s, which signaled the eventual demise of Negro League Baseball, O'Neil became a scout for the Chicago Cubs in 1955, pursuing HBCU talent and others. In 1962, the Cubs made Buck O'Neil the very first African-American coach in Major League Baseball.

*Buck O'Neil*
*Kansas City Monarchs*
*Painting by Graig Kreindler from the collection of Jay Caldwell*

Beginning in the late-1920s and into the mid-1930s, HBCU baseball saw a decline in interest and support. Except for a smattering of games that a handful of schools, such as North Carolina A&T, scheduled against military base teams and area Negro League semi-pro and professional teams, black college baseball remained dormant from the mid-1930s until the mid-1940s. Heightened interest in football and a lack of the financial support necessary to run a baseball program contributed to the downfall of America's national pastime as the top sport among HBCUs. Moreover, the Great Depression took its toll on student enrollment and military service also depleted the pool of student-athletes.

*1929 Easter Monday game between John C. Smith University and Livingston College*

However, before its death and ultimate resurrection following WWII, black college baseball reached a pinnacle of popularity on campuses featuring "Easter Monday" rivalry matchups. These contests of the 1920s and early-1930s had all the hoopla of present-day marquee college sporting events. Of them, none generated more interest than the four-year battle between Livingstone College and Johnson C. Smith University from 1926 through 1929. Livingstone featured ace pitcher Lamon Yokely, who was pitted each year against the Golden Bull's star hurler, Burnalle "Bun" Hayes. Both went on to successful professional careers in the Negro Leagues. Yokely once was the ace of a Baltimore Black Sox pitching staff that included a young Satchel Paige as its number two starter. According to newspaper reports, the games drew anywhere from 3,000 to 10,000 fans for each ballgame, with Johnson C. Smith University and Bun Hayes taking the measure of Livingston College and Lamon Yokely, three of the four Easter Mondays. Almost overshadowed by their rivalry was the fine season Johnson C. Smith University had in 1928 when the Golden Bulls finished with a 12-1 record and reported in the school yearbook as having a record sufficiently impressive enough to cause numerous individuals to designate it as National Collegiate Champions for 1928.[38]

*In their four head-to-head pitching matchups, Bun Hayes and his Johnson C. Smith Golden Bulls held a 3-1 victory margin over Laymon Yokely and the Livingstone College Blue Bears. The Easter Monday games between the two rivals always drew large crowds.*

After the war, there was a revival on the HBCU baseball scene. Enrollment began to increase, and athletic conferences emphasized getting their member's baseball programs up and running again. The handwriting was on the wall, and it was pretty clear that schools should get their student-athletes ready for the integration of Organized Baseball. With that, a renaissance of HBCU baseball was just around the corner.

---

[1] *The Constitution* (Atlanta). "Colored Students at Ball." April 22, 1888, 11.

[2] Bacote, Clarence A. *The story of Atlanta University: a century of service, 1865-1965*, 222-224. Piinceton, NJ: Princeton University Press, 1969

[3] Range, Willard. "The Students and Their Teachers." In *The Rise and Progress of Negro Colleges in Georgia, 1865-1949*, 150. Athens: University of Georgia Press, 2009.

[4] Lucko, Paul M., "Houston, Samuel Walker," Handbook of Texas Online (http://www.tshaonline.org/handbook/online/articles/fhobs), accessed October 18, 2013. Published by the Texas State Historical Association.

[5] Johnson, James W. *Along This Way: The Autobiography of James Weldon Johnson*, 36-37. Cambridge, MA: Da Capo Press, 2000.

[6] Tarry, Ellen. *Young Jim, The Early Years of James Weldon Johnson*, 225. New York: Dood, Mead & Company, 1967.

[7] Kirby, John B. *Black Americans in the Roosevelt Era: Liberalism and Race*, 24. Knoxville: Univ. of Tennessee Press, 1982.

8 "George Alexander Towns, 1870-1960." *The Atlanta University Bulletin*, no. 112 (December 1960), 4.

9 Anderson, Carl E. "James Madison Nabrit, Jr. 1900-1997." *Washington History* 10, no. 1 (1998): 71-73. Accessed June 7, 2021. http://www.jstor.org/stable/40073316.

10 About Charles L. Harper." Charles L. Harper High School International Alumni Association. Accessed April 4, 2019. http://www.charleslharperalumni.com/about-charles-l-harper/.

11 Revel, Dr. Layton, and Louis Munoz. "Forgotten Heroes: Charles Isham "C.I." Taylor." Center for Negro League Baseball Research. Last modified 2016. http://www.cnlbr.org/Portals/0/EP/326615%20Charles%20Isham%20Taylor_1up.pdf.

12 *The Freeman* (Indianapolis). April 21, 1900, 2.

13 Chambers, Ted. *The History of Athletics and Physical Education at Howard University*. New York: Vantage Press, 1986.
(Chambers credits Trinity College as later becoming Duke University, but was actually Trinity College of Connecticut)

14 "Dr Frank Wingate Avant, MD." Find A Grave. Accessed April 8, 2019. https://www.findagrave.com/memorial/27137151/frank-wingate-avant.

15 *The Baltimore Afro-American*. "Wilberforce Joins New Conference." July 7, 1928, 13.

16 *The Golden Bull*, 443. Charlotte, NC: Johnson C. Smith University, 1967. https://archive.org/details/goldenbull1967john.

17 *The Nashville Globe*. "The Intercollegiate Base Ball League of Nashville." March 12, 1909, 8.

18 *The New York Age*. "Howard Claims Baseball Championship." May 16, 1912.

19 Cotter, Holland. "A Language Explorer Who Heard Echoes of Africa." *The New York Times*, September 2010. https://www.nytimes.com/2010/09/03/arts/design/03gullah.html.

20 McKenna, Brian. "Frank Forbes, the Busiest Man in Sports." Baseball History Blog. Last modified September 25, 2011. http://baseballhistoryblog.com/3271/frank-forbes-the-busiest-man-in-sports-part-3-of-3.

21 "Hudson 'Huddy' Oliver | The Black Fives Foundation." Black Fives Foundation. n.d. https://www.blackfives.org/hudson-oliver/.

22 *Official Handbook, Interscholastic Athletic Association of Middle Atlantic States*, 105. New York: American Sports Publishing Company, 1912.

23 Chalk, Ocania. *Black College Sport*, 50. New York: Dodd Mead, 1976.

24 Henderson, Edwin B. "The National Game."*The Negro in Sports*, 187. Washington, D. C.: The Associated Publishers, Inc., 1949.

25 Ibid., 187

26 *The New York Age*. "Shaw Twice Defeats Howard." April 27, 1911, 6.

27 Thomas, Jerry B. "Camp Brock." In *E-WV | The West Virginia Encyclopedia*. 2012. Accessed April 22, 2016. https://www.wvencyclopedia.org/articles/820.

28 Revel, Dr. Layton, and Louis Munoz. "Forgotten Heroes: David "Gentleman Dave" Malarcher." Center for Negro League Baseball Research. Last modified 2014. http://www.cnlbr.org/Portals/0/Hero/Dave-Malarcher.pdf.

[29] Ibid., 4

[30] Henderson, "The National Game."*The Negro in Sports*, 187.

[31] *The Alabama Tribune* (Montgomery, AL). "Newsbeat." May 17, 1957, 6.

[32] Lautier, Louis. "Capital Spotlight." *The Baltimore Afro-American*, May 28, 1938, 7.

[33] *The New York Age.* "At Morris Brown." April 20, 1916.

[34] Downey, William. "Southern Athletic Conference Championship-Baseball-1927-1931." E-mail message to author. June 14, 2011.

[35] *The New York Amsterdam News.* "Wilberforce Defeats Wilmington College." May 6, 1925, 4.

[36] Ashwill, Gary. "Halley Harding." Agate Type. Last modified February 12, 2013. https://agatetype.typepad.com/agate_type/2013/02/halley-harding.html.

[37] Wilson, Lyle K. "The Singing Baseball Team." Last modified 2009. http://www.webcitation.org/mainframe.php.

[38] *The Golden Bull*, 101. Charlotte, NC: The Student Body of Johnson C. Smith University, 1929.

# CHAPTER 3

# Early Black Integrators

# of Historically White

# College Baseball

## (1881-1945)

Before 1945, the world of professional baseball was as different as black and white. On one end of the color spectrum was Negro League Baseball. On the other end was a game that had been denied African-American ballplayers since the 1890s because of an unwritten gentlemen's agreement.

That all changed in the fall of 1945 when Brooklyn Dodgers' General Manager Branch Rickey orchestrated the integration of Major League Baseball by signing Jackie Robinson to a minor league contract. Rickey often cited his time at Ohio Wesleyan University in the early 1900s as his motivation to push for the integration of Organized Baseball. While serving as the school's baseball coach, he experienced firsthand the discrimination cast upon his African-American catcher Charles Thomas.

When Robinson secured a spot on the Dodgers' Major League roster less than two years later, the long history of segregated baseball was forever buried.

The path was opened for other talented African-American ballplayers to follow, but it was a road paved far and wide with obstacles.

The insults, protests, and threats these pioneering integrators endured from baseball fans, opposing ballplayers and even teammates, paralleled those faced by young African-American college students who integrated their schools' baseball programs.

While the process Branch Rickey put in motion took place in the mid-1940s, college baseball's integration began nearly six decades before that.

*Oberlin College's first varsity team featured Moses Fleetwood Walker (6) and Weldy Walker (10)*

The first documented African-American collegiate ballplayer was Moses Fleetwood Walker, a catcher on the first official varsity team at Ohio's Oberlin College in 1881. Joining him was his younger brother Weldy Wilberforce Walker, who technically was still a student in the preparatory program associated with Oberlin. "Fleet" Walker transferred to the University of Michigan the following year and became the first to integrate that program, as well. While brother Weldy had a somewhat less distinguished baseball career,

Fleet Walker became a professional player before the color ban was fully enforced and, until recently, was unquestionably regarded as the first black Major Leaguer.

Two others of note, who at least deserve an asterisk after their names, are Simpson Younger of Oberlin College and William White of Brown University in Rhode Island. Each preceded the Walker brothers in school. However, in Younger's case, he and his Oberlin teammates did not officially represent the school in intercollegiate play. In White's case, while Brown University did field a varsity team, his ethnicity remains a question.

*1868 Oberlin Resolute Club with Simpson Younger (first row, second from the left)*

Simpson Younger enrolled at Oberlin College in 1866. At the time, Oberlin, recognized for having been one of the first American institutions of higher learning to regularly admit black students, did not condone extra-curricular activities such as baseball and did not sponsor a team. Nonetheless, members of the student body assembled one, first as the Oberlin Penfields, more of a recreational team, and then added the Resolutes, a more competitive team.[1]

Younger played outfield with the Penfields then pitched with the Resolutes, which made him the first African American, known by name, to play baseball in the Western Reserve quadrant of Ohio.[2] His teams were acknowledged as being among the best in the area which included the city of Cleveland.

A second African-American student, Josiah T. Settle, joined Younger on the Oberlin Resolute in 1868. After one year, Settle transferred to Howard University in Washington D. C., where he was a member of the collegiate department's first graduating class in 1872. While in Washington D. C., Settle played ball for two of the best all-black teams in town, the Mutuals and the Alerts.[3] One of Josiah Settle's Washington Mutuals Baseball Club teammates was fellow outfielder Charles Redmond Douglass, son of Frederick Douglass. Settle had a distinguished career in both law and politics.

Any assertion that William White was the first African-American college baseball player is based on a controversial story that first surfaced in 2004. Until then, he would never have been considered a candidate because evidence that he was of color did not emerge until that year.

The enigmatic White was a member of the Brown University baseball team in 1879 and 1880. Though there is now compelling evidence that he was the mulatto son of a Georgia slave owner and his house servant, there is also evidence that the light-skinned White played and probably "passed" as a white man.[4]

*1879 Brown University*
*William White (directly behind gentleman in suit)*

In 1879, the professional baseball team in Providence, Rhode Island, where Brown University is located, summoned William White to fill in for an injured ballplayer. Since this was an accepted practice in an era before eligibility rules were established, his participation in this one game has also given rise to a claim on his behalf to being the first African-American professional baseball player.

The claims of William White being the first black collegian and first black professional are most often challenged because he most likely chose to live his life as a white man. Therefore, he did not face the litany of obstacles he would have faced as a true black integrator.

Another black pioneer of college baseball was John Langston Harrison, who studied and played ball at Ohio's Marietta College from 1883-1887. Though he wrote in 1937 of having played for the college team, records do not indicate that baseball was an intercollegiate sport at the time. Instead,

*William White*
*Brown University*
*Painting by Graig Kreindler*
*from the collection of Jay*
*Caldwell*

like at many colleges, baseball was probably a "club" sport supported by a student-run athletic association.[5] Harrison wrote about having teammates Tom Church (another African American and brother of well-known early civil rights activist Mary Church Terrell) and Ban Johnson (founder and first president of Major League Baseball's American League).[6]

In the middle of the nineteenth century, Kansas was one of several territories that were hotbeds for abolitionist activities, and it was during this time that Kansas was admitted into the Union of the United States as a free state. With this designation came the right of both black and white students to be admitted to its state-supported colleges. Therefore, it is not surprising that following the Walker brothers of Oberlin and Harrison of Marietta, Sherman Harvey became one of the next earliest baseball integrators of a historically white college in 1888 at Kansas University. Following his arrival, Harvey's two younger brothers, Grant and Edward, joined the baseball team.

Northeast of Kansas, Hiram Archer attended school and played baseball at Olivet College in Michigan from 1889 through 1892. After graduation, Archer became a professor at what is now Alabama A&M and, later, President of Daniel Payne College in Selma, Alabama.

Around the same time the Harvey brothers and Hiram Archer were integrating their schools' baseball programs, two others were doing so at colleges in Ohio. The two were Edward Christopher Williams at Western Reserve University in 1889 and Carter Barnett at Denison University in 1890.

Following graduation, Barnett began a lifelong career in education. During his teaching career and as principal of Huntington, West Virginia's segregated Frederick Douglass High School, Barnett impacted the lives of countless young students. He had an especially profound influence upon one, his cousin Carter Woodson, who would become known as the father of African-American history for his role in emphasizing and promoting its importance.[7]

Edward Christopher Williams is thought to be the first African American professionally-trained librarian in the United States. Between his career as head librarian at Western Reserve University and Howard University, Williams was principal of M Street High School in Washington D. C., one of the nation's first public high schools for black students.

*1895 Berea College*
*William Miller (top row left), Hume Mathis (next to Miller)*
*and Thomas Routt (top row second from right)*

In 1895, except for those historically black colleges playing baseball at the time, Berea College in Kentucky was the first college in the nation to field a team with as many as three African-Americans on it.[8]

Like Oberlin College, Berea College was deeply rooted in abolitionist activities. Until the enactment of the Day Law in 1904, which outlawed integrated education in Kentucky, the school had a nearly equal number of black and white students. That 1895

Berea College team included African Americans William Miller, Hume Mathis, and Thomas Routt. This was the largest representation of black student-athletes on an integrated college baseball team until Ferris Institute fielded a team with four African Americans in 1919. After leaving Berea, William Miller became a lawyer and served as an aide to Wisconsin governor and one-time presidential candidate, Robert LaFollette. He was also a trusted confidant of prominent Civil Rights activist and educator W. E. B. DuBois. Hume Mathis made a career in education, and Thomas Routt went into the clergy.

According to the 1897 Illinois State Normal University yearbook, *The Index*, spirit was never higher with the anticipation of elevating the standard of the baseball team. A coach had been secured whose knowledge and understanding of the game were expected to help the team exceed all previous efforts. When the Board of Control at what is now Illinois State University hired George Green that year, they unknowingly tapped someone who probably was the first African American to coach a baseball team at a predominantly white college. It would be another 30 years before Illinois State added its first black player to the roster and 75 years before the next African American was hired to coach another predominantly white baseball program.

*1897 Amherst College Baseball Team*
*James Francis Gregory (middle row far right)*

Other pioneers before the twentieth century were Solomon Ford Kingston at Pennsylvania's Geneva College in 1885, Edward Osborne in 1892 at Colby College in Massachusetts, and both Ralph Victor Cook at Cornell University in New York, and James Francis Gregory at Amherst College in Massachusetts, in 1896. Joining them were Merrill Strothers in 1897 at Beloit College in Wisconsin and Gaitha Adolphus Paige of the Kansas State Normal School (now known as Emporia State) in 1898.[9] Gregory, whose father James Monroe Gregory was a member of Howard University's first graduating class along with Josiah Settle, was selected captain of the Amherst College nine in 1896. His selection may have been the first for an African-American ballplayer at a predominantly white school. Before enrolling at Amherst, Gregory was a member of the varsity squad at Howard University in 1894, though he was only a high school student in the college preparatory program.

Two early pioneers of college baseball had close ties to the renowned African-American educator, humanitarian, author, and president of Tuskegee Institute, Booker T. Washington. Frank J. Armstrong integrated the Cornell (Iowa) College baseball program in 1898, and William C. Matthews did likewise at Harvard University in 1902.

*Frank Armstrong*

Frank Armstrong was the second African-American to attend Cornell College and the first to graduate. The popular second baseman served as baseball team captain and was involved in several other student organizations. During his senior year, he was selected to introduce guest lecturer Booker T. Washington and so impressed Washington that he hired Armstrong to be his assistant. [10] After eight years at Tuskegee Institute, Armstrong earned a medical doctorate from the University of Illinois and served with the U.S. Health Department before going into private practice as a physician and surgeon.

William Clarence Matthews was probably the most recognized of all

African-American college ballplayers in the country during the first quarter of the twentieth century. Growing up in Selma, Alabama, Matthews attended Tuskegee Institute (now Tuskegee University). There, he played on the baseball teams managed by Booker T. Washington's half-brother, James and led the club to what the *Washington Bee* described as being the "championship of the state" in 1895.[11] Besides baseball, William Matthews excelled in football and helped organize and coach Tuskegee's first team.

*William C. Matthews*
*Harvard University*
*Painting by Graig Kreindler*
*from the collection of Jay*
*Caldwell*

On the recommendation of Tuskegee president Booker T. Washington, Matthews moved north and attended the prestigious Phillips Andover Academy before enrolling at Harvard in 1902. Like Frank Armstrong at Cornell College, William Matthews was a very popular figure on campus and off. However, at times, he was the subject of ridicule and boycott when facing schools opposed to playing racially integrated teams.

Several well-documented acts of discrimination leveled against Matthews involved opponent Georgetown University of Washington D. C. and its star, Sam Apperious. Besides his boycotts of Harvard games with William Matthews in the lineup, Apperious also led a boycott against Matthews when each played professionally in the Northern League during the summer of 1905.[12]

While the boycotts generally resulted in disfavor towards Apperious and the games went on without him, there is an irony in the relationship between the two. Both William Matthews and Sam Apperious were native Alabamans, Matthews being from Selma and Apperious from Montgomery. Some 60 years later, in 1965, those two cities served as the starting point and destination in a series of civil rights marches that Reverend Martin Luther King Jr. made the focal point to register black voters in the south. The protest, which included violence and bloodshed, brought national attention to the struggle for equality in voting rights and resulted in Congress passing the Voting Rights Act of 1965 later that year.

After missing over half his freshman season with a knee injury, William Matthews returned to lead the Harvard nine in hitting each of the following three seasons. Matthews batted .333 in 1903 with 4 home runs and 12 stolen bases; the next year he hit .343 with 3 home runs and 8 steals; and in 1905, his last year, Matthews batted .400 with 25 stolen bases.[13]

After an outstanding career at Harvard on one of the nation's best college baseball teams, Matthews, who *McClure's Magazine* called "Harvard's best baseball player",[14] went to Boston University to study law. During this time, there was serious talk of William Matthews re-integrating professional baseball when Major League Baseball's Boston Beaneaters of the National League (who still exist today, after several iterations, as the Atlanta Braves) expressed interest in signing him to a professional contract.

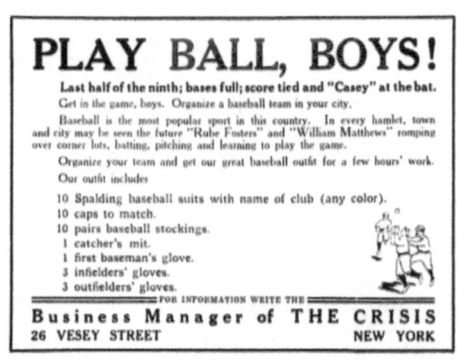

## PLAY BALL, BOYS!

Last half of the ninth; bases full; score tied and "Casey" at the bat.

Get in the game, boys. Organize a baseball team in your city.

Baseball is the most popular sport in this country. In every hamlet, town and city may be seen the future "Rube Fosters" and "William Matthews" romping over corner lots, batting, pitching and learning to play the game.

Organize your team and get our great baseball outfit for a few hours' work.

Our outfit includes

10 Spalding baseball suits with name of club (any color).
10 caps to match.
10 pairs baseball stockings.
1 catcher's mit.
1 first baseman's glove.
3 infielders' gloves.
3 outfielders' gloves.

FOR INFORMATION WRITE THE

**Business Manager of THE CRISIS**
**26 VESEY STREET**      **NEW YORK**

*William Matthews (pictured to the left) was one of the most popular African-American ballplayers of his day. So much so that The Crisis, the official magazine of the NAACP, used his name to promote the game of baseball within its pages.*

As an influential Republican within the African-American community and critical supporter of presidential candidate Calvin Coolidge in 1924, Matthews was rewarded with a position as Assistant Attorney General of the United States. Sadly, William Matthews died prematurely in 1928 at age 51. Obituaries ran in many of the major newspapers in the country and warranted front-page headlines in the nation's African-American papers. *The Boston Globe* called him "one of the most prominent colored members of the bar in this country."[15] In 2006, a trophy named in his honor was created to recognize future Ivy League Baseball champions. In 2014, Matthews was awarded induction into the College Baseball Hall of Fame.

As the twentieth century unfolded, more and more joined the ranks of college baseball integrators. Julian Ware and Adelbert R. Matthews began playing ball at the University of Wisconsin in 1900 and helped the Badgers win its first conference baseball title in 1902. That year, Ware became the first African American to captain a varsity squad in the Big Ten Conference. Before entering Wisconsin, Julian Ware attended and played baseball at Fisk University. Later, Ware became a medical doctor, while fellow Wisconsin integrator "Dell" Matthews played professional baseball with the Chicago Union Giants after leaving school.

Two black pioneers of early twentieth-century college baseball had direct ties to fashioning the racial perspective of Major League Baseball's integrating general manager, Branch Rickey. The two Ohio-based college baseball integrators were Charles Follis of the College of Wooster and Charles L. Thomas of Ohio Wesleyan University.

*1902 College of Wooster*
*Charles Follis (first row right.)*

Follis, who was not officially a student of the College of Wooster, nonetheless, like many others, played with his university's team while still enrolled in the school's preparatory program. As a catcher in 1901 and 1902 on Wooster's baseball team, Charles Follis faced Ohio Wesleyan teams on which Branch Rickey played. Rickey and Follis each excelled in baseball as well as football and played together professionally with the Shelby (Ohio) Blues. Years later, Charles Follis would be recognized as the country's first documented African-American professional football player. Still, Branch Rickey probably remembered Follis for being unshakeable in the face of racial slurs and the physical threat of injury on the playing field.

Like Charles Follis, Charles Thomas of Ohio Wesleyan University played a role in nurturing Branch Rickey's racial beliefs, ultimately leading to his monumental signing of Jackie Robinson to a professional baseball contract.

In 1903, when Rickey was declared ineligible for further collegiate competition after spending a summer with a professional club, he became the baseball coach at Ohio Wesleyan. While there, he recruited former football teammate Charles Thomas to be his replacement as catcher on the school's team. Insults and protests followed Thomas from town to town, but the incident that most impacted Branch Rickey, who years later would be voted the "Most Influential Person in Sports of the 20th Century" by ESPN's SportsCentury panel, occurred when Ohio Wesleyan traveled to South Bend, Indiana for a baseball game versus Notre Dame.

THE Kentucky University baseball team were hooted from the field and pelted with clods and sticks, last week, at Delaware, O., because they refused to play on account of the Ohio boys insisting on playing a negro on their team. That might do in Ohio, they can sandwich in as many negroes on their baseball teams as they please, but when it comes to Kentuckians playing a game with one of their mixed nines you will have to excuse them. It is just natural with them, for they are not built that way. The University boys deserve applause for their manly stand.

*Two different perspectives of a game on June 20, 1905, in Delaware, Ohio between Ohio Wesleyan University and what is now Transylvania University in Lexington, Kentucky. Above is the write-up from the Bourbon News of Paris, Kentucky, and to the right is one from the Cleveland (OH) Gazette.*

**Would Not Play Without Thomas**

Delaware, O. - Arriving in Delaware Tuesday noon for a series of games with Ohio Wesleyan, the University of Kentucky ball-team appeared on the field in their suits in the afternoon for the opening game, but on seeing Thomas, the Afro-American catcher, refused to play with him on the team. The Methodists refused to take him off, so Kentucky left at once for home, paying their own expenses. A crowd of over 1,200 was present, and an alumni team was got up from the old players who were on the bleachers, who defeated the varsity by a score of 6 to 1.

The story Branch Rickey most often relayed was of a downtrodden Charles Thomas who had been denied lodging in the South Bend hotel where his Ohio Wesleyan teammates were staying. Rickey stood up to the hotel manager, insisting that Thomas be allowed to stay in his room. After settling in, Rickey vowed to "Tommy" that someday things would be different. And when things were different, it was noted that the type of individuals Charles Follis and Charles Thomas were, may have been Branch Rickey's model for the character values he found in Jackie Robinson.

*Charles L. Thomas*
*Ohio Wesleyan University*
*Painting by Graig Kreindler*
*from the collection of Jay*
*Caldwell*

Follis and Thomas had at least one opportunity to face each other on a baseball diamond. In 1908, Charles Thomas and his Columbus Black Tourists teammates bested Charles Follis and his Cleveland nine squad in Ohio State Colored League action.

Charles Follis played professional baseball in 1909 with John Bright's Cuban Giants, but unfortunately passed away in 1910 at 31. Charles Thomas played for the nation's black baseball champion, Philadelphia Giants, in the summers of 1904 and 1905. After finishing dental school, Thomas became only the second African American to practice dentistry in New Mexico, where he did so for forty years.

Long before the days of disparity in size, enrollment, and athletic budgets, schools that would in this day and age be considered "Goliaths", regularly scheduled matches against those currently thought of as "Davids". There was far less of an athletic imbalance in the early twentieth century than today. Such an institution was small Washburn University in Topeka, Kansas, which routinely scheduled such contests against the University of Kansas, University of Missouri, and the University of Nebraska. This was true throughout college ranks. In 1903, Washburn welcomed pitcher John Johnson, who integrated its baseball program. While there was some concern over how he'd be accepted, there is little evidence of any specific incidents. Two years later, University of Kansas transfer Thomas McCampbell and his younger brother, Ernest McCampbell, joined the Washburn baseball program. In 1906, both McCampbells and Emporia State baseball integrator Gaitha Page joined the all-black Jenkins Sons Music Company team of Kansas City, one of the city's first.

George Walter Williams integrated the University of Vermont baseball team in 1904 and was joined by Fenwick Henri Watkins the following year. When the University of Alabama team headed north to face Vermont, it discovered that the Catamounts had two Negros on its team and refused to play against "colored men". Alabama was forced to forfeit $300 for canceling its scheduled games with Vermont. One African-American newspaper, the *Cleveland Gazette*, provided editorial commentary suggesting that Alabama should have forfeited more like $3000.[16]

The year 1904 saw three others integrate their schools' baseball programs. Arthur Butler did so at Northwestern University in Evanston, Illinois, Bobby Marshall at the University of Minnesota, and John Davis Smith at Connecticut's Wesleyan University. When Thomas Jarvis Taylor made the Wesleyan varsity nine the following year, the Cardinals joined the University of Vermont as possibly the only two predominantly white schools at this time whose rosters included more than one African American ballplayer. Taylor later became head baseball coach of the powerhouse Tuskegee Institute clubs in the early 1910s.

Bobby Marshall was a well-known name in sporting circles throughout Minnesota, not only for baseball, but also as a star in football and hockey. In 1971, his legendary football career for the university's Golden Gophers earned him a permanent spot in the College Football Hall of Fame. As a first baseman, in 1907, Marshall led Minnesota to the championship of the Western Conference (forerunner of the Big Ten Conference). Though he earned a law degree from Minnesota and practiced for a short time, a good amount of Bobby Marshall's professional career was in baseball. At one time, he played, coached, and owned the Saint Paul Colored Gophers, a popular barnstorming team of his day.

During the next decade, three previously all-white baseball programs welcomed black pioneers who would become nationally recognized figures in the African-American community. Cleveland "Cleve" Abbott played ball at South Dakota State University from 1912-1916, Paul Robeson played varsity baseball beginning in 1916 at Rutgers University in New Jersey, and Cumberland Posey (also known as Charles Cumbert) played at Pennsylvania's Duquesne University in 1916.

A four-sport letterman in college, Cleve Abbott will be remembered as Tuskegee University's most successful football coach, having led the Tigers to nine mythical national black titles in his 32 years of coaching. Besides serving as the school's athletic director, Abbott coached women's track for 32 years and was inducted into the USA Track and Field Hall of Fame in 1996. Abbott was elected to the South Dakota State Hall of Fame in 1968, the Tuskegee University Hall of Fame in 1975, the Southern Intercollegiate Athletic Conference Hall of Fame in 1992, and the Alabama Sports Hall of Fame in 1995. In recognition of his outstanding contribution to athletics, the Tuskegee University Football Stadium was renamed the Cleveland Leigh Abbott Memorial Alumni Stadium in 1996.

*1914 South Dakota State*
*Cleveland Abbott (top row second from right).*

Paul Robeson was one of the most gifted individuals of the twentieth century. A three-sport star at Rutgers, Robeson excelled in football (twice earning All-America honors), basketball and baseball. As an undergraduate, he was selected class valedictorian and then went to Columbia University, earning a law degree in 1923.

Though Paul Robeson practiced law for a short time, he is most remembered for his resonant baritone voice, which afforded him a long career as an internationally acclaimed singer and actor. Robeson's rendition of his most identifiable song, "Ol' Man River", from the 1927 musical Show Boat, was inducted into the music industry's Grammy Hall of Fame in 2006.

*Paul Robeson (pictured in catcher's gear) was a Rutgers star in both baseball and football.*

Robeson is also remembered as a lifelong social and political activist. His outspoken opinions resulted in disfavor among many groups and led to his being blacklisted from scores of potential engagements and performances, mainly during the 1950s. Even though he is still remembered as a controversial figure, in death, Paul Robeson's accomplishments far outshine any negatives that may still be associated with his name.

Cumberland "Cum" Posey was a talented basketball and football player, but is most often recognized as the owner and driving force of the Homestead Grays, one of the most successful teams in Negro Leagues history.

Posey played baseball at Duquesne University and later with the Homestead Grays. He also played basketball at both Penn State and Duquesne, where he led the team in scoring for three years. After his playing career ended, Posey became the business manager of the Grays, then manager, and finally the owner of the team.

During his tenure with the Homestead Grays, Cumberland Posey directed his teams to nine consecutive Negro National League pennants (1937-1945) and two Negro League World Series titles. Posey had a knack for recognizing and acquiring talented players, including over ten who would be inducted into Major League Baseball's Hall of Fame. Posey, too, was voted into the hall in 2006.

*1919 Ferris Institute*
*School president, Woodbridge Ferris is pictured in the middle row, center and Maceo Clarke*
*is pictured in the top row, second from right.*

By 1919, Ferris Institute (now known as Ferris State University), located in Big Rapids, Michigan, already had a tradition of welcoming minority students. Around 1910, the school's founder and president, Woodbridge Ferris, who later became governor of Michigan, arranged for students from

Hampton Institute in Virginia to take special preparatory courses at Ferris before transferring to other schools. Of the four African-American student-athletes on the 1919 baseball team, one of those Hampton Institute transfers was Maceo Clarke. Clarke, who became a physician, later transferred to Howard University, where he also played baseball. While living in the Washington D. C. area, Dr. Clarke played a short time with Negro League teams such as the Washington Potomacs, Homestead Grays, and the Atlanta City Bacharach Giants. After settling down to practice medicine in Dayton, Ohio, Maceo Clarke became president of the local NAACP in 1961 and served on the Ohio Higher Education Board of Regents from 1966 through 1975.

Other notable black pioneers of college baseball during the mid-1910s to early-1920s were William Kindle at the International YMCA College in Massachusetts (now known as Springfield College) and Fred Long at Millikin University in Illinois, both in 1915, Harold D. Martin at Norwich University in Vermont in 1917, John Prim at the University of Washington and Charles Howard at Iowa's Drake University, both in 1920, Douglas Sheffey (a Negro Leagues pitcher for the Hillsdale Daisies in 1915-1917) at the University of Pennsylvania, also in 1920, John Riddle at the University of Southern California in 1923 and Bazz Smaulding at the University of Idaho in 1924.

*Fred Long*
*Millikin University*

William Kindle played football and baseball in his home state of Tennessee at Fisk University, then migrated to Springfield College (known for being the school where professor James Naismith invented basketball in 1891) to play both sports. Like many lone black athletes on college baseball rosters before and after him, Kindle faced protests by opponents' teams. Most notably was a game in 1915 when the United States Military Academy at West Point refused to play with Kindle on the field.[17] After a stint with the Negro League's Brooklyn Royal Giants, Kindle became a professor and athletic director at Talladega College in Alabama.

Fred Long, like William Kindle, had a brief career in the Negro Leagues with the Detroit Stars and Indianapolis ABCs after being the first African American graduate of Millikin University. Skilled at baseball and football, Long then chose to go into college coaching after his playing career ended. During his 45-year career, mainly at Wiley College in Texas, his teams captured three national black college football titles. In 1962, Fred Long was inducted into the National Association of Intercollegiate Athletics Hall of Fame.

Harold Martin became the first African-American student at Vermont's Norwich University when he enrolled in college in the fall of 1916. A multi-sport athlete, including baseball, Martin played Negro League baseball for the Pittsburgh Keystones and Homestead Grays. He coached football at Virginia Union and Virginia State, and became the first appointed commissioner of football officials in the CIAA (in 1939). Harold

*Harold Martin of Norwich University-the Military College of Vermont devoted much of his professional career to HBCUs.*

Martin was also a professor at Miner Teachers College (an HBCU now known as the University of the District of Columbia) and later was the ground school director at Tuskegee Air Field for the celebrated Tuskegee Airmen.

On the west coast, John Prim and John Riddle integrated their college baseball programs in 1920 and 1923, respectively. Each starred in both football and baseball while in school. Prim graduated from the University of Washington and went into the legal profession. He holds the distinction of being the very first African-American judge in the state of Washington. John Riddle became an architect and is the very first African American to appear in the Rose Bowl, while playing football at the University of Southern California.

Bazz Owen Smaulding was the son of a pioneering African-American family in New Mexico and a baseball, basketball, football and track star athlete. After graduating high school in Albuquerque, Smaulding enrolled at the University of Washington, where he played football, and ran track. Smaulding then transferred to the University of Idaho in 1923, where he was the lone African American on the football and baseball teams. Bazz Smaulding continued his baseball career playing for the Gillkerson Union Giants and Kansas City Monarchs before becoming a teacher and coach at the Piney Woods School in Jackson, Mississippi.

Also, in 1923, Joe Washington most likely became the integrator of New York University baseball. Though he was not taken on the team's initial southern tour of games, upon return, Washington became a regular for the Violets playing all three outfield positions, as well as both shortstop and third base. On April 3rd of that year, he was the leadoff hitter in the game versus Columbia University and played left field. Batting third and playing first base for the opposing Columbia Lions was Lou Gehrig. Joe Washington played only the one season for NYU, and little is known of him after that. On the other hand, Gehrig joined the New York Yankees and ended up starting 2,130 straight games on his way to Major League Baseball's Hall of Fame.

In the days when eligibility rules were still evolving, Charles Howard integrated Iowa's Drake University baseball team after starring on the powerful Tuskegee Institute ball clubs of 1912 and 1913. At Tuskegee, Howard was selected to the All-Southern baseball team in 1913 and was said to have no peer at first base. Charles Howard became a successful lawyer and is credited with being one of the founders of the Negro Bar Association, later renamed the National Bar Association. Like fellow black pioneer of college baseball and friend Paul Robeson, Charles Howard left a legacy of civil rights and political activism.

In the 1930s, probably the most recognizable individual to integrate his college's varsity baseball team was Kenny Washington at UCLA, where he was Jackie Robinson's football teammate.

By the time Jackie Robinson transferred from Pasadena Junior College in 1939, Kenny "Kingfish" Washington had already established himself as the football and baseball hero on the Los Angeles, California campus of UCLA. As a senior on the football team, Washington led the country in total offense and was named All-American in 1939. On the diamond, his .397 batting average in 1938 paced the UCLA nine almost the entire season, and Washington's four home runs and 17 RBIs led the squad. In his lone year playing baseball for the Bruins in 1940, Jackie

*Kenny Washington*
*UCLA*

Robinson, who, like Washington, was a UCLA shortstop, hit a mere .097. Even so, Robinson showed the promise of things to come. In his first game at UCLA, Jackie Robinson collected four hits in four times at bat and stole four bases, including one of home.[18] Kenny Washington helped re-integrate professional football, which had been segregated since 1934, playing for the Los Angeles Rams in 1946. In 1950, he had an unsuccessful tryout with the New York Giants baseball team. Kenny Washington was inducted into the College Football Hall of Fame in 1956.

Slightly more than a decade before Kenny Washington became a big man on campus, Ralph Bunche integrated UCLA's basketball program in 1925 and played freshman baseball the year before. Bunche would become a long-time professor at Howard University. However, his name is far more recognized as a civil rights activist and as the Under Secretary for Special Political Affairs of the United Nations. In that capacity, Ralph Bunche was awarded the Nobel Peace Prize in 1950.

Two brothers who made their marks in different professional athletic endeavors were the earliest integrators of baseball at Indiana Central College (now known as the University of Indianapolis). Ray Crowe joined the baseball team in 1939, and younger brother George enrolled shortly thereafter. Ray

Crowe became one of the most celebrated coaches in Indiana high school basketball history with his state championship teams of the 1950s at all-black Crispus Attucks High School in Indianapolis, which featured future professional basketball Hall of Famer Oscar Robertson. After leaving Indiana Central, Ray Crowe's brother George played baseball for a short time in the Negro Leagues with the New York Black Yankees and the Philadelphia Stars. Moving on to Organized Baseball, George Crowe played an additional nine years with the Boston and Milwaukee Braves, Cincinnati Reds, and the Saint Louis Cardinals.

Three years before Jackie Robinson's historic signing, catcher John Ritchey integrated the San Diego State College (now San Diego State University) baseball team in 1942. The following year, Ritchey was drafted into the Army, but returned to school and the team in 1946. At the end of the following year, John Ritchey signed a Minor League contract with the San Diego Padres, and with the 1948 season opener, Ritchey became the first African American to play in the Pacific Coast League of professional baseball.

While John Ritchey was integrating San Diego State baseball in 1942, just about 90 miles to the north, Emmett Ashford was doing likewise at Chapman College (now Chapman University). Ashford became an umpire and was an early integrating umpire in the late-1940s of the Pacific Coast

*Emmett Ashford (left) at Chapman College and John Ritchey (right) at San Diego State*

Conference, which at the time included UCLA, the University of Southern California, Stanford, and the University of California. In 1954, Ashford became the first African-American umpire in the Pacific Coast League, and in 1966 Emmett Ashford broke the color barrier of umpiring in Major League Baseball.

Following the lead of Jackie Robinson and Branch Rickey, more and more African-American ballplayers stepped over the color line and onto the playing field of what was commonly known as Organized Baseball. On the college scene, it would still be over two decades before southern schools slowly began fielding their first integrated teams.

[1] Dixon, Phil, and Patrick J. Hannigan. *The Negro Baseball Leagues, 1867-1955: A Photographic History*, 41. Mattituck, NY: Amereon House, 1992.

[2] James M. Egan, Jr. "The Early Years/1867." In *Base Ball on the Western Reserve: The Early Game in Cleveland and Northeast Ohio, Year by Year and Town by Town, 1865-1900*, 21. Jefferson, NC: McFarland & Co., 2008.

[3] Brunson, James E. *Black Baseball, 1858-1900: A Comprehensive Record of the Teams, Players, Managers, Owners and Umpires (3 vol set)*, 1123. Jefferson, NC: McFarland & Company, 2019.

[4] Husman, John R. "June 21, 1879: The Cameo of William Edward White." Society for American Baseball Research | Society for American Baseball Research. Accessed May 1, 2019. https://sabr.org/gamesproj/game/june-21-1879-cameo-william-edward-white.

[5] Showalter, Linda. "John Langston Harrison and Ban Johnson." E-mail message to author. January 27, 2015.

[6] "John Langston Harrison - Class of 1887." Pioneer Prologue. Accessed January 9, 2015. http://pioneerprologue.blogspot.com/2012/02/john-langston-harrison-class-of-1887.html.

[7] Goggin, Jacqueline. *Carter G. Woodson: A Life in Black History*. Baton Rouge: LSU Press, 1997.

[8] Bond, Gregory. "Jim Crow at Play: Race, Manliness, and the Color Line in American Sports, 1876-1916." 441. PhD diss., University of Wisconsin-Madison, 2008.

[9] Ibid., 559-578.

[10] *Iowa State Bystander* (Des Moines). "Cedar Rapids Budgetarian." June 22, 1900, 6. https://chroniclingamerica.loc.gov/lccn/sn83025186/1900-06-22/ed-1/seq-6/.

[11] *The Washington Bee* (Washington, District of Columbia). "Alabama Notes." August 24, 1895, 1.

[12] Lindholm, Karl. "William Clarence Matthews." In *The Cooperstown Symposium on Baseball and American Culture, 1997 (Jackie Robinson)*, edited by Peter M. Rutkoff and Alvin L. Hall, 34-36. Jefferson, NC: McFarland & Company, 2000.

[13] Ibid., 33.

[14] Needham, Henry B. "The College Athlete." *McClure's Magazine*, June 1905.

[15] *The Boston Globe*. "W. C. Matthews Dies Suddenly in Capital." April 11, 1928, 4.

[16] *The Gazette* (Cleveland). June 15, 1907, 2.

[17] *The Springfield Daily Republican* (Springfield, MA). "Springfield College is Fast." May 17, 1915, 12.

[18] *California Daily Bruin* (Los Angeles). "Bears Rule Slight Favorites Over Locals Despite Double Loss to Troy." March 11, 1940, 3.

# CHAPTER 4

# The Renaissance Era

## (1945-1959)

The resurgence of black college baseball is commonly linked to a single event in 1945, which profoundly impacted the sport and helped spark greater social change. It energized HBCU baseball when, for several years prior, leadership at collegiate conferences had failed to accomplish.

During its baseball depression and dating back to at least 1938, black college athletic conferences such as the Southern Intercollegiate Athletic Conference (SIAC) and the Colored Intercollegiate Athletic Association (CIAA) brought the matter of reinstating baseball to the attention of member schools regularly. While some schools were willing to work towards fielding teams, those efforts never seriously came to fruition until October 1945. That's when Brooklyn Dodgers' general manager Branch Rickey signed Jackie Robinson of the Negro League's Kansas City Monarchs to a professional baseball contract and integrated Organized Baseball. As much as anything else, this one event served as a catalyst for black college baseball's resurrection.

The Southern Intercollegiate Athletic Conference annual meeting, held at year's end in 1945, was highlighted by an earnest conversation about restoring baseball to the conference calendar of sporting events. It was the opinion of officials that "Inasmuch as opportunities are arising for wider participation in organized baseball, colleges should undertake the preparation of young men possessing talent in this sport, and they should be encouraged to make baseball a career."[1]

At its annual meeting in December 1946, William Nunn, the managing editor of the *Pittsburgh Courier*, speaking to members of the Colored Intercollegiate Athletic Association, urged conference schools to develop baseball teams immediately, saying "Jackie Robinson's development as a member of the Montreal team shows clearly that a Negro athlete, if he is good, can make big money in organized baseball."[2]

Louis Lautier, a Washington correspondent for the National Negro Publishers Association, penned a story in 1947 stating that "as a consequence of the opening of organized baseball to the colored player, colleges are expected next spring to revive baseball as a major sport." He went on to say that college campuses are the logical place for the development of ballplayers and concluded that a revival of the sport among colleges will produce the players that eventually will make the grade in the big leagues.[3]

On April 5, 1947, ten days before Jackie Robinson played in his first Major League game, the headline of *The Ohio State News* sports section (an African-American newspaper in Columbus, Ohio) read, "Baseball Revival Expected." Penned by Edwin B. Henderson, prominent athletic administrator, educator, and writer, he began by recognizing that "Black colleges are again beginning to take up baseball." He noted that "Many a high school boy will find his chance, as well as get a higher education, and in fours year from now, if it is in the cards, colored professionals will have cleared the way for some more of our athletes to play organized baseball."[4]

Also acknowledging the relationship between the integration of Organized Baseball and the revival of black college baseball, the 1949 Howard

University yearbook stated, "The impact of organized baseball on educational institutions is in evidence at Howard University. It has been to a large degree responsible for the revival of baseball on the campus after a lay-off of about twenty years."[5]

While schools were motivated to jump-start their baseball programs, obstacles for some included neglected playing fields in disrepair from lack of use. Others faced ball diamonds now occupied by school buildings or used for other purposes. Many schools did not immediately have the means to resurrect playing fields or the ability to fund the ongoing expenses of intercollegiate baseball.

Nonetheless, in 1946, baseball came back to the SIAC with Morehouse College, Tuskegee Institute, Alabama State, and Florida A&M fielding teams. It was observed that play was spotty and awkward, but was impressive in the sense that schools put teams on the field the same academic year that the conference voted to resume the sport.[6]

One year after the SIAC, the Colored Intercollegiate Athletic Association brought baseball back in 1947 with North Carolina A&T, Johnson C. Smith College, North Carolina College at Durham (now known as North Carolina Central University), Howard University, Virginia Union, Shaw University, and Lincoln University. That same year, the SIAC and CIAA again began naming conference champions, with Alabama State claiming the SIAC crown and North Carolina A&T topping the CIAA.

***

In the Bayou State, big things were on the horizon for the Louisiana Negro Normal and Industrial Institute in 1946. That year, the school changed its name to Grambling College. The football program, under the guidance of future College Football Hall of Fame coach Eddie Robinson, and the baseball team, under the direction of school president and future College Baseball Hall of Famer Ralph Waldo Emerson "Prez" Jones, were building dominant programs and molding professional athletes.

Grambling College completed the 1946 season, winning 36 of 37 games, losing only to Tuskegee Institute, while defeating all other college, semi-pro, and professional teams it faced. According to sports information director Collie J. Nicholson, by the end of the 1949 baseball season, the Tigers had won 120 of its last 137 games against both college and professional teams.[7] Interestingly, during these seasons, when the office duties of President Jones kept him off the baseball diamond, the reins were often handed over to football's Coach Eddie Robinson.

*1946 Grambling College Tigers with Coach Eddie Robinson (standing on left)*

When Jackie Robinson broke the "color barrier" and with the revival of HBCU baseball, the door also opened up for black Major League scouts. The first African-American, full-time scout was former Negro League standout John Donaldson, who the Chicago White Sox hired to usher talent from the Negro Leagues and black college campuses into Organized Baseball.

In the days before the advent of the Major League Baseball draft, which was instituted in 1965, professional prospects were free to sign contracts with any organization of their choosing. In 1949, Branch Rickey and the Brooklyn Dodgers established another milestone with the signing of three Grambling pitchers, Mackie Freeze, Gussie Williams, and Mack Hall, the latter finishing the season for the Tigers going 17-2. It marked, as Collie Nicholson wrote, "the initial invasion of a Negro college campus by scouts from big league clubs seeking first-rate talent."[8]

Soon after, more scouts were dispatched to Grambling, like John Donaldson of the White Sox, who was responsible for the signing of Frank Ensley and Crawford Neal. From the time the first scout visited Grambling in 1949 until the Major League draft was established in 1965, no less than 22 Tigers were signed to professional baseball contracts.

*Major League scouts, like Buck O'Neil (standing far left in Chicago Cubs uniform), regularly scouted HBCU baseball programs. Here he, along with Cubs' star Ernie Banks (seated in Chicago uniform), visit Grambling. Shown along with the team are head coach, R.W.E. Jones (in glasses to the right of Banks) and assistant coach, Eddie Robinson (standing on the far right in uniform).*

The Southwestern Athletic Conference restarted baseball in 1949 and named its first champion in 17 years, with Bishop College garnering the honor. That same year, Howard University won its only Colored Intercollegiate Athletic Association title, and in the Southern Intercollegiate Athletic Conference, Morris Brown College collected its first of two straight championships. Howard was directed by former Springfield College pitching ace Dr. Thomas Johnson, while A. J. Lockhart guided Morris Brown, where he starred on the baseball diamond years before.

During Morris Brown's two-year run of championships in 1949 and 1950, the strength of the Wolverines could be found in its pitching, led by Henry Franklin and Richard Phillips. Franklin would go on to pitch in the Brooklyn Dodgers organization, while Phillips' star shined brightest at Morris Brown

College when he, as the conference's only unanimous all-star pick, was unofficially tabbed the SIAC's most outstanding player.[9]

*** 

At many HBCU schools, it was not unusual to find multi-sport athletes participating in baseball. During this era, two such student-athletes, better known in basketball circles, were Earl Lloyd at West Virginia State College and Davey Whitney at Kentucky State. In 1950, Lloyd, formerly a pitcher for the Yellow Jackets of West Virginia State, became the first African American to play in a National Basketball Association game, which started his decade-long professional basketball career. In 2003, Earl Lloyd was inducted into the Naismith Memorial Basketball Hall of Fame. Davey Whitney, on the other hand, made his name in basketball as a college coach. Though Whitney did get tabbed as an all-conference shortstop at Kentucky State and played professionally for the Kansas City Monarchs from 1952 to 1954, he'll be remembered as the longtime basketball coach at Alcorn State. While there, he guided the Braves to the first-ever NCAA Division I postseason tournament win by a historically black university with a 70-62 victory over South Alabama in 1980. In 2010, Davey Whitney was inducted into the National Collegiate Basketball Hall of Fame.

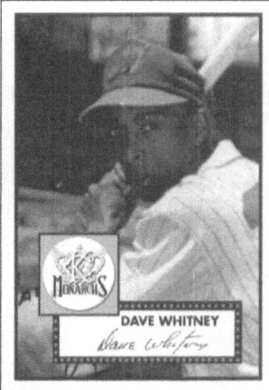

Another multi-sport college athlete, who became one of the all-time greats in Canadian professional football, was Rollie Miles of North Carolina's Saint Augustine's College. Miles was a .403 hitting middle-infielder in the spring of 1950. Later that winter, he was named a *Pittsburgh Courier* football All-American. In prior school off-seasons, Miles had been a member of the Raleigh Tigers and helped them win a Negro American Association baseball crown in 1948. Though newspaper reports indicated that the Cleveland Indians were interested in offering Rollie Miles a baseball contract in June 1950, he returned to school to play his last season of football. Then, in late November, Miles signed a professional baseball contract with the Boston Braves of the National League. However, he went to Canada instead to play baseball with the integrated Regina Caps. While in Canada, Miles was persuaded to play football for the Edmonton Eskimos. Though he continued to play semi-pro baseball in Canada, his future was in professional football. It was a future that led Rollie Miles into the Canadian Football Hall of Fame.

***

By 1950, of the "big four" conferences (SIAC, CIAA, SWAC, and MWAA), only the Midwestern Athletic Association had yet to name baseball champions again. That would soon change as the MWAA was about to expand with the addition of Grambling College, Jackson College, Tillotson College, and Texas State (renamed Texas Southern University in 1951).

Grambling, which had never been affiliated with a conference before 1952, and Jackson College, having recently parted ways with the South Central Athletic Conference, along with both Texas Southern and Tillotson College, were all eagerly welcomed into the Midwestern Athletic Association. In 1952, with enough schools fielding teams, a baseball champion was first crowned. Before leaving the MWAA after just six years, to join the Southwestern Athletic Conference in 1958, Grambling College ruled the baseball diamond, claiming five titles outright and a share of the title in 1953 with Texas Southern.

***

In 1950, the Colored Intercollegiate Athletic Association became the Central Intercollegiate Athletic Association. It also marked the beginning of a four-year run by North Carolina A&T as CIAA champion and titlist in five of the first six years in the decade. During that stretch, Felix Long coached teams won 103 games against just 10 losses, and in conference play, won 93 and lost 5. The Aggies were led by four future professionals: Hubert Simmons, Robert Smith, Jim Robinson, and Tom Alston. Simmons, NCA&T's ace pitcher, who once estimated that he went 35-7 on the mound, later pitched for the Baltimore Elite Giants. Smith signed with the Boston Braves after hitting over .350 each of his four years at school and then spent three seasons in the low Minor Leagues. Robinson, an infielder with A&T, played in the Negro Leagues with the Philadelphia Stars, Indianapolis Clowns, and Kansas City Monarchs. In 1990, South Carolina State University selected Jim Robinson as its head coach and assigned him the task of resurrecting Bulldog baseball, which had been dormant for 15 years. Unfortunately, the once-strong program could not jump-start itself, and the reincarnation of South Carolina State baseball lasted only four years under Coach Robinson.

*1950 North Carolina A&T*
*Pictured in the front row are Tom Alstom (sixth from right), Robert Smith (fifth from right) and Jim Robinson (second from right). In the rear is Hubert Simmons (fifth from left).*

The biggest name in the North Carolina A&T University lineup was unquestionably Tom Alston. A physical specimen, scouts liked his 6' 4", 210 lb. frame. In 1954, the Saint Louis Cardinals made the can't-miss prospect its first African-American Major Leaguer. Sadly, a career that got off to a slow start in Saint Louis and lasted only 91 games, stretching over four years, was cut short by a mental disorder triggered by stress and anxiety.

Just as Grambling dominated the MWAA for a good part of the 1950s and North Carolina A&T did likewise in the CIAA winning six titles, Florida

A&M College (renamed Florida A&M University in 1953) also ruled its conference, the SIAC, claiming six titles during the decade of the 1950s.

***

The Rattlers of Florida A&M won its first-ever Southern Intercollegiate Athletic Conference crown in 1951 under the guidance of head coach Oscar Moore and team captain Costa Kittles. Kittles returned in 1953 to assist Moore and succeeded him in 1960 as head coach. Between them, Florida A&M won 12 SIAC titles, one co-championship and had a combined overall record of 595-188. In 1962, Coach Costa Kittles' Rattlers squad qualified for the NAIA College World Series.

*Florida A&M Coaching Staff*
*Oscar Moore (l) and Costa Kittles (r)*

One of the team leaders of Florida A&M in the early-1950s was shortstop William "Bill" Lucas. While he had a sterling career with the Rattlers, hitting over .350 in each of his four years and spent seven years in the Milwaukee Braves organization, Lucas is most often remembered for his role in management within the Braves organization.

When his playing career stalled, in 1965 the Braves asked Bill Lucas to trade in his uniform for a suit and take a position in the front office. Though Lucas was initially reluctant, he impressively advanced within the organization. He was first assigned to serve on a transition team during the year before the Milwaukee Braves' permanent move to Atlanta, Georgia. In 1968, Lucas was named the assistant farm director; in 1972, he was named Director of Minor League Operations.

The year after media tycoon Ted Turner purchased the Atlanta Braves in 1975, Bill Lucas was Turner's choice for the position of vice president of baseball operations. His duties were those of other Major League teams' general managers, but Braves owner Ted Turner reserved that official title for himself. With his promotion to vice president, Bill Lucas became the highest-ranking African-American front office administrator in Major League Baseball, and in essence, became the first black general manager in league history. The entire professional baseball community was heartbroken when, just three years later, in 1979, Bill Lucas suffered a massive cerebral hemorrhage and died one day later.

*Bill Lucas*
*Florida A&M*

\*\*\*

In the Southwestern Athletic Conference, Southern University won or shared league titles in 1950, 1952, 1953, 1954 (tie with Wiley College), 1957, and 1959. The decade started with future Kansas City Monarch infielder Bill Breda and two-time no-hit pitcher Johnny Davis leading the Jaguars and ended with future Major League Baseball Hall of Famer Lou Brock leading Southern University to the National Athletic Intercollegiate Association College World Series title in 1959.

\*\*\*

During the mid-1950s, box scores in black newspapers like the *Chicago Defender, Pittsburgh Courier, Baltimore Afro-American,* and *Atlanta Daily World* were filled with the names of college ballplayers who would go on to successful careers in Major League Baseball.

In 1954, Tennessee A&I State College (renamed Tennessee State University in 1968), having just resurrected its baseball program, supplemented its roster with recruits from both the football and basketball squads. From the gridiron came quarterback Fred "Memphis Kid" Valentine and from the hardcourt, forward George "Jo Jo" Altman.

As a freshman in 1954, Fred Valentine was the regular center fielder for the Tigers, hitting .310 for the season. The following year, Valentine upped his batting average to .328. A football-related shoulder separation limited his participation on the diamond in 1956, but at the end of the summer, Valentine signed a professional baseball contract with the Baltimore Orioles. His seven-year Major League playing career was split between the Orioles and the Washington Senators.

Like Fred Valentine, George Altman came to Tennessee A&I to play a sport other than baseball. While Valentine's was football, Altman starred in basketball for the mighty Tiger five. Though each chose a career playing professional baseball, both Fred Valentine and George Altman were members of Tennessee State teams that were proclaimed mythical Black College National Champions in football and basketball, respectively.

*Fred Valentine*
*Tennessee State*

*George Altman*
*Tennessee State*

Even before baseball resurfaced at Tennessee A&I, the school had a strong, respected athletic program. With the encouragement of a president who was a fan of the game, officials deemed it time to start up its dormant baseball program. George Altman eagerly joined the team since he always had a love of baseball, and though he had not seriously played the game since high school, he quickly became a team leader. In 1954, Altman led the Tigers in home runs, runs batted in, and batting with a hefty .428 average. Rain plagued the season of 1955, yet the Chicago Cubs recognized his potential. After a very short stint with the Negro Leagues' Kansas City Monarchs, George Altman signed a professional baseball contract with the Cubs of the National League. Altman spent nine years in the Majors, where he was an all-star in 1961 and 1962, and then an additional eight years playing professional baseball in Japan.

In 1955, Tennessee A&I traveled to Raleigh, North Carolina to face the Shaw University Bears on March 31$^{st}$. Fred Valentine hit third in the lineup for the Tigers, and George Altman was the cleanup hitter, batting fourth. On the other side of the box score, hitting third for the Bears and catching was Chuck Hinton.[10]

Hinton went to Shaw University and played football, basketball, and baseball in 1954 and 1955, then entered professional baseball. He was a catcher in college, but with such good foot speed, Hinton was moved to the outfield once he turned pro. Chuck Hinton's time at Shaw was not the only stint at an HBCU school. From 1972 to 1999, Hinton was the head baseball coach at Howard University.

In between his college playing career and coaching career, Chuck Hinton played twelve years in the Major Leagues and represented the Washington Senators in the 1964 Major League Baseball All-Star Game.

Besides George Altman, Fred Valentine, and Chuck Hinton, other HBCU alums from the mid-1950s who played in the Major League included Al Jackson, Jake Wood, Bubba Morton, and Donn Clendenon.

*Alvin Jackson*
*Wiley College*

Al Jackson spent only one year pitching for Wiley College in 1955. His 17 strikeout performance against the Texas College Steers on April 5$^{th}$ and his 9-1 record for the season surely caught the eye of Pittsburgh Pirates scout Buster Chatham, who signed Jackson to a pro contract two months later. "Little Al", as he was known, was an accomplished hitter at Wiley and once hit two home runs in a doubleheader versus Grambling

College. However, it was his left arm that took him to the Major League where he pitched for the original New York Mets in 1962 and later with the Saint Louis Cardinals.

Like Al Jackson, Jake Wood only played one year of college baseball as the starting shortstop at Delaware State College (now Delaware State University). In his 1957 debut for the Hornets, Wood was the batting hero, collecting a hit in each of his five at-bats. In the spring of his sophomore year, just before the start of baseball season, Jake Wood signed a contract with the Detroit Tigers and became only the second from Delaware State to turn pro (pitcher George Brown was the first, signing with the Cleveland Indians in 1951). Wood wasn't the first black player to crack the Detroit Tigers' lineup, but he was the first to play his way through the Tigers' minor league system and make it with the Major League club as a regular.[11]

Before his nine-year career in professional baseball with the Detroit Tigers, Milwaukee Braves, and California Angles, Wycliffe "Bubba" Morton was the starting shortstop during his first year at Howard University in 1955. Like Chuck Hinton, who became a college head baseball coach after his Major League career ended, Morton also went into college coaching. In fact, when Bubba Morton was selected coach of the University of Washington Huskies, he missed out by only months being named the first African-American baseball coach at a non-HBCU NCAA Division I institution. That honor went to Dave Baker, who was selected as Creighton University's head coach for the 1972 baseball season.

*Donn Clendenon*
*Morehouse College*

Another news headliner of the mid-1950s was Morehouse College all-around athlete Donn Clendenon. During his time at Morehouse, where he was mentored as a freshman by a family friend and fellow "Morehouse Man" Martin Luther King Jr., Clendenon earned 12 combined varsity letters in football, basketball, and baseball from

1952 to 1956. Good enough to be considered for professional football by the Cleveland Browns and basketball by the Harlem Globetrotters, Donn Clendenon's future would be in baseball. In 1957, Clendenon signed a contract with the Pittsburgh Pirates and began a 16-year career in professional ball, highlighted in 1969 with his selection as the World Series Most Valuable Player while playing for the champion New York Mets. Donn Clendenon is one of four baseball representatives of HBCU institutions enshrined in the National Association of Intercollegiate Athletics Hall of Fame. The others selected were George Altman of Tennessee A&I, Coach R.W.E. "Prez" Jones of Grambling, and Coach Robert Lee of Southern University.

\*\*\*

In the decade of the 1950s, when North Carolina A&T and Florida A&M were not winning CIAA and SIAC titles, respectively, Maryland State (which joined the CIAA in 1954) and Alabama State were conference titlists. The Hawks of Maryland State (now known as the University of Maryland Eastern Shore) won CIAA titles in 1954 and from 1956 through 1958. Alabama State won SIAC titles in 1952 and then again in 1957 and 1958.

*The Hawks of Maryland State won four CIAA titles in the fifties, including a run of three straight in 1956-1959.*

The leader of those championship Maryland State ball clubs in the mid-to-late 1950s was Johnny "Red Ball" Sample, who was also a two-time *Pittsburgh Courier* Black College All-American football player.

A multi-sport athlete, Johnny Sample led the Maryland State football squad to glory as an offensive and defensive standout. His football talent was validated with his selection by the Baltimore Colts in the seventh round of the 1958 National Football League draft. During his two seasons with the Colts (which became the Indianapolis Colts years later), Sample was part of two NFL championship teams. His eleven-year career was further highlighted with both an American Football League championship and a Super Bowl title with the New York Jets during the season of 1968.

On the baseball diamond, Johnny Sample was equally blessed with talent. His Maryland State squads captured CIAA championships in three of his four seasons with the Hawks (1956, 1957, and 1958). In 1957, Sample finished with a .394 batting average, and his .682 slugging percentage ranked among the top national small school leaders. The following year, Sample upped his batting average to .418 and again ranked high among the national slugging leaders with an average of .764. Additionally, he used his speed (9.6 seconds in the 100-yard

*Johnny Sample*
*Maryland State*

dash) to finish fifth in the country with 17 stolen bases, averaging 1.31 steals per game. In 1958, Johnny Sample was the most outstanding player and a unanimous all-star selection at second base in the CIAA. And though he was offered a baseball contract with the Philadelphia Phillies, Sample's professional future was to be in football.

After Maryland State's fourth Central Intercollegiate Athletic Association title in five years, the Hawks were invited to represent the combined NAIA Districts 29 & 6 in its second annual national tournament in 1958. But because of distance and final examinations, Maryland State was unable to make the trip to Alpine, Texas for the 12-team series.[12]

The following year marked the defining moment in black college baseball's renaissance when Southern University was crowned the National Association of Intercollegiate Athletics College World Series champion of 1959.

Only six years after the NAIA's groundbreaking decision to accept its first historically back institutions and in only the third year of the organization's sponsorship of a national championship baseball tournament, Southern University became the first HBCU to be crowned champion.

Guided by NAIA Hall of Fame coach Robert Lee and assisted by Emory Hines, who would succeed Lee as head coach in 1961, the title-winning Jaguars were led on the baseball diamond by right fielder Louis C. "Lou" Brock. After an unimpressive freshman season of adjusting to college life and college baseball, Brock returned strong as a sophomore in 1959, hitting a resounding .524 in 22 games with eight doubles, six triples, and five home runs, while collecting 27 runs batted in and scoring 30 runs. His three-run home run in the seventh inning against Omaha University, to give the Jaguars its first lead in the title game, helped Southern University claim the 1959 NAIA championship and

*In the top photo, Southern University receives its 1959 NAIA championship trophy. Pictured are Head Coach Bob Lee (third from right), Assistant Coach Emory Hines (second from the right) and Captain Harry Levy (far right). In the bottom photo are members of the 1959 all-tournament team, including Lou Brock (far right).*

earned Lou Brock a spot on the all-tournament team. Shortly after the season ended, Brock was selected to the NCAA All-District 3 team, the only small school representative on a team made up of ballplayers primarily from the Southeastern Conference (SEC) and Atlantic Athletic Conference (ACC). Lou Brock's sophomore season was capped off with his selection to the USA National Team, which finished third in the Pan-American Games of 1959.

*Lou Brock*
*Southern University*

*Robert Williams*
*Southern University*

*McVea Griffin*
*Southern University*

Southern University (19-3 during the regular season and 23-4 overall) was more than just one man, though. Besides Lou Brock, other leaders included left fielder Robert Williams, who hit .394, was second on the team with 21 runs batted in and tied Brock for the team lead in doubles with eight. Second baseman Harry Levy led the Jaguars and the Southwestern Athletic Conference with 27 stolen bases while hitting .365. First baseman Herman Rhodes hit .361, and pitcher McVea Griffin, who had a perfect 7-0 won-loss record with five shutouts and 58 strikeouts in 61 innings pitched. In addition to these All-SWAC selections, catcher Roy McGriff (father of former Major Leaguer Terry McGriff) was also an all-conference pick in 1959. Two years later, the NAIA began the practice of selecting All-American teams, and both Levy and Griffin were honorees that first year.

After one more year at Southern University, a year in which he hit .351 during the 1961 baseball season, Lou Brock signed a professional contract with the Chicago Cubs and was assigned to its Minor League franchise in Saint Cloud, Minnesota. It would be his only season in Minor League Baseball as Brock was promoted to the parent Chicago Cubs in September 1961. After what has been described as a mediocre two-plus season stay in Chicago, Lou Brock was traded to the Saint Louis Cardinals in June 1964. Now considered one of the most lopsided trades in baseball history (in the Cardinals' favor), Brock helped elevate Saint Louis, from its eighth-place standing at the time of the trade, to the National League pennant at the conclusion of the regular season.[13] The 1964 season, which culminated in a World Series title for Brock and his Cardinals, was the turning point in a 19-year Major League career that was rewarded in 1985 with his selection into the Major League Baseball Hal of Fame. At one point in his playing career, Lou Brock was both the Major League record holder for stolen bases in a season with 118 and in a career with 938. His career total remains the most in the National League and the second most ever in the history of Major League Baseball.

***

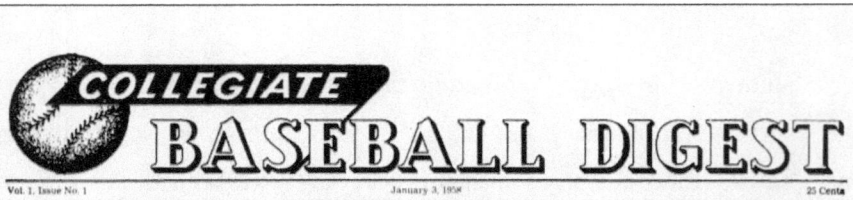

In 1958, the first regularly issued publication dedicated solely to college baseball hit the newsstand with the January 3rd distribution of *Collegiate Baseball Digest*. Now known simply as *Collegiate Baseball*, it remains the oldest continuing publication of college baseball news.

For the vast majority, it was the only source of HBCU baseball-related news for years. To its credit, *Collegiate Baseball* began publishing feature stories, statistics, schedules, and standings of black college teams from its earliest of issues and continues to do so.

The first mention of an HBCU came in March 1958 with a brief overview and schedule of West Virginia State University baseball. April and May issues contained the stories "Allen U. Pulls Off No-Hitter, Triple Play" and "Gardner Pitches No-Hitter For Florida A. & M.", respectively. Still, in 1958, *Collegiate Baseball* reported "Maryland State Wins CIAA Loop" and included a listing of the league's all-conference team. The first feature story related to HBCU baseball came in June with a story and picture of Grambling State University president and head coach R.W. E. Jones entitles "School President Doesn't Worry This College Coach".

The significance of *Collegiate Baseball* should not be minimized. It brought current news on, and publicity for, black college baseball programs when there was little else available for the college baseball fan.

*** 

When Southern University's 1959 NAIA championship pennant was hoisted, it marked a subtle transition in the timeline of black college baseball. With the raising of that pennant, down came a metaphorical banner symbolizing the rebirth of black college baseball, and up went another heralding what some might argue to be the heyday of HBCU baseball.

---

[1] *Atlanta Daily World*. "SIAC Officials Hold Annual Meeting at New Orleans, La." December 27, 1945, 5.

[2] *The Pittsburgh Courier*. "Bill Nunn Urges CIAA to Stress Major Sports." December 26, 1946, 29.

[3] Lautier, Louis. "Writer Sees Colleges Producing New Stars for Baseball Majors." *Afro-American* (Baltimore), September 6, 1947, 13.

[4] Henderson, Edwin B. "Baseball Revival Expected." *The Ohio State News* (Columbus), April 5, 1947, 24.

[5] Howard University, "The Bison: 1949" (1949). *Howard University Yearbooks*, 201. https://dh.howard.edu/bison_yearbooks/201

[6] Jackson, Marion E. "High Schools and Colleges Eye Baseball as Majors Sport." *Atlanta Daily World*, July 25, 1947, 5.

[7] Nicholson, Collie. "3 Hurlers to Report Next Year." *New York Amsterdam News*, July 23, 1949, 25.

[8] Ibid., 25.

[9] *Atlanta Daily World*. "Richard Phillips Cited as Outstanding Player." May 21, 1950, 7.

[10] *Atlanta Daily World.* "Shaw Bears Trip Tenn. State 7 to 5." April 1, 1955, 7.

[11] "African-American Heritage." Detroit Tigers. Accessed June 21, 2016. http://detroit.tigers.mlb.com/det/community/aa_heritage.jsp.

[12] *Afro-American* (Baltimore). "Third Title in Row for Maryland." May 31, 1958, 11.

[13] Gold, Eddie. "These Were the Ten Most Lopsided Player Trades." *Baseball Digest*, August 1996, 32-33.

# CHAPTER 5

# The Next Wave of Integration

## (1946-1969)

Taking inspiration from groundbreaking integrators of professional baseball like Jackie Robinson and Larry Doby (who broke the Major League color barrier in the American League only months after Robinson made history with the Brooklyn Dodgers of the National League), the next wave of African-American collegians did the same at predominantly white college baseball programs. Like Robinson, Doby, and other integrators of that era, some would face the same racist issues as their professional brethren.

*Billy Harrell*
*Siena College*

Near the end of this historical decade of the 1940s, future Major Leaguers Brooks Lawrence and Billy Harrell became baseball integrators of Miami (OH) University in 1948 and Siena College of Loudonville, New York in 1949, respectively.

Brooks Lawrence enjoyed a seven-year Major League Baseball career, punctuated with his selection as a pitcher onto the 1956 National League All-

Star team representing the Cincinnati Reds. Billy Harrell, who starred in basketball and baseball at Siena College, logged four seasons in the Major League playing infield for the Cleveland Indians and Boston Red Sox. Lawrence was inducted into the Cincinnati Reds Hall of Fame in 1976, and Harrell was similarly honored by Siena College in 1966.

The decade of the 1950s opened with athletes such as Benjamin Veal at Seton Hall University in New Jersey, Earl Woods at Kansas State College (now known as Kansas State University), and Bob Gibson at Nebraska's Creighton University breaking the color barrier at their respective colleges.

Benjamin Veal, the brother-in-law of American League integrator Larry Doby, was himself an integrator. In 1950, Veal was the first African American to play baseball at Seton Hall University. Following the 1952 college season, in which he had a .409 batting average, Ben Veal signed a professional baseball contract with the National League's New York Giants.

*Earl Woods*
*Kansas State University*

Baseball at Kansas State University and its conference, the Big Seven Conference (now called the Big 12 Conference), were both integrated in 1952 by catcher Earl Woods. Woods had a distinguished career in the military and was once offered a contract with the Negro League Kansas City Monarchs. He is best known for being a driving force in fashioning the career of his son Tiger Woods, one of professional golf's all-time greats. While traveling with the baseball team in college, Woods faced the same racist tactics from opponents that fellow integrators faced. And like most others, Earl Woods had the full support of his ball-playing teammates.[1]

In 1953, three years after moving to its present home in Omaha, Nebraska, the NCAA College World Series welcomed its first black participants in Don Eaddy and Frank Howell, both from the University of Michigan. Infielder Eaddy, and Howell, an outfielder, were vital components of the College World Series-winning National Champion University of

Michigan baseball team. During the series, Frank Howell hit .429 (6 hits in 14 at-bats), and Don Eaddy hit .318 (7 hits in 22 at-bats), with each appearing in all five of Michigan's tournament games. Two years later, Don Eaddy became a 1955 American Baseball Coaches Association All-American and, in 1959, had a brief 15-game stay in the Major League with the Chicago Cubs.

*Don Eaddy (l) and Frank Howell (r)*
*1953 University of Michigan*

While the academically prestigious University of Chicago admitted African-American students before the turn of the twentieth century, it was not until 1954 that baseball became an integrated program at the university. In 1954 and 1955, Walter L. Walker was a catcher for the Maroons and later became the university's vice-president. From there, Dr. Walker was named president of HBCU LeMoyne-Owen College in Memphis, Tennessee, where he served from 1974 to 1986.

*Thelton Henderson*
*University of California,*
*Berkeley*

Thorough research provides compelling evidence that Thelton Henderson, at the University of California, Berkeley in 1954, and Bob Gibson at Creighton University in 1955, integrated their college varsity baseball programs.

The University of California, Berkeley had African Americans on its junior varsity and freshman teams before Thelton Henderson's arrival. Yet, it appears that in 1954, Henderson was the first to don a uniform with the Golden Bears' varsity. After a two-year stint with the baseball team, Thelton Henderson later earned a law degree, and in 1962 served as an attorney with the civil rights division of the United States Department of Justice under Attorney General Robert Kennedy. In that capacity, Henderson was sent on assignment to investigate and monitor civil rights abuses in the

South. One task included monitoring the infamous 16th Street Baptist Church bombing in which four young black girls were killed in Birmingham, Alabama on September 15, 1963.[2] Later in life, Thelton Henderson became a federal court judge and today, his alma mater's Center for Social Justice is named in Henderson's honor. In 2020, Judge Henderson was named a recipient of the George H.W. Bush Distinguished Alumnus Award by the College Baseball Hall of Fame.

Another significant early integrator of his school's baseball program was Bob Gibson at Creighton University. Though he wanted to play basketball at Indiana University, according to Gibson, the school's unofficial quota of black ballplayers had already been filled, so the Omaha Tech High School multi-sport athlete ended up at his hometown Creighton University.[3]

At Creighton, Gibson was primarily recognized for his basketball talent. By the time he graduated, Bob Gibson was the Blue Jays' all-time leading scorer and, as of this writing, still ranks fourth all-time in career points per game. While sorting out his career path, Gibson spent another year playing basketball with the world-famous Harlem Globetrotters.

*Bob Gibson*
*Creighton University*

In the days when Bob Gibson was in school, baseball at Creighton was considered a minor sport, and being under-emphasized helps explain why his talent was not widely recognized.[4] Nonetheless, Bob Gibson had three outstanding seasons of baseball. In 1955 Gibson, who was primarily a center fielder, finished second in his conference by hitting .418 and recorded two home runs. On the mound, he had a 2-1 won-loss record. In an April game, Bob Gibson came close to pitching his first and only college no-hitter. Gibson went into the seventh inning without yielding a hit versus Midland College of Fremont, Nebraska. Though looking strong through the first sixth inning, Gibson's coach relieved him, citing an attempt to save his arm. However, Bob Gibson surmised that it really may have been due to the coach's lack of confidence in him. Admittedly, he tended to be wild at times back then.[5]

During the remainder of Bob Gibson's college career, highlights included a 16-strikeout game in 1956 versus Concordia University of Nebraska. According to Gibson, he led the Nebraska College Conference in hitting in 1957 with a .333 batting average while accumulating a 6-2 pitching record.

Soon after turning his full attention to professional baseball, Bob Gibson's talent blossomed. His well-documented 17-season career included being named an all-star nine times, twice a World Series champion, a two-time Cy Young Award winner, and in 1968 he was named the National League Most Valuable Player. Bob Gibson's baseball career was validated with his induction into Major League Baseball's Hall of Fame in 1981.

It is not particularly noteworthy that Gary Mays integrated the tiny College of Idaho baseball program in 1955. Nor is it significant that he came cross-country from Washington, D. C. to do so. Though it's an interesting story why African Americans such as R. C. Owens (later an All-Pro football player with the San Francisco Giants), Elgin Baylor (later an All-NBA and Naismith Memorial Basketball Hall of Famer with the Los Angeles Lakers) and Gary Mays were a handful of black classmates at an Idaho based school of about 500 students, this is not why it is notable. What is most noteworthy about Gary Mays, the integrator, is that he did so as a catcher with only one arm.

When he was a youth, Mays lost his left arm just below the shoulder in a shooting accident. Nonetheless, he had an outstanding high school career in both baseball and basketball. His story and accomplishments were documented by both *Jet* and *Ebony* magazines while still a student at Washington, D. C.'s Armstrong High School.

Gary Mays, who also played basketball at the College of Idaho, left after the 1955 school year and did not return. He had a tryout that summer at the

*Washington Daily News*-sponsored Baseball Talent Hunt, where Mays was named the camp's most outstanding player. However, he was never offered a professional contract. The year 1956 found Gary Mays on the baseball team at Howard University in his hometown of Washington, D. C. where he was primarily an outfielder. Later, an opportunity came about to join the Harlem Globetrotters basketball team, but Gary Mays declined the offer, thus ending any professional athletic aspirations.[6]

With little exception, until the mid-1960s, most all college baseball integration took place at schools north of the nation's historic cultural divide known as the Mason-Dixon Line.

*Hal Greer*
*Marshall University*

One exception occurred at Marshall University in Huntington, West Virginia, where Hal Greer integrated the varsity baseball and basketball programs during the 1955-1956 school year. Like Bob Gibson at Creighton University, Greer too was more accomplished at basketball in college, but unlike Gibson, Hal Greer's professional career path was, in fact, basketball. Greer played 15 years with the Syracuse and Philadelphia Warriors and, in 1982, was inducted into the Naismith Memorial Basketball Hall of Fame.

Bob Hoover enrolled at Penn State University in 1956 and integrated the Nittany Lions baseball program the following spring. In 1957, Hoover and his Penn State teammates participated in the NCAA College World Series, making him one of the earliest African-American participants in the series. In 1959, Bob Hoover's Penn State Nittany Lions team returned to the College World Series. Later that summer, Hoover and Lou Brock of Southern University were picked to compete in the Pan American Games. Their selections made them among the first blacks selected to represent the United States in international amateur baseball competition.

In 1957, The National Association of Intercollegiate Athletics introduced baseball as a championship sport. The following year, Bill Gilkey of Indiana State Teachers College (now known as Indiana State University) was most likely the tournament's first African-American participant. Nearly a decade before, another Indiana State Sycamore, Clarence Walker, was the first African American to participate in the association's basketball version of a national tournament in 1948. Interestingly, the year before, Indiana State's basketball coach declined an invitation from the National Association of Intercollegiate Basketball, the forerunner of the NAIA, citing the organization's policy banning African-American players from the tournament.[7] This action, as well as protests presented to tournament directors by other schools, led to a shift in policy in 1948 and ultimately in the admittance of HBCU institutions into the National Association of Intercollegiate Athletics, beginning in 1953. The basketball coach at Indiana State credited with this bold move became one of the game's most respected coaches. His name was John Wooden.

Two more multi-sport athletes, best known for football, integrated college baseball programs at the University of Louisville in 1958 and Purdue University in 1960. Ernie Green was a star running back for the Cardinals of Louisville and later became a supporting backfield mate of Cleveland Browns Pro Football Hall of Famers Jim Brown and Leroy Kelly. Like Ernie Green at Louisville, Clyde Washington starred on the football team at Purdue University in Indiana. After a stellar collegiate career, Washington went on to a five-year professional career in the American Football League. Though Clyde Washington's emphasis at Purdue was football, he played one year of baseball for the Boilermakers in 1960 as an outfielder.

In 1966, tiny Texas Western University, which changed its name to the University of Texas at El Paso in 1967, became the first school to win an NCAA college basketball national title with a starting lineup of five African Americans. Three years before, in 1963, the first baseball team was formed, and it included three black ballplayers. Of the three, one was outfielder Nolan Richardson, best remembered as the head coach of the 1994 National

Collegiate Basketball Champion, University of Arkansas. Richardson led the Razorbacks to two additional "Final Fours" and has the distinction of being the first African-American coach at a major university in the South. In his only season with the Miners baseball team, Nolan Richardson had a .376 batting average and tied for the team lead with five home runs.

*Steve Martin
Tulane University
Courtesy of Tulane
University Athletic
Department*

Following the lead of Marshall University ten years before, another southern school integrated its baseball program in 1966, and then three additional schools did likewise the following year. Steve Martin of Tulane University in New Orleans, Louisiana, was not only the first black baseball player for the Green Wave in 1966, but was also the first African-American student-athlete in the Southeastern Conference (Tulane's last year of membership in the SEC). Years later, Martin became the Chief Financial Officer at Tuskegee University.

As the pace of integration accelerated in Dixie, Vincent Colbert at East Carolina University, Arthur Speakes at Old Dominion University (in Virginia), and Ed Harris at Florida State University integrated southern college baseball programs in 1967. Colbert was drafted by the Cleveland Indians in 1968 and spent three seasons on its Major League roster.

In 1968, the National Collegiate Athletic Association instituted a postseason baseball tournament for smaller schools classified as "college division" programs. This College Division World Series became known as the Division II World Series when, in 1973, the NCAA divided the college division into Division II and Division III. In the first tournament of 1968, California's Chapman College was crowned champion. and the team included the first two African Americans to participate in the NCAA Division II College World Series. The two were John Young and Chuck Stone.

John Young was an outfielder, and Chuck Stone was an infielder. Both were drafted and ended up playing in the Detroit Tigers organization. And while each had a short stay playing professionally, both contributed to the sport long afterward. Chuck Stone became a minor league manager, scout, and head of a baseball instructional service. Like Stone, John Young was a baseball instructor and scout. As a scout, Young noticed in 1986 that few African Americans were drafted in the annual Major League Players Draft. This was the impetus for his founding a youth outreach baseball program in his hometown of Los Angeles in 1989 named Reviving Baseball in Inner Cities (RBI). With the support of Major League Baseball, the program has established upward of 200 leagues in the United States and around the world.

---

[1] Tramel, Jimmie. "Tiger Was Raised by a Wildcat." *Tulsa World*, August 3, 2007. http://www.tulsaworld.com/sports/article.aspx?articleID=070803_2_B1_hPlay11047.

[2] Egelko, Bob. "Judge Thelton Henderson Ending Long Career Rallying for Oppressed." *SFChronicle.com*. Last modified January 15, 2017. https://www.sfchronicle.com/bayarea/article/Judge-Thelton-Henderson-ending-long-career-10859424.php?psid=7YdxU.

[3] Gibson, Bob, and Lonnie Wheeler. *Stranger to the Game*, 23. New York: Penguin Group USA, 1994.

[4] Ibid., 38.

[5] Ibid., 39.

[6] Hruby, Patrick. "The Legend of Gary Mays is No Legend." ESPN.com. Last modified September 28, 2017. http://www.espn.com/espn/news/story?page=hruby/110228_gary_mays.

[7] "Remembering a Legendary Coach." NAIA.org. Last modified June 4, 2010. http://www.naia.org/ViewArticle.dbml?DB_OEM_ID=27900&ATCLID=205298260.

# CHAPTER 6

# When Stars Shined Bright

# in the NAIA

## (1960-1973)

The National Association of Intercollegiate Athletics was founded in 1940 as the National Association of Intercollegiate Basketball, though the organization first sponsored a national tournament in 1937. In 1952, the NAIB became the National Association of Intercollegiate Athletics and, over the course of the year, took a giant leap forward by admitting HBCU schools into its membership. Starting with Ohio's Central State University, 36 black colleges secured memberships in the NAIA within a year. As the organization grew, the group voted to expand its championship series to include a baseball tournament, starting in 1957.

To date, no HBCU has won an NAIA baseball title since Southern University claimed the College World Series crown to close out the decade of the 1950s. Yet, the next era of black college baseball proved to be a memorable period, with many outstanding individual performers and near-miss championship teams.

In 1960, the NAIA tournament representative from the districts of 6A,

6B, and 29 was to be determined by a playoff of Southwestern Athletic Conference champion Southern University, Southern Intercollegiate Athletic Conference champion Allen University, Central Intercollegiate Athletic Association champion North Carolina A&T and Midwestern Athletic Association champion Tennessee State. However, the latter three schools bowed out because of prohibitive expenses, and Southern University was selected to represent the combined districts.[1] While Southern University returned most of its team members who contributed to the previous year's title, and the team had a slightly better won-loss record than the '59 team going into the postseason tournament, the 1960 contingent fell short of winning back-to-back championships, losing in the semi-finals of the NAIA College World Series. Lou Brock was selected to the all-tournament team, as he was the year before, and was joined in 1960 by fellow Jaguars Harry Levy, and Henry Triplett.

That same year, the NAIA began compiling and recording individual and team statistics. In 1960, Southern University freshman, Charles Gray, was the national pitching leader with an earned run average of 0.56, while teammate McVea Griffin ranked eighth with an ERA of 1.54. As a team, Southern University ranked third in pitching with a 2.01 ERA and third in hitting with a team batting average of .335. Southern's Robert Williams led the nation with

*Tommie Agee*
*Grambling College*

23 stolen bases in 24 games, and Charles Gray collected a second individual statistical title, striking out an average of 12.3 batters per game.

The following year, it was Grambling College's turn to show off its baseball muscle, leading the country in hitting with a .362 average, fielding with a .964 average, and nearly pulling off the Triple Crown finishing third in pitching with a team ERA of 1.79. The Tigers finished third in the 1961 NAIA College World Series and were led by freshman Tommie Agee, later of New York Mets World Series fame. Agee finished third in the country, hitting an even .500, third in home runs with seven, and seventh in runs batted in with 37. In his only year at Grambling, the 12-year Major League outfielder hit a then record-setting four home runs in one game on March 14th versus Philander Smith College of Arkansas.[2] While equaled many times, that benchmark stood for 42 years until broken in 2003.

Of the country's top ten leading NAIA hitters in 1961, ballplayers representing HBCU schools finished third, fourth, fifth, seventh, eighth, and 10th in batting. Besides Tommie Agee, one of those was Archie Wade of Stillman College. A former minor leaguer in the Saint Louis Cardinals organization and coach at Stillman, Dr. Wade later became the first African-American professor hired at the University of Alabama.[3]

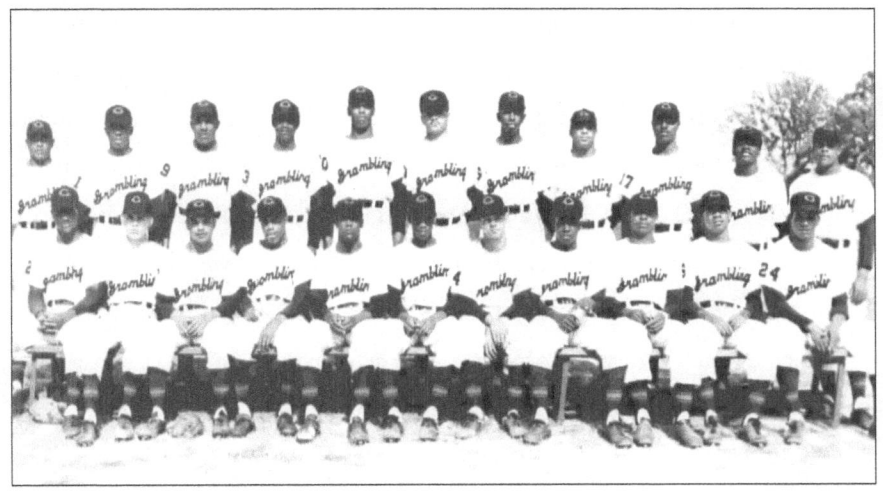

*1961 Grambling College*

On the pitching side of the NAIA's best of 1961, Clyde Parquet of Grambling ranked first in the country with a 0.66 ERA, aided by three no-hitters, while the Tiger staff finished fourth with a team ERA of 1.79. The year 1961 marked the first year the National Association of Intercollegiate Athletics awarded All-America status in baseball. Besides Clyde Parquet, the inaugural class included Tommie Agee and Southern University's Harry Levy and McVea Griffin. Southern's head coach, Bob Lee, who was nearing the end of a successful coaching career, was named Coach of the Year, and Tennessee

State University baseball alum George Altman was inducted into the NAIA Hall of Fame.

In 1962, Florida A&M became the third different HBCU school to participate in the NAIA College World Series. Going into the tournament, the Rattlers ball club had accumulated a 22-2 record, but after two straight one-run losses, it was eliminated without a victory. Florida A&M was led offensively by outfielder Phillip Malcolm, who finished fifth in the country hitting .529, and on the mound by Johnny Davis, who had an earned run average of 1.07 to finish sixth nationally. The nation's pitching leader in 1962 represented Grambling College for the second year in a row. Hillary Bossier recorded an ERA of 0.53 and earned All-American status.

For the next two years, Grambling College took part in the College World Series and each year finished as the national runner-up, losing in 1963 by the score of 2-1 to Sam Houston State Teachers College of Texas and in 1964 by the score of 3-2 to West Virginia's West Liberty State College. Grambling's third baseman Frank Garnett and catcher Donald Welch garnered All-American honors in 1963 and their teammates, pitcher Candy Robinson and outfielder John Wyatt, did likewise the following year. Robinson later became the head baseball coach at Texas Southern University and, during his 19 years at the Houston-based school, led them to NCAA Division I postseason regional tournaments in 2004 and 2008.

Another member of the 1963 and 1964 Grambling tournament teams was outfielder Johnny Jeter, who played six seasons in the Major Leagues with the Pittsburgh Pirates and three other teams. Also, in 1964, head coach R.W.E. "Prez" Jones was selected for induction into the NAIA Hall of Fame.

In 1963, Grambling College won 26 of its 28 games and led the country in team hitting with an average of .370 and in team pitching with an earned run average of 0.61. Offensively, the Tigers were led by four who each hit above the .400 mark in John Wyatt (.469), Jesse Jones (.466), Frank Garnett (.427), and Donald Welch (.405). For the third straight year, the Tigers had a pitcher with the lowest ERA in the land. Smallish Alex Pero did not yield an earned run in 61 innings pitched for an ERA of 0.00.

Southern University took the baton back from Grambling College by winning the Southwestern Athletic Conference and representing HBCUs in the following two NAIA College World Series tournaments of 1965 and 1966. The Jaguars finished third in the latter tournament to duplicate its finish in 1960.

Coming off two stellar seasons at Grambling in 1963 and 1964, Alex Pero was named an All-American in 1965, leading the country with a perfect 10-0 won-loss record, striking out 143 batters in 70 innings pitched, while recording a 0.90 ERA. Allen University of Columbia, South Carolina, led the country in team batting with an average of .368 and Grambling College finished third in team pitching with a 1.28 ERA.

The leader of the Southern University's back-to-back World Series participants in 1965 and 1966 and then again the team leader in 1967 was Pete Barnes. An outfielder for the Jaguars from 1964 to 1967, Barnes earned All-Southwestern Athletic Conference honors each of his four years in school. As a sophomore in 1965, he finished fourth in the country, hitting a robust .506 and also ranked high among the NAIA leaders in home runs with seven and runs batted in with 41. At the end of the season, Barnes became the first HBCU ballplayer ever selected in

*Pete Barnes*
*Southern University*

a Major League Baseball draft when he was picked by the Los Angeles Dodgers in the sixth round (110th player overall) of the 1965 MLB Draft. The following year, Pete Barnes was again nationally ranked, hitting .436 with eight doubles and 26 RBI. He finished his college career hitting .432 with a nation-leading eight home runs and 43 RBIs as a senior in 1967. A two-time NAIA baseball All-American in 1966 and 1967, Pete Barnes was twice awarded the same honor in football by the *Pittsburgh Courier* and then embarked upon an eleven-year professional football career.

In the spring of 1966, two more Grambling College Tigers were ranked among the NAIA's elite pitchers. Jim Jackson finished the season with a 0.82 ERA, and teammate Jophrey Brown followed up close behind with an ERA of 1.05. Brown was named an All-American in 1966, and the following year, Jim Jackson, with an even lower ERA of 0.79, earned All-American honors in 1967.

Jim Jackson was a draft pick of the Saint Louis Cardinals in 1967 and spent three years in its minor league system. Jophery Brown was drafted by the Chicago Cubs in 1966 and pitched in its organization for four seasons, including one game in the Major Leagues.

While still in school, Jophery Brown followed in the footsteps of his older brother, Calvin, as a pioneering African-American movie stuntman. After his baseball career ended, Brown devoted the rest of his professional career serving as a stunt double to such renowned actors as Morgan Freeman, Denzel Washington, James Earl Jones, and Sidney Poitier. Besides the long list of movies in which he served as a stuntman and often as the stunt coordinator, Jophery Brown had minor acting roles in over 40 television programs and films. Among his well-known movies are *Foul Play, Rocky III, Jurassic Park,* and the 1976 movie based upon a fictional black barnstorming team of the 1930s, *Bingo Long Traveling All-Stars & Motor Kings.* Filmed with several former ballplayers, besides Grambling's Jophery Brown, the cast also included former South Carolina State Bulldog James "Rico" Dawson.[4]

With the NCAA opening its door to HBCU institutions in 1956, as a reaction to the NAIA's policy of inclusion, and with many switching affiliations in the mid-1970s, 1967 would be the next to last time, to date, that a black college has qualified for the championship round of the NAIA World Series (Kentucky State University participated and was a semi-finalist in the 1976 tournament). Nonetheless, there would still be years of great team and individual performances ahead.

*1967 Grambling College*

Arguably one of the very best team performances in the history of HBCU baseball may have been that of Grambling College in 1967. The Tigers finished its regular season with a 33-1 record. The only blemish was a mid-season loss to archrival Southern University. In the NAIA tournament, Grambling placed third and finished the season with an outstanding 37-3 record. As a team, Grambling led the country in hitting with a .355 batting average, followed by Southern University and Maryland State, who tied for second with averages of .341. Six HBCU ball clubs finished in the top 13, including Texas Southern, Winston-Salem State College, and Fort Valley State, each hitting above .300. Grambling College also led the country in team pitching with an earned run average of 0.88.

Guided by school president and NAIA Coach of the Year Ralph W.E. Jones, the 1967 Grambling Tigers were led by two All-Americans, pitcher Jimmie Jackson, and infielder Ralph Garr. But Grambling was more than a two-person team. Six of the

*Ralph Garr*
*Grambling College*

regular eight position-players hit .300 or better. Included in the group was third baseman Matt Alexander who hit .377. A future Major Leaguer of nine seasons, Alexander led the Tigers with 17 stolen bases and was among the team leaders in doubles, triples and home runs.

While it was a team effort that took Grambling to the NAIA College World Series in 1967 and undoubtedly compiled its best record ever, without question, the star of the Tiger nine was Ralph Garr. His exploits were nationally heralded in the June 26, 1967 issue of *Sports Illustrated's* "Faces in the Crowd" segment. Garr's .582 average led the country in hitting, as did his 11 triples. To date, Garr holds the record for the highest single-season batting average in NCAA Division II history. During his four years at Grambling, Ralph Garr compiled a batting average of .418, and his Tigers amassed a record of 103-11. Garr was drafted in the third round of the 1967 Major League Draft by the Atlanta Braves and, during his 13 years in the big leagues, had a career batting average of .306. Among his many post-career baseball honors, Ralph Garr was inducted in 2013 into the College Baseball Hall of Fame.

*** 

In the Southwestern Athletic Conference, Grambling and Southern Universities were the dominant programs of the 1960s. The only exception was Jackson State, SWAC champion in 1968. Breaking the stronghold of those two, Jackson State won its first title after joining the conference ten years prior. However, in the decades to follow, the Tigers would join Grambling and Southern as elite baseball programs. Also, in 1968, Walter Thompson, representing fellow conference member Alcorn A&M College (now Alcorn State University), was the nation's top-ranked NCAA Division II hitter with a .508 batting average. The following year, Arthur Jones, from Shaw University and representing the CIAA, claimed the same laurels with a .580 batting average.

***

In the decade of the 1960s, after Allen University captured the initial crown, Florida A&M produced Southern Intercollegiate Athletic Conference champions from 1961 through 1966. Besides those standouts on the 1962

NAIA World Series team previously referenced, a few of the more notable Rattlers during that span included Moses McCray, Hal McRae, and Harriet Adderley.

Moses McCray pitched on Florida A&M's 1962 NAIA tournament team his freshman year and, over his four years at school, won 26 games and struck out a reported 400 batters in 320 innings pitched. Before signing a professional contract with the St. Louis Cardinals organization in 1965, McCray compiled a 9-1 record, struck out 102 batters, and had an ERA of 1.56 his senior year.[5]

Hal McRae, a FAMU Rattler in 1964 and 1965, signed professionally with the Cincinnati Reds in 1965 (the second HBCU ballplayer ever drafted) and began a 19-year career as an outfielder in Major League Baseball with the Reds and Kansas City Royals. However, while at Florida A&M, McRae was the Rattlers' regular shortstop both years. In his second season there, he hit .358 with five home runs and 28 runs batted in. Later, after his playing career ended, Hal McRae became a Major League manager in Kansas City and Tampa Bay.

*Harriet Adderley*
*Florida A&M*

In 1963, infielder Harriet Adderley was the first female to appear in a game for Florida A&M. She possibly was the first female, African-American or other, to play college varsity baseball in the United States. Like many blacks who integrated their predominantly white college baseball programs, this integrator also faced discrimination. In a 2013 interview, Adderley recalled Allen University pulling its team from the field and forfeiting a game with the Rattlers rather than play a team with a woman on it. And like a number of her college baseball playing black brethren who preceded her, Harriett Adderley too was active in seeking social change.[6] A 1966 United States Supreme Court case bearing the name *Adderley, et al. v. Florida* (based on her name being alphabetically listed atop the group of 32 petitioners), examined a 1963 protest march on a segregated Tallahassee theater during a time when similar civil rights protests in the south were escalating; the resulting incarcerations dealt with the interpretation of the First Amendment right to peaceably assemble.[7]

Ending Florida A&M's string of six straight baseball titles, Southern Intercollegiate Athletic Conference charter member Fisk University won its first league title in 1967. Rounding out the decade, South Carolina State and Tuskegee University claimed SIAC championships in 1968 and 1969, respectively.

The 1968 Bulldogs of South Carolina State topped the NAIA in hitting with a .362 team batting average. Leading hitters were all-conference selections sophomore Samuel Leaphart (.517), freshman Dennis Bailey (.474), and junior Willis Ham (.468). Catcher Dennis Bailey would be named All-SIAC in each of his four years at South Carolina State and, in 1970, was one of the NAIA's leading home run hitters, averaging .41 home runs per game. After the season, outfielder Paul Johnson was selected in the third round (45th player picked) of the 1968 June Major League Baseball Draft.

\*\*\*

In the Central Intercollegiate Athletic Association, the sixties opened and closed with North Carolina A&T being crowned CIAA champions. In between, the Aggies added two more, making four titles in the decade. Maryland State won two titles and shared one, while Shaw University won two crowns. Delaware State claimed one title outright and shared another.

In the early-1960s, leaders of the NCA&T Aggies championship teams included Sim Bowden, Jim Rouse, Cornell Gordon and pitchers James Baten and Joe Cotton.

Shortstop Sim Bowden led the Aggie squad with a batting average of .437 in 1960, followed by outfielder Jim Rouse close behind with an average of .424. Two years later, Bowden led the CIAA in hitting with an average of .516 and was named the loop's most outstanding player of 1962. Teammate Cornell Gordon, the future National Football League defensive back of eight years, hit .425 for NCA&T. Also in 1962, conference champion Delaware State was led by pitcher Al Lawson with a league-leading 1.06 earned run average and his 54 strikeouts was another league best. Lawson concluded the season being tapped as the league's most outstanding pitcher.

*Charles Stukes*
*Maryland State*

Like Johnny Sample in the late-1950s, Charles Stukes was one of several Maryland State gridders who not only went on to have pro football careers, but also starred on the Hawks baseball teams in the decade of the 1960s. Others who either led the country or were highly ranked in various statistical categories within the National Association of Intercollegiate Athletics included Harold Gray, who in 1960 lead the country in slugging with a percentage of 1.000 and was second in hitting with an average of .524, Curtis Gentry (later of the NFL's Baltimore Colts) and William Thompson (later of the Denver Broncos). In 1966, Charles Stukes, who played professional football with the Baltimore Colts, led the nation in runs batted in and finished fourth nationally in hitting with an average of .492. Teammate Pennington "Tick" Hebron finished sixth, hitting .484, and combined with Stukes to lead the Hawks to second place nationally in team hitting with a .352 batting average. Charles Stukes followed up in 1967, hitting .489, ranked fifth in the country, and was the national leader in stolen bases in 1966 and 1967. His average of 2.73 stolen bases per game in 1967 remains an NCAA Division II record.

Shaw University's two CIAA championships came in 1964 and 1965. Leading the squads, among others, were shortstop Willie French, outfielder Bobby Height, and pitcher Nathan Walton. Willie French hit .553 in 1964 to lead the CIAA and followed up by hitting .385 in 1965. Bobby Height's .414 batting average led the Bears hitters in 1965. The following year, Height was drafted by the New York Yankees. Nathan Walton, who served as Shaw

University's catcher when not pitching, was 4-0 in 1964 on the mound and in 1965 was 6-1 with an earned run average of 1.98.

The last two CIAA titles of the decade were claimed by North Carolina A&T. Leading the Aggies of the late-1960s were pitchers Wilson Stallworth and Richard Cummings, as well as outfielders Carl Hubbard and Clarence Williams, two-time All-CIAA second baseman Steve Parson and infielder Lloyd Lightfoot. In 1967, Lightfoot became the first African American to play in the prestigious Shenandoah Valley League, a summer developmental league for collegians with professional baseball potential.[8] There, he was named the league's co-MVP. After the 1968 school year, Lloyd Lightfoot was drafted by the Baltimore Orioles in the tenth round of the MLB Draft. Clarence Williamson was the nation's leader in stolen bases in 1968, with 28 for an average of 1.75 per game. In doing so, he set a present-day record by stealing nine bases (including three of home) in one game. The following year, Clarence Williamson finished fourth nationally in stolen bases and led the country that year in triples averaging .29 per game.

Al Bumbry of Virginia State was another star performer at a CIAA member institution in the decade of the 1960s. Bumbry, who came to Virginia State as a heralded high school basketball player, led the Trojan varsity on the hardwood for three years. After his final basketball season, Bumbry was recruited to play baseball in 1968 and hit .378 while earning All-CIAA honors. Following his success on the diamond at Virginia State, Al Bumbry played 13 seasons of professional baseball in the Major Leagues, primarily with the Baltimore Orioles.

Joining Al Bumbry in the outfield of the Central Intercollegiate Athletic Association's all-conference team of 1968 was Marty Miller of Norfolk State.

Marty Miller played baseball at Norfolk State from 1965 through 1968 and graduated with a bachelor's degree in mathematics in 1969. As a freshman, Miller hit .357; the following year, as a sophomore, he raised his batting average to .380. During his final two seasons at Norfolk State, Miller hit .438 with eight doubles, two triples, and three home runs as a junior in 1967. He then concluded his college career hitting .409 as a senior while earning NCAA College Division All-American honors.

Following a short professional baseball career with the Minnesota Twins, Marty Miller returned to Norfolk State in 1972 as an assistant baseball coach. The following year, he was promoted to head coach and kept the position for the next 33 years. During that time, Marty Miller had an overall coaching record of 718-544-3 with 17 CIAA conference titles. Miller led his teams to 12 postseason appearances and was named the CIAA Coach of the Year 15 times. He produced six All-Americans, and 22 of his former players signed pro contracts.

\*\*\*

The last conference, which historically composed one of the top four baseball-playing conferences, the Midwestern Athletic Conference, was in the final phase of its existence. With membership dwindling via school migration to other conferences, the MWAA finally ceased to exist after the 1966 school season.

Beginning in 1969, representatives from several CIAA and SIAC member institutions, who shared a similar desire to achieve Division I status in athletics, met in discussion and ultimately agreed in December 1970 to form the Mid-Eastern Athletic Conference. Charter members were former CIAA schools Howard University, Morgan State, Delaware State, University of Maryland Eastern Shore, North Carolina A&T, North Carolina Central, and from the SIAC, South Carolina State. In 1980, the MEAC joined the SWAC in gaining NCAA Division I status.

In the early-1970s, Southern University (in 1970 and 1972) and Jackson State University (in 1971 and 1973) traded Southwestern Athletic Conference championships annually. In the Southern Intercollegiate Athletic Conference, four different teams won titles (Alabama A&M in 1970, South Carolina State University in 1971, Alabama State in 1972, and Tuskegee in 1973). Central Intercollegiate Athletic Association championships were shared in 1970 by North Carolina A&T and Shaw University and in 1971 by Delaware State,

North Carolina A&T, and Virginia State. Hampton Institute claimed the CIAA title outright in 1972, and Virginia State did likewise in 1973. Sadly, following one of its most successful seasons, baseball at Hampton Institute was suspended in 1972 due to financial difficulties. The Pirates have yet to step back onto a ball diamond since.

The neophyte Mid-Eastern Athletic Conference awarded Howard University its first championship in 1972. In coming to the league from the CIAA, the Bison of Howard had won only one prior title in the nearly 40 years that its former conference crowned baseball champions. And in 1973, the MEAC championship was awarded to South Carolina State University, which had previously claimed SIAC titles in 1968 and 1971.

The leaders of Southern University's 1970 SWAC championship team were shortstop Lee Richard and third baseman Henry Baker. Richard earned NAIA All-American honors and was named All-American by the *Sporting News*, which selected all-star teams from 1964 to 1992. Lee Richard was drafted in the first round of the 1970 June Regular Phase by the Chicago White Sox (sixth player picked overall) and played all or part of five seasons in the majors between 1971 and 1976.

Henry Baker, like Lee Richard, was a high Major League Baseball Draft pick in 1970 but did not sign until 1971, when he was drafted in the third round by the Boston Red Sox. In 1970, Baker finished third in the country, hitting .487 for the Southern University Jaguars.

When Southern University wasn't winning baseball crowns, Jackson State was claiming titles and doing it at the plate and on the base paths. The Tigers led the National Association of Intercollegiate Athletics in team hitting in 1970 (.369), 1971 (.389), and again in 1973 (.372). Individually, outfielder Russell Stephen finished fourth in the country by hitting .479 in 1970 and first baseman Isadore Peyton finished sixth, hitting .471. Outfielder Cliff Hayes led the country stealing (a then NAIA record) 45 bases. Peyton ranked third in the country the following year by hitting .500, while teammate James Marshall finished fifth, hitting .485. Jackson State's third team batting crown of the early 1970s was again spearheaded by leading hitter James Marshall, who finished third in the country with a .495 batting average in 1973. Challenging Marshall for SWAC hitting laurels was Steve Henderson of Prairie View A&M. A fifth-round draft pick in 1974 of the Cincinnati Reds and 12-year Major Leaguer, Henderson hit .488 in 1973, the fifth-best in the NAIA that year.

In 1973, Robert Braddy, a former Jackson State all-conference pitcher in 1962 and 1963, took over the head coaching position at his alma mater and began a 28-year coaching career at the school. Over the years, Braddy accumulated a record of 824-546, 12 conference titles, and coached 52 student-athletes who signed professional baseball contracts. In 2003, Robert Braddy became the first African American to be inducted into the American Baseball Coaches Association Hall of Fame, and in 2016 was inducted into the National College Baseball Hall of Fame.

*1972 Howard University*
*with Coach Chuck Hinton (front row center)*

Howard University's MEAC championship in 1972 was facilitated by first-year head coach, ex-Major Leaguer Chuck Hinton, and team leaders catcher Glenn Harris, infielder Eugene "Rock" Newman, outfielder Robert Woodland, outfielder-pitcher Sylvester Wright, and pitcher Steve Powell, among others.

As a college coach, Hinton upgraded the Howard University baseball program by taking on anyone and everyone, no matter where it took his team. The Bison faced premier NCAA Division I baseball programs even though his program was only in its own Division I infancy. On his way to 471 career victories, Hinton's Bison faced national powers such as Arizona State, Clemson, the University of Miami (FL), North Carolina, Wichita State, Georgia Tech, and South Carolina. When Howard University entered the newly formed Mid-Eastern Athletic Conference, Hinton's teams were dominant, winning six titles, which included the very first MEAC title. Though only two of his former players became major leaguers (Milt Thompson and Jerry Davis), 13 others were drafted and played professionally.

Besides his coaching, Hinton continued his relationship with Major League Baseball and was a founding father in 1982 of the Major League Baseball Players Alumni Association which, among other goals, promotes baseball to young people and raises money for charity.

In 1972, two freshmen, one who attended Southern University and the second who attended North Carolina A&T, began prolific college careers that

*Danny Goodwin*
*Southern University*

years later landed each a spot in the National College Baseball Hall of Fame.

Danny Goodwin came to Southern University after turning down a professional baseball contract as the number one overall pick in the 1971 Major League Baseball Draft following his senior year of high school. He left Southern being the only individual in MLB draft history twice selected number one overall when the Minnesota Twins chose Goodwin first in the 1975 draft. During his four years as a catcher at Southern University, Danny Goodwin was a three-time All-American, twice at the NAIA level and once at the NCAA level. In 1975, he was selected National Player of the Year by the *Sporting News*. Goodwin had a .394 career batting average and compiled 20 home runs and

166 runs batted in.

Besides Danny Goodwin, the second bright rookie star of 1972 was Al Holland, who pitched at North Carolina A&T from 1972 through 1975 before beginning a 10-year Major League Baseball career. Holland threw four no-hitters in college, one in each year he pitched. His no-hitter in 1972 against North Carolina Central included 25 strikeouts. As a freshman, Al Holland led the nation in strikeouts (143) and was second in earned run average (0.54). The following year, the Aggies final one in the NAIA, he recorded an earned run average of 1.03 and added another 102 strikeouts. Though North Carolina A&T moved to NCAA status, Holland continued to dominate the competition during the next two years with a 0.95 earned run average and 105 strikeouts in

*Al Holland*
*North Carolina A&T*

1974 and a nation-leading 0.26 earned run average and 118 strikeouts in 1975. Al Holland was a two-time NAIA All-American in 1972 and 1973.

***

Tuskegee University, in 1969, was the first HBCU baseball program to participate in an NCAA Division II postseason tournament, which was established the year before. The Golden Tigers appeared again in 1972 and then became the first HBCU to win an NCAA postseason tournament game by defeating Bellarmine College, 6-4 in the 1973 South Regional.

The '69 squad was led by All-SIAC performers, second baseman Obeadiah Threadgill, shortstop Woody Draper, who hit .378, and pitcher Kenneth Soares, who had a won-loss record of 10-3 with a 1.35 earned run average. Outfielder Kenneth Threadgill led the team in hitting with a .413 batting average.

In 1972, the 21-8 Tuskegee University made its second postseason appearance but was eliminated in regional play with two straight losses. Junior third baseman Richard Shaw (.422), senior first baseman Lorenzo Ogden

(.415), and freshman outfielder Mac Shivers (.409) were the team's leading hitters, and each earned All-SIAC honors. Joining them on the all-conference squad was sophomore pitcher Lucious McDade, owner of a 5-0 record and a 1.12 earned run average.

*1972 Tuskegee Institute*

The 1973 Tuskegee team finished the season with a record of 22-7 with one tie. All-SIAC third baseman Richard Shaw was the team's leading hitter with a batting average of .440. He also led the country with 42 stolen bases and was drafted by the Saint Louis Cardinals at the end of the season. Fellow teammates and All-SIAC honorees, shortstop Curtis Crump hit .426, and outfielder McArthur Shivers (who later coached Tuskegee in 2002-2003 and 2006-2008) hit an even .400. Freshmen Tyrone Phinnessee and Roy Lee Jackson, who would have huge careers at Tuskegee, also contributed in 1973. Jackson led a strong contingent of SIAC pitchers that year with a 7-1 record, 0.87 earned run average, and 131 strikeouts, which ranked second in the country. Steve Barlow of Morehouse finished second in the country with an earned run average of 0.37 and led the nation in strikeouts per nine innings pitched with an average of 16.5 strikeouts. Joining the two 1973 all-conference pitchers was Larry Bradford of Clark College in Atlanta, Georgia, a three-time All-SIAC pitcher and conference Pitcher of the Year in 1972. Bradford was drafted in the 19th round of the 1973 Major League Draft and played with the Atlanta Braves for four years.

At the conclusion of the 1973 regular season, Tuskegee University head coach, Jim Martin, arranged for a game versus an elite group of Southern Intercollegiate Athletic Conference ballplayers in what was to be the only such "all-star" game of its kind in SIAC baseball history. According to Tuskegee centerfielder Harold Michael Harvey, who scored the winning run and made the run-saving catch to end the game, the contest was organized to enhance Tuskegee's chance to receive a regional tournament bid in the days when there were no automatic bids for HBCU conference champions.[9]

*Roy Lee Jackson*
*Tuskegee Institute*

Tuskegee University's Roy Lee Jackson was not only the ace of the Golden Tigers' pitching staff, but was also its regular designated hitter and one of its leading hitters. In 1974, Jackson's .404 batting average placed him second on the team to teammate and the nation's leading hitter, Ty Phinnessee. The following year, Jackson led the Tigers in hitting with a .431 average, ranking fifteenth nationally in the NCAA Division II (finishing twentieth in the country was Ty Phinnessee with a .418 batting average). Pinenessee led the country in 1975 with 18 doubles, and Jackson's .718 slugging average finished eighth nationally. Roy Lee Jackson was even more impressive on the mound in 1975 than in 1974, with his 0.98 ERA and nation-leading 160 strikeouts. After the season, Jackson signed a contract with the New York Mets and played 10 seasons in the Majors with four different teams.

Looking back, the decade of the seventies is sometimes characterized as a "pivot of change" for America politically, economically, and socially.[10] While the changes within the HBCU baseball community understandably had no global significance, the ramifications of change were equally impactful. A significant number of schools with either NAIA ties or dual membership in both the NAIA and NCAA were dropping NAIA affiliations and migrating to the NCAA. As well, 1974 marked a significant change throughout all of college baseball... the transition from wooden bats to ones made of aluminum, implemented in order to minimize the escalating cost associated with the less durable wood bats.

---

[1] Jackson, Marion E. "Sports of the World." *Atlanta Daily World*, June 4, 1960, 5.

[2] Nicholson, Collie J. "Grambling Tigers Win 24 to 2." *Ruston Daily Leader* (Ruston, LA), March 15, 1961, 19.

[3] "UA Honors Dr. Archie Wade, UA's First African American Faculty Member." *The University of Alabama*. June 13, 2013. https://www.ua.edu/news/2013/06/ua-honors-dr-archie-wade-uas-first-african-american-faculty-member/.

[4] Costello, Rory. "Jophery Brown." Society for American Baseball Research | Society for American Baseball Research. Last modified August 2017. https://sabr.org/bioproj/person/8107c727.

[5] *The Philadelphia Tribune*. "St. Louis Cards Sign A&M Hurler." July 17, 1965, 15.

[6] Abrams, Michael. "Harriett Adderley Went to Bat 50 Years Ago in Civil Rights Protest that Resulted in Landmark Case." The Tallahassee News. Last modified September 25, 2013. http://www.thetallahasseenews.com/index.php/site/article/harriett_adderley_went_to_bat_50_years_ago_in_civil_rights_protest_that_res.

[7] Ibid.

[8] *Chicago Defender*. "Orioles Tab A&T Star." July 6, 1968, 17.

[9] Harvey, Harold M. *Freaknik Lawyer: A Memoir On the Craft of Resistance*, 78-79. Atlanta: Cascade Publishing House, 2019.

[10] "The Many Pivots of the 1970s." Visualizing Wonder | Building and Exploring a Database of Fairy Tales in TV. Last modified December 19, 2015

# CHAPTER 7

# Integration Takes Hold in the South

## (1970 and beyond)

Though only a handful of colleges in the south had integrated baseball programs prior, the seventies ushered in an era of desegregation at southern institution baseball programs. It also marked the time when the first African Americans became head baseball coaches at the NCAA Division I level.

In 1970, James Lee Robinson, a dual-sport performer (football and baseball), integrated the baseball program at Southern Methodist University in Texas. That same year, Henry LeBoyd integrated Louisiana State University baseball and Ansel (Jackie) Brown, another dual-sport performer in football and baseball, did likewise at the University of South Carolina. The following year, Mickey Hickerson integrated baseball at the University of North Carolina, Derek Bryant, who later played professionally in the Oakland Athletics organization, integrated the University of Kentucky's program, and W. D. Jennings integrated baseball at the Citadel in South Carolina.

The 1971-1972 school year welcomed a major barrier-breaking event: hiring the first two African Americans to lead NCAA Division I baseball programs. Both Dave Baker and Wycliffe "Bubba" Morton were hired within months of each other in 1971 to head the baseball programs at Creighton University and the University of Washington, respectively, for the 1972 spring college season.[1]

Dave Baker grew up in Manhattan, Kansas, and as a youth saw first-hand the desegregation of his hometown's baseball program at Kansas State. Shortly after graduating from Emporia State University (then named Kansas State Teachers College), Baker was hired to assist his former Emporia coach, Larry Cochell, who by then had become the head coach at Creighton University. When Cochell left Creighton in 1971, Dave Baker was selected to lead the Blue Jays. Baker spent six years at Creighton University before moving to Kansas State University, where he was the head coach for six more years. Dave Baker concluded his college coaching career, spending 12 more years at NAIA-level Bacone College in Oklahoma.

Bubba Morton had been an infielder at Howard University in the mid-fifties. But when he signed with the Detroit Tigers representing the team's third-ever African American, Morton began a seven-season career as a Major League outfielder. In 1972, Bubba Morton became the head coach at the University of Washington and remained there for five years.

*Dave Baker*
*Creighton University*

*Bubba Morton*
*University of Washington*

Also, in 1972, former Shaw University catcher turned Major League outfielder Chuck Hinton took over NCAA Division II Howard University and would then guide them into an NCAA Division I HBCU powerhouse.

Miles McAfee, in 1973, became the third black head coach at a Division I program when he took over the reins at Saint Mary's College in California. McAfee, who had been a star football and baseball athlete at Tuskegee University in the mid-1950s, played professionally in the Pittsburgh Pirates organization and was a professional scout for the Pirates for 12 years before being tapped by Saint Mary's.

*Condredge Holloway*
*University of Tennessee*

Condredge Holloway, born and raised on the campus of Alabama State University in Montgomery, has the distinction of being the first African-American member of the University of Tennessee baseball team in 1972 and the first black football quarterback in the Southeastern Conference (SEC) later that fall. In his three seasons as a starter on the football team (1972-1974), Holloway directed the Tennessee Volunteers to three postseason bowl games and an overall record of 25-9 with two ties. Condredge Holloway left the Knoxville, Tennessee campus and then played 13 seasons in the Canadian Football League, earning league MVP honors in 1982 and ultimately a place in the CFL Hall of Fame.

As impressive of a career Condredge Holloway had in football, his best sport may have been baseball. A first-round draft choice of the Montreal Expos in 1971 (fourth pick overall) out of high school, Holloway earned All-SEC and All-American honors as a shortstop while at Tennessee and finished his college career with a .353 batting average. Holloway's 27-game hitting streak remains a school record and, years later, was named to the University of Tennessee's All-Twentieth Century Baseball Team.

The same year that Condredge Holloway integrated baseball at the University of Tennessee, about two hours west on I-40 at David Lipscomb College (now David Lipscomb University) in Nashville, Jacob Robinson joined the Bisons' initial integrator from 1969, Ted Jamison, in Lipscomb's outfield. The two were vital components of David Lipscomb's runner-up finish at the 1972 NAIA College World Series. After graduation, Jacob Robinson coached baseball at Tennessee State University, Kentucky State University, and then Wiley College.[2]

Of the three service academies, the U.S. Air Force Academy in Colorado was the first to field an integrated baseball team when Clarence Smith played for the Falcons in 1972. Five years later, both the U. S. Military Academy and the U. S. Naval Academy integrated their programs in 1977, Patrick Landry with the Army Silver Knights and Warren Lewis with the Navy Midshipmen.

In 1973, Clarence Poitier integrated baseball at the University of Miami in Coral Gables, Florida, and further north, but still in the deep southeast, Georgia Southern University baseball was integrated by Carl Person. In his first season after transferring to Georgia Southern, Person participated in the 1973 NCAA Division I World Series and made the all-tournament team.

Freshman outfielder Otis Foster integrated High Point University in 1973. He would become an NAIA All-American and later was a first-round selection (15th player selected overall) of the Boston Red Sox in the 1975 Major League Draft. During his three-year college career, Foster hit 60 home runs.

Twenty years after the NCAA College World Series was integrated by University of Michigan ballplayers Don Eaddy and Frank Howell, two African-American arbiters umpired college world series games for the first time. Bob Motley, who had worked college games in what is now the Big 12 Conference, was named chief umpire for the 1973 series and his crew included Gene Agnes, another African American who had been an early integrating umpire in the Western Athletic Conference.

*From 1973 College World Series souvenir program*

Ever the showman, Bob Motley had a distinguished career as a baseball umpire at many levels, though never making it to the Major Leagues. He began umpiring in the amateur Ban Johnson Summer League in Kansas, its first African-American umpire. In 1948, Motley began a decade-long career in the Negro American League and often traveled with the famous Kansas City Monarchs. Then, in 1957, Motley was invited to and became the first African-American to graduate from the Al Somers Umpire School, the most highly regarded of its day. From there, Bob Motley worked his way up to the Pacific Coast League. He became the league's second full-time African-American umpire in 1958, following Emmet Ashford in 1954. Motley was a lifelong fan of baseball and, in 1990, helped establish the Negro Leagues Baseball Museum, based in Kansas City, Missouri.[3]

Notre Dame, based in South Bend, Indiana, where Branch Rickey supposedly gained motivation in 1903 to someday integrate professional baseball years later, first accepted African-American students around the same time Jackie Robinson integrated Major League Baseball. However, the baseball program's own color line was not broken until 1974, when football letterman Ron Goodman joined the Fighting Irish baseball team. That same year, Virginia Tech, Vanderbilt University, and the Universities of Alabama and South Alabama also integrated their baseball programs.

In 1975, Jerry Gaines of Western Carolina University added baseball to the list of sports he excelled at for the Catamounts. It not only made him the first black baseball player there, but also earned him his third small-college All-America honor, adding to the football and track laurels he had already achieved.

Transfer Ellis Meredith integrated baseball at South Carolina's Clemson University in 1975 after his former school, South Carolina State University, unexpectedly terminated baseball before the 1974-1975 school year. The following year, the University of Maryland, University of Virginia, University of Arkansas, Auburn University, and the University of Mississippi all saw their baseball programs welcome their first African Americans in 1976. That same year, Larry Doby Jr. (whose father integrated the American League three months after Jackie Robinson integrated the National League and whose uncle, Ben Veal, integrated baseball at Seton Hall in 1950) integrated baseball at Duke University.

Though some schools were latecomers integrating their baseball programs, a number had long before abolished the policy of barring African Americans from enrolling. For example, the first African-American baseball player at the University of Florida was Jim Watkins in 1968, but the first black student enrolled at Florida, ten years prior, in 1958. In the early 1960s, the city of Nashville, Tennessee, was a hotbed of civil rights activity. The focal point was a series of nonviolent sit-ins in early 1960 initially aimed at integrating the town's segregated lunch counters. At Nashville's Vanderbilt University, the first undergraduate African Americans were admitted in 1964, but the baseball team remained segregated until Steve Chandler joined the team ten years later. The University of Mississippi desegregated in 1962 with the contentious, well-publicized admission of James Meredith, and in 1976, the Ole Miss baseball program included Roy Coleman, its first black ballplayer.

| *Larry Doby Jr.* | *Roy Coleman* | *Andre Robertson* | *Steve Chandler* |
|---|---|---|---|
| *Duke University* | *University of* | *University of Texas* | *Vanderbilt* |
| | *Mississippi* | | *University* |

Like so many others, the University of Texas reluctantly integrated its undergraduate population in 1956, and in 1977 Andre Robertson became the Longhorns' first African-American baseball letterman. Mississippi State University recruited its first two black ballplayers in 1980 (Glenn Young, who later was a wide receiver in the National Football League, and Harold Myers). However, the school's first African-American students were accepted 15 years before, in 1965. Likewise, the University of Georgia's baseball team was integrated in 1980 by Guy Stargell. But the first blacks enrolled in school nearly 20 years prior, in 1961.

By 1985, most all historically white institutions had integrated baseball programs. For the first time in College World Series history, one school featured five black starters in its lineup when the 1985 University of Arkansas series entrant included All-American outfielder Mike Loggins, outfielder Norm Roberts, shortstop Derrick Richardson, outfielder Mark Jackson and second baseman Ellis Roby.

*University of Arkansas African-American Starters in the 1985 College World Series*

*(from left are Mike Loggins, Norm Roberts, Derrick Richardson, Mark Jackson and Ellis Roby)*

During this era of integration, both the Southeastern Athletic Conference (SEC) and the now-defunct Southwest Conference (SWC) integrated their umpiring corps. One of the earliest in the SEC was Eddie Payton, who, along with his National Football League Hall of Fame brother Walter, played football at Jackson State. Eddie Payton also played in the NFL and later became Jackson State's longtime golf coach. Besides becoming an SEC arbiter in 1983, Payton also umpired in both the Sun Belt Conference and in the Southwestern Athletic Conference.[4]

Among the earliest umpires to integrate the SWC were John Winters and Jacob Robinson in 1989. In his 27 years as a baseball

*Eddie Payton (l) and Dr. John Winters (r)*

umpire, Dr. Winters also worked in the Southland Conference and Mid-Continent Conference (now known as the Summit League) before becoming a college professor. Winters was the first supervisor of umpires in the NCAA Division II Lone Star Conference and was also named one of 14 Big 12 Conference umpire observers.[5] Jacob Robinson, one of the earliest integrators of David Lipscomb University baseball and former head coach at a trio of HBCUs, like John Winters, also umpired in the Southland Conference.[6]

---

[1] "Creighton Tabs Baker Head Baseball Coach." The Manhattan Mercury, [Manhattan, KS], 7 June 1971, p. 7

[1] "Bubba Morton Washington Coach." *Colorado Springs Gazette-Telegraph*, 11 Dec. 1971, p. B3.

[2] Jamison, Ted. Facebook Messenger Interview. Nashville, TN November 9, 2020.

[3] Motley, Bob, and Byron Motley. *Ruling Over Monarchs, Giants & Stars: Umpiring in the Negro Leagues & Beyond.* Sports Publishing LLC, 2007.

[4] Payton, Eddie. Phone Interview. Jackson, MS October 20, 2020.

[5] Winters, Dr. John. Phone Interview. Muskogee, OK November 10, 2020.

[6] Robinson, Jacob. Phone Interview. Marshall, TX November 10, 2020.

# CHAPTER 8

# The Current Era of the Aluminum Bat

## (1974-present)

The current chapter in the history of HBCU baseball can be defined by the introduction of aluminum bats into college baseball in 1974. Metal bats were intended to eliminate the necessity and expense of replacing wood bats, which frequently broke, while replicating the dynamics of wood. However, advancements in the development of aluminum bats proved them to dramatically outperform wood ones. After years of record-breaking hitting performances, a series of bat standards were implemented, beginning in 1999, to make bats perform more "wood-like".

The adjustment to aluminum in 1974 proved to be no problem for three ballplayers at HBCU schools, Artis Stanfield of North Carolina A&T, Tyrone Phinnessee of Tuskegee Institute, and Nate Chapman of Jarvis Christian College. Stanfield, a junior, topped the NCAA Division I national hitting charts in 1974 with a .500 batting average. In NCAA Division II, sophomore Ty Phinnessee was the leading batter in the country, hitting .482, and junior Nate Chapman topped the NAIA by hitting .551. Artis Stanfield also won the individual stolen base crown stealing an average of 1.32 bases per game in

1974. In 1975, Nate Chapman was named a National Association of Intercollegiate Athletics All-American and then became a third-round draft pick of the New York Yankees.

*Nate Chapman*
*Jarvis Christian College*

*Artis Stanfield*
*North Carolina A&T*

*Ty Phinnessee*
*Tuskegee Institute*

\*\*\*

In the Mid-Eastern Athletic Conference, expectations were high at South Carolina State for the 1974 season. A program that won SIAC titles in 1968 and 1971, and the MEAC title in 1973, the Bulldogs welcomed back all-conference selections John Hargrove and dual-position pitcher/outfielder Eugene Richards, who hit .450 the year prior. Also returning were 1972 NAIA All-American catcher Ben Samuels and his football teammate, outfielder Donnie Shell. Newcomers to the team included junior college transfer Ellis Meredith and first-year catcher Willie Aikens. Though the Bulldogs fell short of retaining its MEAC title, falling one game behind both Howard University and North Carolina A&T, South Carolina State finished with a respectable 20-7 record. Individually, Willie Aikens led the team, hitting .473, which placed him second nationally in the NCAA Division I classification behind NCA&T's Artis Stanfield, followed by Gene Richards with a .419 batting average (19th highest in the country) and Ellis Meredith at .397 (40th highest). Aikens recorded a team-high 11 home runs (placing him second nationally) and 50 RBIs. Ben Samuels, the former catcher who moved to third base to accommodate Aikens behind the plate, contributed six home runs. On the mound, Gene Richards had a 7-1 record with an earned run average of 2.79 and 89 strikeouts in 69 2/3 innings pitched, which ranked seventh in the country, averaging 11.2 strikeouts per game.

Following the '74 spring season at South Carolina State, both Willie Aikens and Gene Richards were in the midst of impressive summers playing in high-level amateur leagues and were looking forward to reclaiming a MEAC title in 1975. That's when they got an abbreviated, but dramatic, lesson on a 1972 federal amendment to the Civil Rights Act of 1964. The amendment, commonly known as Title IX, but formally named the Patsy T. Mink Equal Opportunity in Education Act, provided that "no person in the United States shall, on the basis of sex, be excluded from participation in, be denied the benefits of, or be subjected to discrimination under any education program or activity receiving Federal financial assistance."[1]

*Gene Richards*
*South Carolina State*

*Willie Aikens*
*South Carolina State*

Title IX required gender parity in athletic opportunities at federally funded educational institutions. At some schools, this equity meant adding a sport or sports for women by reallocating funds to meet equity. At some, reaching gender parity in athletic participation meant eliminating one or more men's sports. At South Carolina State, with funding being a stumbling block, it was the latter. It was announced in July 1974 that the school would eliminate its baseball program.

Team member Donnie Shell was a senior, and cutting the program had no impact on his athletic future. Shell signed a football contract with the Pittsburgh Steelers as an undrafted defensive back and had a very successful fourteen-year pro career as a member of Pittsburgh's famed "Steel Curtain" defense. In 1998, Shell was inducted into the College Football Hall of Fame and, in early-2020, was voted into the Professional Football Hall of Fame.

Teammate Ellis Meredith still had eligibility remaining and chose to transfer to Clemson University, where he integrated the Tigers' baseball program.

Caught off guard by South Carolina State's move, Gene Richards and Willie Aikens were left with their plans in limbo. As it turned out, opportunities were waiting to be seized less than six months later. Until 1986, Major League Baseball held a draft in January as well as the June draft, which continues today. On January 9, 1975, the baseball community was surprised to learn that two little know student-athletes from the same small school, a school that also few knew of, were the first two ballplayers selected in the January Phase of the 1975 Major League Baseball Draft. Once Gene Richards' name was called first by the San Diego Padres and Willie Aikens' name was called second by the California Angles, it marked the first and only time to date that ballplayers from the same school were selected with the first two picks in a regular phase of the Major League Baseball draft.

Both Gene Richards and Willie Aikens enjoyed eight-year careers in Major League Baseball. Richards spent all but one year with the San Diego Padres and the other with the San Francisco Giants, while Aikens split time with the California Angels, Kansas City Royals, and Toronto Blue Jays. Aikens later played six seasons in the Mexican League, where he was a prolific hitter and fan favorite.

In the Mid-Eastern Athletic Conference, with South Carolina State no longer supporting baseball, Howard University claimed MEAC titles from 1975 through 1977. Leading the Bison during this period were infielders Michael Banks, who doubled as a quarterback on the football team, and Burt Herron, who, during those three seasons, stole 116 bases. In 1975, Edward

Holland, Winford Copeland, and Herron finished second, third, and fourth nationally in NCAA Division I stolen bases. On the mound, John Chestnut and Gene Fleet were aces of the pitching staffs. Chestnut threw opening day no-hitters in 1974 and 1975, and in 1976 Gene Fleet threw an impressive two-hitter in a complete game victory versus a Florida State University team that finished the season ranked fourteenth in the country.

From 1978 through 1983, the MEAC did not sponsor conference play because of a depleted number of participating schools. Nonetheless, member schools fielding baseball teams continued to play non-conference schedules. Once the MEAC reinstated conference play, Howard University picked up where it left off, winning the title in 1984.

*1979 Jackson State University*

\*\*\*

In the Southwestern Athletic Conference, Southern University and Jackson State continued to dominate the league, just as each had done in the early 1970s. Southern won titles in 1974-1976 and 1979, while Jackson State claimed SWAC crowns in 1977 and 1978. The Southern University champions of 1974 and 1975 were led by All-American Danny Goodwin and another future major leaguer, Joseph Pittman, who had a team-high .446 batting average in 1975. Southern University made its only NCAA Division II regional tournament appearance that year and was one victory shy of advancing to the College World Series.

In 1976, Mississippi Valley State University had one of its better conference finishes, going 12-5. As a team, the Delta Devils led the country in hitting with a season's average of .370. Individually, Willie Powell won the hitting crown with a nation's best .563 batting average, followed by his teammates Richard Mobley and Roy Hazzle, who finished fourth and fifth, respectively, with averages of .535 and .526. MVSU recorded a team earned run average of 1.79 to also lead the country, and individually, Fredrick Akon's 0.71 earned run average ranked second lowest nationally.

Following Danny Goodwin and Joe Pittman, the next Southern University Jaguar star in a long line of great hitters was Michael Woods Sr. (father of Michael Jr., who also starred at Southern University and became a first-round MLB draft selection of the Detroit Tigers in 2001). The senior Woods established a then NCAA Division II record in 1978 by collecting at least one base hit in 45 consecutive games.[2]

Jackson State's championship teams were led offensively by Huey Gayden, Kevin Hinds, Kelvin Moore, and Mike Godley. In 1978, the Tigers finished with a 52-12 record led by designated hitter Huey Gayden's .412 batting average and first baseman Kelvin Moore's 17 home runs. In 1977, Moore belted 13 home runs and led the team with a .388 batting average. On the mound, Jim McBride recorded 103 strikeouts while going 10-2 in 1977. The following year, he finished with a 1.54 earned run average, winning another 10 games against a lone loss. Fellow starting pitcher Charlie Scott also recorded a 10-1 record in 1978.

***

From 1973 through 1975, with fifteen baseball-playing institutions, the Southern Intercollegiate Athletic Conference divided competition into the Eastern and Western Divisions. Each division held a round-robin playoff, and then the division winners faced off for the SIAC championship. Tuskegee claimed the 1973 title by defeating Morehouse; in 1974, Bethune-Cookman bested Tuskegee for the crown. The following year, division champs Morehouse and Fisk University shared the 1975 title when weather halted the tournament.[3]

Beginning in 1976, the SIAC restructured its two baseball divisions based on schools' NCAA-designated classification. For the next three years, divisional champs continued to face off to determine the SIAC title. That first year, Division II Champion Bethune-Cookman beat Division III Champion Miles College for the title. However, in 1977 Division III turned the table on Division II when Savannah State University topped Bethune-Cookman to win the conference title.[4] Leading the Tigers of Savannah State was two-time All-SAIC catcher Lee Blitch. That year, LeMoyne-Owen College outfielder Anthony Johnson led the entire NCAA Division III in hitting with a .574 average, home runs per game with an average of .41 per game, and slugging percentage with an average of 1.096. He was also selected as an All-American in 1977.

In 1978, Florida A&M topped Morehouse, and then in 1979, the SIAC dispensed with pitting the two divisional leaders against each other and named a champion in each of the two divisions. In 1979, Tuskegee claimed the Division II crown, while Ft. Valley State claimed the Division III title.[5]

*1978 Florida A&M University*

Leading the FAMU Rattlers' title team of 1978 was a talented group of three freshmen, two of whom had famous baseball fathers. The top hitter on the team was Bill Lucas Jr., whose father, of the same name, was the first African-American front office executive to obtain the status of general manager in Major League Baseball. Bill Lucas, the son, led the Rattlers' offense, hitting .394. Lary Aaron, son of Major League Baseball Hall of Famer Hank Aaron, and James LeCount were the other two freshmen stars of the 1978 Florida A&M team. LeCount finished a close second to Lucas, hitting .390. Upperclassmen Danny Pendleton, FAMU's third baseman, and pitchers Robert Lavine and Melvin Gilliam, who led the NCAA Division I pitchers nationally in 1979 averaging 12.5 strikeouts per game, also paced the 1978 Rattler nine.

The 1979 SIAC crown of Tuskegee Institute began a reign that lasted late into the 1980s. The title run of nine straight was orchestrated by head coach James "Jim" Martin.

Martin was the head baseball coach at Tuskegee Institute from 1971 through 1982 and from 1984 to 1988. During his tenure at Tuskegee, Coach Martin had an overall record of 291-121 with three ties and was honored as the Southern Intercollegiate Athletic Conference (SIAC) Baseball Coach of the Year ten times. Martin took eight of his fifteen teams to NCAA Division II Regional Tournaments and sent nine players to Major League Baseball. Among them were Roy Lee Jackson, Ken Howell, and Alan Mills.

*Andre Dawson*
*Florida A&M University*

Another notable ballplayer from the Southern Intercollegiate Athletic Conference in the first decade of the aluminum bat era and one of the greatest HBCU alums to play in Major League Baseball was Andre Dawson. Dawson, who hit .352 as a junior in 1975, earned All-SIAC First-Team honors that year after claiming a spot on the second team the year before. In 1974, Andre Dawson finished third in the NCAA Division II rankings in doubles with an average of .41 per game (11 doubles) and 10th in slugging with a .695 average. His FAMU squad collected a monumental victory in 1974 against the University of Miami Hurricanes, which finished its season ranked second in the country and runner-up to the University of Southern California in the College World Series. During his three years at Florida A&M, Dawson led squads to big wins in three of the four games played against the perennial national power Miami Hurricanes, and the Rattlers' doubleheader sweep of Miami in 1973 was one of the highlights of his college years.

Dawson was selected by the Montreal Expos in the 11th round (250th player picked overall) of the 1975 Major League Baseball Draft. He had a brilliant 21-year career, primarily with the Expos and the Chicago Cubs. His efforts were rewarded when, in 2010, Andre Dawson was chosen for enshrinement into the Major League Baseball Hall of Fame in Cooperstown, New York. In 2019, Dawson received the additional honor of selection into the National College Baseball Hall of Fame.

While Florida A&M's Andre Dawson was honing his skills in college for a career in professional baseball, Greg "Boomer" Wells was doing the same at Albany State College in Georgia. In 1974, Wells was one of the nation's "college division" leaders in hitting with a .420 batting average and seven home runs, and like Dawson, was an All-SIAC pick in 1975. But unlike Andre Dawson, who built a hall of fame career in Major League Baseball, Greg Wells' stardom came to him playing professionally in Japan.

After very short stints with the Toronto Blue Jays and Minnesota Twins for 47 Major League games, Greg Wells began a "hall of fame-like" career in Japan, lasting 10 seasons. In 1984, his MVP-winning season, Wells became the first foreigner ever to claim Japan's version of the Triple Crown (with a .355 batting average, 37 home runs, and 130 runs batted in). Boomer Wells' legendary 531 ft. home run is one of the longest in Japanese baseball history, if not the longest. In 2012, Wells fell just 13 votes shy of induction into the Japanese Baseball Hall of Fame. Nonetheless, it was a testament to a successful career overseas.

\*\*\*

During the mid-to-late 1970s, another HBCU baseball program finding great success was the NAIA's Kentucky State University. From 1974 to 1978, the Thorobreds amassed a record of 157-56 and, after the 1976 regular season, participated in the National Association of Intercollegiate Athletics World Series, finishing in a tie for third place.

Individually, in 1974, right-handed starting pitcher Anthony Roberson finished third in the NAIA with an earned run average of 0.81 and also third nationally in winning percentage with an average of .929 (a 13-1 record). Offensively, Kevin Threatt finished second in the country by hitting .445, tied for fourth in the nation in runs batted in (57), and fifth in doubles (16).

The following season, Kentucky State led the entire NAIA in hitting with a .375 team batting average, and individually, Greg Carter's .487 batting average placed him fifth in the country. Teammate Jerome Williams was not far behind with an 11th-best average of .459. Freshman outfielder Richard Phillips supplied the power with 11 home runs.

*1976 Kentucky State University*

In its banner season of 1976, Kentucky State finished with an overall record of 55-6, including a 30-game winning streak. On the mound, Hilton Napoleon finished with a perfect 9-0 record and a 1.11 earned run average. Teammate Anthony Roberson added 11 wins against three losses. At the plate, Jerome Williams led the Thorobreds in hitting with a .407 average while being named a first-team NAIA All-American at third base. And on the base paths,

Cedric Collins stole 38 of 40 base attempts.

Besides Kentucky State, Tennessee State University also competed without conference affiliation in the 1970s. It was not until 1986 that the Tigers joined the Ohio Valley Conference. Due to its independent status as an NCAA Division I school, the 1979 Tennessee State squad did not qualify for postseason play, but had a record-setting season going 30-12. An impressive 16-7 victory over Vanderbilt University was included in the win column. Offensively, the team was led by Terry Blocker, Curtis Burke, and Kirk Forbes. Blocker, a future first-round selection of the New York Mets in 1981, led Tennessee State in hitting with a .360 batting average. His 40 stolen bases in 42 attempts contributed to the team's nation-leading average of 4.21 stolen bases per game. Team Captain Greg Goodwin stole 41 of 44 attempts while leading the Tigers with five triples. Kirk Forbes, a 13th-round pick of the Montreal Expos in 1979, stole 43 bases in 46 attempts, and Curtis Burke, a third-round pick in 1981 of the Houston Astros, was second on the team, hitting .348. Roy Johnson only collected 55 at-bats in 1979, but hit .400 in 1980 and then became a fifth-round selection of the Montreal Expos that year.[6]

*1979 Tennessee State University*

Stillman College was a third school in the late-1970s playing an independent schedule, due to having no conference affiliation. The Tigers twice played in the NCAA Division III Southern Regional postseason tournament in 1978 and 1979. The 29-10 team of 1978 was led by Leon Farmer, who hit .415 and had 11 home runs, and by Edward Harper, who had a team-leading .467 batting average. The following year, Stillman nearly duplicated the previous season's record by accumulating a record of 28-10-1. Its tournament team was led by Jimmy Rochell, who hit .371 with nine home runs, and Danny Garland, a freshman who led the team with a .448 batting average.

By the end of the 1970s, aluminum bats had already changed the complexion of the college game, skewing the balance towards hitting. But in the 1980s and 1990s, the onslaught of offense and the gaudy numbers it produced would be the impetus to tweak the characteristics of bats in a series of adjustments that were implemented dating from 1986 and most recently in 2011.[7]

***

In the Southwestern Athletic Conference, the 1980s saw the continued domination by Southern University and Jackson State. However, for three years, the Grambling Tigers returned to its former glory of the Sixties claiming titles in 1983-1985. Beginning in 1981, the SWAC went to a four-team tournament to determine the league champion. Before that, from 1977 through 1980, the conference championship was determined by a two-team playoff. And before 1977, the SWAC crown was claimed by the regular-season champion.

Jackson State University claimed the league title in 1980 and then again in 1982, 1986, and 1989. Between 1980 and 1989, 20 different Tigers were drafted into professional baseball, beginning with Dennis "Oil Can" Boyd. In 1979, Boyd had a 1.87 earned run average and followed up in 1980 with an ERA of 2.11, helping lead Jackson State to the SWAC title. His 10.3 strikeouts per game ranked 10th nationally in the NCAA Division I. In the June 1980 Major League Baseball Draft, Dennis Boyd was selected in the 16th round by the Boston Red Sox and spent eight of his 10 MLB seasons with them.

The 1982 edition of Jackson State baseball completed the regular season with a 34-18 record. With the SWAC now receiving an automatic postseason bid, Jackson State became the first HBCU baseball program to participate in an NCAA Division I regional tournament. The Tigers were led that year by sophomore third baseman David Clark who topped the regulars by hitting .363, and by two talented freshmen, shortstop Julius McDougal and pitcher Marvin Freeman. After the 1982 season, Clark was selected as a *Sporting News* All-American.

*Julius McDougal*
*Jackson State University*

*Dave Clark*
*Jackson State University*

*Marvin Freeman*
*Jackson State University*

David Clark returned to Jackson State in 1983, hitting an even higher .378 and adding 13 home runs. After the season, Clark was a first-round MLB draft pick of the Cleveland Indians. His 13 years in Major League Baseball as an outfielder preceded a career as a Minor League manager, Major League coach, and, for a short stint, the interim manager of the Houston Astros in 2009.

Following David Clark's first-round MLB Draft selection in 1983, Marvin Freeman and Julius McDougal became early-round draft selections in 1984. Freeman was picked by the Philadelphia Phillies in the second round (49th selection overall), while McDougal was chosen by the Chicago Cubs in the third round (57th selection overall). Marvin Freeman pitched 10 years in the Major Leagues, primarily with the Phillies and the Atlanta Braves. Julius McDougal, an infielder, never made it to the Majors but enjoyed a nine-year minor league career.

*Earl Sanders*
*Jackson State University*

Jackson State cruised to the 1986 SWAC championship on both the arm and bat of Earl Sanders. After a successful 1985 sophomore season in which he hit .402 with 13 home runs as an outfielder and an 8-1 record with a 2.88 ERA as a right-handed starting pitcher, Sanders followed up the next season by hitting .432 with 17 home runs and as a pitcher, had an 11-2 record with a 3.32 ERA and 109 strikeouts. Earl Sanders was selected an All-American in 1986 by both *Baseball America* and the American Baseball Coaches Association. Like David Clark three years prior, Sanders was a first-round draft pick. With the 26th pick in the 1986 draft, the Toronto Blue Jays selected Earl Sanders, who was primarily used as both a starting and relief pitcher during his pro career. Presently, Sanders serves as head coach at Tougaloo College.

Other Jackson State University Tigers drafted into professional baseball during the 1980s, and whose careers included playing time in the Majors, counted Curt Ford (drafted in the fourth round by the Saint Louis Cardinals in 1981), Wes Chamberlain (drafted in the fourth round by the Pittsburgh Pirates in 1987) and Harold Farmer (drafted in the seventh round by the Montreal Expos in 1987).

*Wes Chamberlain*
*Jackson State University*

Jackson State's Southwestern Athletic Conference baseball rival, Southern University, won conference laurels in 1981, 1987, and 1988. The 1981 Jaguar squad, which finished with a 41-20 record, featured five teammates who were drafted into professional baseball between 1981 and 1983. Of them, only outfielder Reggie Williams, who hit .361 for the Jags in 1981, reached the Major League level (with the Los Angeles Dodgers) as a ballplayer. Another,

DeMarlo Hale, never advanced above Double-A baseball during his playing career, but became a respected Minor League manager and Major League coach with the Boston Red Sox, Baltimore Orioles, and Toronto Blue Jays.

In 1985, Roger Cador became head coach of his alma mater, Southern University. But in 1972, as an outfielder leading the Jaguars with a .393 batting average (two years before aluminum bats came on the scene), Roger Cador had dreams of pro baseball, not coaching. As a tenth-round draft selection of the Atlanta Braves in 1973, Cador spent five seasons in the minor leagues before turning to coaching as an assistant at Southern University in 1978. Once he took the reins as head coach in 1985, Cador guided the Jaguars to 14 SWAC titles, 11 NCAA regional appearances and, upon his retirement in 2017, had accumulated a record of 913-597-1.

*1987 Southern University*

The 1987 and 1988 championship Southern University teams were built with several vital underclassmen from the 1986 Jaguar nine. The 1986 team included freshmen Brian Cornelius and Adell Davenport, who hit .391 and .366, respectively, with Davenport additionally contributing 13 home runs. Sophomore shortstop Tim Stargell hit .365 and junior outfielder Kenneth Clarke hit .345 with four saves as a pitcher. The only key loss going into 1987 was senior second baseman Trent Hubbard, the future major leaguer, who hit

.373 in 1986.

*Adell Davenport (above)*
*Brian Cornelius (below)*
*both of Southern University*

The 1987 Southern Jaguars became the first HBCU to win an NCAA Division I regional tournament game defeating Cal State Fullerton 1-0. They were again led by, now sophomores, Brian Cornelius and Adell Davenport, and junior Tim Stargell. Cornelius contributed 22 doubles and a .415 batting average. Davenport, a *Baseball America* All-American in 1987, added 20 home runs and a .393 batting average and Stargell contributed 19 doubles and a .364 batting average. Senior Kenneth Clarke led the Jaguars in hitting with an average of .434 and was named an All-American by the American Baseball Coaches Association. Aces of the pitching staff included Jeff Swain and Allan Ratliff, who threw that complete game shutout for the regional tournament win against the Titans of Cal State Fullerton.

With Tim Stargell moving on to the Seattle Mariners organization, Adell Davenport and Brian Cornelius were tasked with leading Southern University to a second straight SWAC title in 1988. On the strength of Davenport's .394 batting average and 16 home runs, as well as Cornelius' 12 home runs, Southern retained its league crown.

Sandwiched between Southern University's and Jackson State's titles in the 1980s, Grambling State University put together back-to-back-to-back SWAC crowns in 1983-1985 (the only one of the three schools to win three straight titles in the decade).

Going into the 1983 season, Grambling no longer had first baseman Derrick Smith, the SWAC's leading hitter (.452 batting average) and conference MVP in 1982, nor ace pitcher Thaddeus Walker, who had an 8-2 record and a conference-leading 3.00 earned run average. The Tigers returned Juan McWilliams and Orlando Watkins, who, as freshmen, finished third and fifth respectively among the conference's leading hitters in 1982. McWilliams, a third baseman, hit .402, and Watkins, a shortstop, hit .363.

The 1983 Grambling Tigers' regular lineup included just one senior, outfielder Don Reed, and one junior, outfielder Moses Clerk. Of the remaining six, all but one, freshman catcher Lenny Webster, were sophomores. Two of the three primary starting pitchers, freshman Martin Foley and sophomore Tony Bailey, were also underclassmen. The third was junior Marty Gulley. Despite a relatively young squad, the Tigers won the conference crown with a 15-3 record and a 30-12 overall record.

*1984 Grambling State University*

Grambling's second straight SWAC title in 1984 was accomplished with the underclassmen of 1983, who now had a year of championship baseball to build upon, and the Tigers' last title in its three-year run was crafted with a solid junior and senior-laden roster. In 1985, Grambling was powered by the long-ball hitting of Eric Taylor's 12 home runs, Juan McWilliams' 11 home runs, DeForrest Young's nine home runs, and both Ira Tieuel and Lenny Webster with eight home runs each. The pitching staff was paced by junior Gary Eave, who went 10-2 with a 2.05 ERA. Overall, the '85 Tiger diamondmen went 36-16-1 on the season and 15-3 in the SWAC.

From the Grambling teams of 1983-1985, eight members were drafted into professional baseball and three, Gary Eave, Lenny Webster, and outfielder Gerald Williams, played in the Majors. The other five drafted were Ira Tieuel, Tony Bailey, John Lewis, Juan McWilliams, and Marty Foley.

*Gary Eave, Juan McWilliams, Eric Taylor and Lenny Webster (left to right)*
*1985 Grambling State University*

Managing the Grambling championship teams during that stretch was head coach Wilbert Ellis. However, his association with the school went back much farther. A self-proclaimed "average ballplayer" for the Grambling Tigers in the late 1950s, Ellis became an assistant to his College Baseball Hall of Fame coach, R.W.E. "Prez" Jones, and remained in that position for 17 years. When Coach Jones retired, Wilbert Ellis moved into the head coaching position in 1978 and remained there until his retirement after the 2003 season. During those 26 years, Coach Ellis accumulated a winning record of 745-462-1 and in 2007, the seven-time SWAC Coach of the Year was inducted into the American Baseball Coaches Association Hall of Fame.

Other superlative performances in the SWAC during the 1980s included those of Greg Daniels of Alcorn State, who in 1983 led the entire NCAA Division I in hitting. His .545 batting average remains the second highest single-season average since the NCAA began recording statistics in 1957. Prince Cousinard of Texas Southern, also in 1983, led the country in stolen bases per game stealing 53 of 55 attempts for an average of 1.63 per game. His 53 stolen bases were the second-most in NCAA Division I, and his .496 batting average ranked fourth in the country. As a team, the Alcorn State

Braves finished third nationally with an overall batting average of .360. The following season, Prince Cousinard's Texas Southern teammate, Greg Charlot finished second in the country in hitting with a .468 batting average.

*Greg Daniels*
*Alcorn State University*

*Robert Williams*
*Prairie View A&M*

Two seasons later, in 1985, Alcorn State again finished third in the country in hitting with a team batting average of .368. Two of its teammates, Jesse Jackson and Steve Brown, finished 11th and 15th, respectively, in individual batting. However, the top hitting honors among all HBCU NCAA Division I hitters went to Robert Williams of Prairie View A&M, who hit .464 to finish ninth in the country. Williams, a 1985 College Sports Information Directors of America (COSIDA) Academic All-American, who hit well over .400 in three of his four years at Prairie View and just under .400 in his other season there, currently is ranked sixth nationally in career batting with an average of .450. Unofficially, for Division I ballplayers who played four years of varsity baseball, no one in the country owns a better career average than Robert Williams.

The coach of that 1985 Alcorn State team, as well as coach of 37 other Braves baseball teams, was Willie "Rat" McGowan. McGowan, a former football and baseball player at Alcorn, took over the baseball program in 1972 and, over his 38 years as head coach, accumulated a 720-663-7 record. McGowan was named SWAC Baseball Coach of the Year four times (in 1978, 1979, 1981, and 1988). His 1981 team, with a 21-6 record, was Coach McGowan's most successful. Stanley Barker, a fifth-round selection of the

Detroit Tigers in the 1981 Major League Baseball Draft, was the leader of the Braves' offense that year. His .456 batting average was the sixth-highest in the country. On the mound, Richard Pickett (10-1 with a 1.24 earned run average) and Al Jones (7-2 with a 2.06 earned run average) were the leading pitchers. Jones was a 13th-round pick in the same MLB draft as Stanley Barker and pitched for three years with the Chicago White Sox.

***

When the decade of the 1980s opened, the Mid-Eastern Athletic Conference was still four years away from re-instituting a conference baseball schedule. Nonetheless, six MEAC schools (Bethune-Cookman, Delaware State, Florida A&M, Howard University, North Carolina A&T, and beginning in 1981, the University of Maryland Eastern Shore) continued to field teams and play non-conference schedules. No schools received at-large bids to postseason tournaments during that time, but there were plenty of individual stars and record-setting performances.

*Cousins Lary Aaron (left), son of MLB Hall of Famer Hank Aaron and Bill Lucas, Jr. (right), son of the first MLB African-American front office executive, Bill Lucas, Sr. starred at Florida A&M in the late-1970s through early-1980s.*

At Florida A&M, infielder Bill Lucas Jr. led the 1980 team in hitting with a .432 average, placing him in the top 25 nationally. Outfielder Tony Gresham finished second on the team, hitting .392 and his 31 of 34 stolen bases ranked eighth in the country. Between the two, Bill Lucas Jr. and Tony Gresham stole 55 of 62 base attempts. In the following two seasons, future major leaguer Vince Coleman led the Rattler nine in hitting with a .374 average in 1981 and .407 average in 1982. His 65 stolen bases led the country in 1981, and his average of 1.56 stolen bases per game (42 in 27 games) did likewise in 1982.

In 1981, FAMU teammates Bill Lucas Jr. and Lary

*Vince Coleman
Florida A&M*

Aaron were both drafted by the Atlanta Braves (in the 31st and 32nd rounds, respectively), and each had brief careers in professional baseball. Vince Coleman was also drafted in 1981. However, he didn't sign that year and was then drafted a second time, in 1982, by the St. Louis Cardinals in the tenth round and played 13 seasons in the Majors. An outfielder known for his stolen base prowess, Vince Coleman currently ranks sixth all-time in stolen bases for a Major League career with 752, holds the record for most stolen bases in a season by a rookie with 110 in 1985, and also holds the MLB record collecting 50 consecutive stolen bases without being caught stealing. Additionally, Vince Coleman has three of the top six single-season stolen base totals (third-most with 110 in 1985, fourth-most with 109 in 1987, and sixth-most with 107 in 1986).

In 1983, Bethune-Cookman's Stan Jefferson hit a team-best .408 and led the country stealing 67 bases (in 68 attempts). At season's end, Jefferson was selected both a *Sporting News* and *Baseball America* All-American and was drafted in round one (20th overall selection) of the Major League Draft by the New York Mets. After a six-year career in the Majors, Stan Jefferson became a New York City police officer and was on duty the infamous day that came to be known simply as "9/11". In the weeks that followed the September 11, 2001 terrorist attack on the city's World Trade Center, Jefferson worked long shifts at Ground Zero and, sadly, like many of the first responders, experienced prolonged mental and physical effects of that traumatic experience.[8]

When the Mid-Eastern Athletic Conference re-instituted league play in 1984 after a six-year hiatus, Delaware State University went into the postseason tournament with the best overall record in the conference. However, Howard University walked away with the MEAC crown. As they did in 1983, Barry Jackson and Rozier Jordan led the 1984 championship Bison squad offensively.

Barry Jackson, the son of former Wiley College and Major League pitcher Alvin Jackson, led the 1983 team in hitting with a .432 batting average, which also placed him atop all unaffiliated conference teams' hitters in the

Mideast/East Independents Region.[9] Teammate Rozier Jordon, just a sophomore, was second on the team with a .407 average and his 12 home runs led both the team and the Midwest/East Independents.[10] The duo of Jackson and Jordan again led the MEAC champion Bison on offense in 1984 with Rozier Jordan hitting a team-best .412 and Barry Jackson hitting .342. After the season, Rozier Jordan was drafted in the eighth round by the Cleveland Indians.

Bethune-Cookman College (which became Bethune-Cookman University in 2007) claimed the 1985 MEAC title. Howard University re-claimed the title in 1986, and then Florida A&M was crowned MEAC champs in 1987 and 1988. Delaware State closed out the decade winning its first tournament championship in 1989.

*Marquis Grissom*
*Florida A&M*

Leading those Florida A&M Mid-Eastern Athletic Conference championship squads was outfielder/pitcher Marquis Grissom. As a freshman in 1987, Grissom hit .393 with eight home runs. The next season, he followed up by hitting a team-leading .448, with 10 doubles, 10 triples, and 12 home runs. On the mound, Marquis Grissom threw 12 complete games with a 9-3 record and a 2.40 earned run average. In 86 innings pitched, Grissom struck out 93 batters. In 1988, his 10 triples tied for most in the country, his .448 average ranked sixth nationally, he finished with the 18th-best earned average among all NCAA Division I pitchers and tied for the seventh-most complete games.

Drafted as an outfielder/pitcher in the third round of the 1988 MLB draft (76th player drafted overall) by the Montreal Expos, Marquis Grissom ended up being groomed solely as a position player. Grissom played 17 seasons in the Major Leagues with six different teams, twice was a National League All-Star, won four Gold Gloves for excelling defensively in the outfield and, in both 1991 and 1992, led the National League in stolen bases. Following his playing career, Marquis Grissom had a short career as a coach with the Washington Nationals. He currently runs a nonprofit baseball academy for underprivileged youth in the Atlanta area.

From 1984 and until the end of the decade, Delaware State University finished first in the regular-season, single-division MEAC four of the six years. Still, it did not collect its first conference tourney championship until 1989.

The Hornets of 1989 were led by five players who each hit above .400 and contributed to the current NCAA Division I team single-season record batting average of .396. The five who helped guide Delaware State to an overall record of 18-8-1 included first baseman Elmore Briggs, with a team-best .467 batting average, which ranked third in the country. Outfielder Ron Probst finished second on the team and fourth in the country with a batting average of .457, while infielder Jeff

*Leaders of the 1989 Delaware State Hornets included Jarvis Smith, Pedro Swann, Eric Gass (rear) and Elmore Briggs, Tony Alston (front).*

Greenly hit .453, placing him third on the team and sixth in the nation. Freshman Pedro Swann hit .449, the country's seventh-highest while leading Delaware State in home runs with five and RBIs with 44. Swann was drafted by the Atlanta Braves in the 26th round of the 1991 Major League Baseball draft and left school as its all-time hitting leader with a career average of .421. The fifth Hornet hitter with a batting average over .400 in 1989 was Tony Alston, a junior infielder who hit .402.

Even with all the heavy hitters at Delaware State, the Mid-Eastern Athletic Conference had another representative who ranked even higher. The University of Maryland Eastern Shore's Ira Smith led the country in hitting with an NCAA Division I best of .488. In fact, seven of the country's top 15 hitters in 1989 came from the MEAC.

\*\*\*

The Southern Intercollegiate Athletic Conference was dominated in the decade of the 1980s by two schools in Alabama, approximately 2-1/2 hours apart on US Route 82. During this era, the SIAC was comprised of both NCAA Division II and Division III schools, and the conference was divided into two divisions designated as such. Tuskegee University won nine of the ten SIAC Division II titles, interrupted only by Benedict College in 1988. Farther north in Tuscaloosa, Stillman College won five of the eight Division III SIAC crowns before the conference eliminated the division's baseball tournament in 1988 after the conference attained NCAA Division II status. The other three Division III champions in the '80s were Fort Valley State in 1980, Fisk University in 1981, and Lane College in 1982.

For Tuskegee Institute (which became Tuskegee University in 1985), the decade opened with the baseball team winning 32 games against just six losses in 1980. The Golden Tigers were led by outfielder Harold Carter, MVP of the pre-conference season Tuskegee Baseball Tournament, which featured teams from Jackson State, Tennessee State, Texas Southern, Florida A&M, and Tuskegee. After the season ended, Carter was named an NCAA Division II All-American and was drafted in the 16th round of the Major League Draft by the Detroit Tigers.

Ken Howell
*Tuskegee Institute*

In 1982, pitcher Ken Howell's 17-0 mastery of Albany State gave the Golden Tigers its third SIAC title of the decade. In the title game, Howell struck out 13 Albany State batters while walking just one and threw a complete game shutout for the victory. Even so, Ken Howell's won-loss record of 3-6-1 left him fearful he wouldn't be drafted. However, scouts liked his performance in the prestigious Cape Code League the summer prior with the Cotuit Kettlers, and loved his 95 miles per hour fastball.[11] So highly regarded was Ken Howell that he was drafted by the Los Angeles Dodgers in the third round of the 1982 Major League Draft. As a professional baseball player, Howell pitched for seven years in Major League Baseball, and then later served as a pitching coach for the Dodgers from 2008 through 2015.

From 1982 to 1987, the Tuskegee Golden Tigers produced several All-SIAC performers including pitcher Ray Stevenson (the 1982 SIAC Tournament Most Valuable Pitcher who was all-conference in both 1982 and 1983) and catcher Derek Crum (who earned conference honors all four years from 1983 through 1986). In 1984, the champion Golden Tigers featured Shaun Crayton, the SIAC tournament MVP pitcher, and teammates Bernard Anderson (who hit .349), Antonio Garrett (.333), Danny Clark (.372), and Cecil Clark (.311), the latter four each having earned All-SIAC honors at least once between the years 1984 and 1986.

Tuskegee University claimed a second 32-win season and its sixth straight division title in 1985. Two freshmen, outfielder Darren Fudge and pitcher Alan Mills, earned all-conference honors and were selected Southern Intercollegiate Athletic Conference Tournament MVPs. Fudge earned the most outstanding hitter award, and Mills claimed most outstanding pitcher.

Alan Mills left Tuskegee that year after the school eliminated baseball scholarships and transferred to Polk Community College.[12] After one season there, Mills was drafted in 1986 by the California Angles in the first round of the secondary phase of the June Major League Baseball Draft. He then pitched 12 seasons split between the New York Yankees, Baltimore Orioles, and Los Angeles Dodgers.

At Stillman College, junior first baseman Thomas Wesley hit .451 in 1980, which ranked seventh in the country in the NCAA Division III. His 11 triples topped the country while averaging the nation's best .28 triples per game. His teammate, pitcher Roger Clark, finished third in the country in earned run average with a 1.07 ERA. In June, the Cincinnati Reds selected Thomas Wesley in the seventh round of the 1980 Major League. Following a short playing career, Wesley moved into coaching and served as the head coach at Alabama A&M (an HBCU institution based in Normal, Alabama) for 16 years, beginning in 1991. Two years later, infielder Carl Hollis became the second Stillman Tiger in the decade of the 1980s to be selected in the Major

League Draft when he was picked in the 18th round of the 1982 draft by the New York Mets. That same season, Hollis was named a second-team NAIA All-American.

In 1983, Stillman College featured two teammates who later joined Thomas Wesley in the college coaching ranks. Mark Salter (who hit .468 as a junior outfielder and .382 as a senior) coached at Talladega College and Jackson State University. Randy Jennings (who hit .375 and a team-best seven home runs for the Stillman Tigers as a senior) headed HBCU programs at Alabama A&M, LeMoyne-Owen College, and Stillman College.

Two others added to the legacy of SIAC baseball in the decade. Reggie Jackson, a pitcher from Fisk University, had the highest strikeout ratio per nine innings in the NCAA Division II (15.4) in 1980. Reggie Zinn, of Division III Rust College in Mississippi, lead the country in triples for a season (10), stolen bases for a season (58) and most stolen bases per game played (averaging 1.38 steals per game), all coming in 1986.

***

Led by head coach Marty Miller, Norfolk State University won Central Intercollegiate Athletic Association titles every year from 1974 through 1993, except for 1979 and 1986 when Saint Augustine's College of North Carolina claimed CIAA baseball crowns, and in 1983 when Shaw University, also in North Carolina, won the championship. In 1976, there were not enough schools fielding teams to name an official conference champion, though Virginia State held the best record in league play. The Trojans were led by three-time All-CIAA outfielder Rey Bradley, whose father William Bradley coached Virginia State from 1967 to 1970.

Leaders of those Norfolk State University Spartans teams in the late-1970s and early-1980s included pitcher Jarrell Wilkerson, who had a career earned run average of 2.42 from 1976 through 1979, and infielder Ron Dillard, who had a career batting average of .374 from 1978 through 1980. Dillard was later a fifth-round Major League Draft selection of the Baltimore Orioles. Catcher Eugene Hawkins hit .440 in 1981 and followed up the next year hitting an even higher .443. Hawkins, a career .410 hitter at Norfolk State, was drafted by the New York Mets in 1982.

Jamaican-born Andrew Dixon was the next leader at Norfolk State. During his four years as a Spartan, from 1983 through 1986, Dixon, an outfielder, had a career batting average of .418. His .958 career successful stolen base average currently ranks as an NCAA Division II record. At the end of his collegiate career, Andrew Dixon was drafted by the San Francisco Giants in the 17th round of the 1986 Major League Draft and played five seasons of Minor League baseball.

*Andrew Dixon (left) and Mel Wearing (right) starred at Norfolk State University from the mid-1980s through the late-1980s. Each was a national statistical leader while in school and both were Major League Draft selections.*

The last star at Norfolk State in the 1980s was possibly the Spartans' brightest star of the decade and one of the best in the Central Intercollegiate Athletic Association. Melvin Wearing was the conference Player of the Year in 1988 and 1989 and an NCAA Division II All-American in 1989. As a sophomore, Wearing finished fourth in the country, hitting .497, and the following year finished fifth with a .454 batting average. Also, in 1989, his average of 1.65 runs batted in per game (66 in 40 games) led the entire nation, and his 17 home runs (for an average of .43 per game) ranked second nationally. Mel Wearing was drafted after his junior year by the Baltimore Orioles in the 25th round of the 1989 Major League Draft and then played professionally for 13 seasons.

\*\*\*

In 1975, future major leaguer of nine seasons, Eddie Milner, led the Central State Marauders of Wilberforce, Ohio to one of its best-ever records of

36-11. Though he fell just short of the number of required plate appearances to qualify as a leading hitter in the National Association of Intercollegiate Athletics that year, his .509 batting average would have placed him second in the country. And while fortunes turned for Central State, with only one winning season in the 1980s (finishing 24-23 with one tie in 1985), during the decade, three Marauders led the country in hitting, seven were drafted, and one earned All-American honors. Unfortunately, after the 1993 spring baseball season, the Central State University baseball program was terminated.

*Eddie Milner*
*Central State University*

Toney Howell was the first of the three Central State ballplayers to win a batting title, leading the NAIA in hitting in 1981 with a .524 average. Howell was drafted by the Cincinnati Reds organization in the 16th round of the '81 MLB Draft and became a longtime baseball scout and administrator after a short playing career. Two years later, in 1983, Terry Edwards, an All-American and a fourth-round selection of the Chicago Cubs, topped the NCAA Division II in hitting with a .514 average, and teammate Sammy Ruiz duplicated that effort the following year by hitting .509 in 1984. Ruiz was then drafted by the Chicago White Sox in 1985.

The four other Central State University draft selections in the decade were Jeff Smith (in 1983 by the New York Yankees), Thelanious "Laney" Prioleau (in 1985 by the Detroit Tigers), Ernie Radcliffe (in 1986 by the Saint Louis Cardinals), and Henderson Mosley (star quarterback of the Mauraders' football team) in 1989 by the Baltimore Orioles.

Laney Prioleau was one of the most successful dual-position baseball players to ever play for the Maroon and Gold of Central State. In 1983, his 1.39 earned run average was the fourth-lowest in the NAIA. As a sophomore in 1984, Prioleau's .412 batting average ranked in the nation's top 30; the following year, his .452 average was fifth-best in the country. In 1985, Laney Prioleau led the nation with 53 stolen bases, and from the mound, his 53 strikeouts, for an average of 8.8 strikeouts per game, ranked second. Primarily a pitcher and shortstop, in a game versus Walsh University in May 1984, Prioleau played all nine positions.[13]

In 1954, after the landmark U. S. Supreme Court case *Brown v. Board of Education of Topeka*, ruling that racial segregation in public schools is unconstitutional, West Virginia State College, an HBCU designated institution, underwent a significant transformation by implementing "reverse integration". Around the same time, West Virginia State left the Central Intercollegiate Athletic Association and joined the integrated West Virginia Intercollegiate Athletic Conference.

By 1980, the Yellow Jackets were two years into the tenure of head coach Calvin Bailey. A former star athlete at the school, Bailey would turn West Virginia State into a baseball powerhouse, winning 17 conference titles in the now defunct WVIAC and in the Mountain East Conference. In his 37 years coaching WVSU, Bailey amassed a record of 1063-523-4 and took two of his squads to the NCAA Division II World Series. A draft selection himself in 1966, Coach Bailey produced four draft picks in the 1980s and three All-Americans during the decade.

Though membership of HBCU institutions within the NAIA was shrinking in the decade of the 1980s, those remaining schools still dotted the pages of national statistical leaders. Eddie White, an outfielder from Saint Augustine's College, Calvin Green, an outfielder from Texas College, and Vince Loggins, a third baseman from Harris-Stowe State College, each finished second in the country in batting in 1982, 1984, and 1986, respectively. In 1988, dual-position player Earl Carter of Paul Quinn College in Texas led the nation in hitting with an average of .562 and on the mound, finished in the top 20 with a 2.25 earned run average. Carter also finished sixth in strikeouts, averaging 11.25 strikeouts per game. Earl Carter's teammate at Paul Quinn, Mike Foster, led the country in stolen bases, swiping all 24 of his attempts, while Carter finished ninth, stealing 21 of his 22 attempts. Earlier in the decade, Calvin Green led the country in stolen bases, swiping a total of 46 bases in 1983. That same year, Texas College teammate Reginald Cuington topped the nation in stolen base percentage, stealing a perfect 27 of 27. Cuington eked out fellow Steer Lee Powell, who finished second nationally, stealing all 26 of his base attempts. Four years later, Texas College was even more prolific on the base paths, setting the current NAIA standard for stolen bases in a season with 328 (in 362 attempts). The 1987 Steers were led by Eland Rhodes, who successfully stole 52 of his 54 attempts, and Kenny Bridges, who stole 60 of 63.

***

In the last decade of the twentieth century, Southern University won six Southwestern Athletic Conference titles, Jackson State won three, and the two shared the title in 1993 when field conditions made it impossible to play the championship game. In those ten years, thirty-seven ballplayers were drafted out of the SWAC, led by Jackson State and Southern University, with 12 each.

Jackson State's 1990 league crown was won with pitching and speed. That year, the Tigers finished second in the country in pitching with an overall earned run average of 2.69. On the base paths, Jackson State led the NCAA in stolen bases, averaging 4.82 steals per game, while leading the nation with 241 total steals. Over the next two years, Coach Roger Cador and his Southern University Jaguars went 60-24 overall and 36-8 in conference play to claim the SWAC titles of 1991 and 1992. After sharing the 1993 crown with Southern, Jackson State won the next two league championships before Southern University closed out the decade of the nineties, winning the final four titles.

Though Southern and Jackson State dominated the SWAC by winning all ten league titles between them, it was Grambling State University that produced the majority of conference most valuable players, claiming five. Beginning in 1992, third baseman Kevin Nalls garnered MVP honors for the Tigers, followed by pitcher Courtney Mitchell in 1993, outfielder Marlon Stewart in 1996 (finishing third in the county in both hitting and slugging), second baseman Rickie Miller in 1998, and then shortstop Gilbert Lanoix to close out the decade and century in 1999.

From 1977, when the SWAC created a two-team playoff to determine a conference champion, through the end of the twentieth century, when the conference had grown to a four-team playoff, Southern University and Jackson State University combined to win 20 of the 23 league crowns. Only Grambling broke the two-team stronghold, winning SWAC titles from 1983 through 1985. However, the next decade would usher in an era of more parity in the conference.

\*\*\*

In the Mid-Eastern Athletic Conference, the SWAC's fellow HBCU NCAA Division I conference, Florida A&M claimed four of the first five conference titles in the decade of the 1990s, with North Carolina A&T interrupting the streak in 1993. During this stretch, University of Maryland Eastern Shore outfielder Ira Smith became the first Division I ballplayer to repeat winning a national batting crown. In 1990, Smith was the nation's leading

*Ira Smith*
*University of Maryland Eastern Shore*

hitter with a .519 average after claiming the title in 1989, hitting .488. Interestingly, since then, a repeat national batting title has only been duplicated once, when another HBCU ballplayer, Southern University's Rickie Weeks, won the hitting crown in 2002 and repeated in 2003.

Beginning in 1994, the MEAC was granted an automatic bid to the NCAA postseason tournament and by winning its league title, Florida A&M became the first conference team to play in the College World Series qualifier.

While Florida A&M was winning most of the MEAC's postseason tourneys in the first half of the 1990s, Delaware State had the conference's best overall record in 1991 and 1992. Then when the MEAC split into two divisions in 1993, the Hornets had the top winning record in the North Division in 1993 and again in 1994. In 1991, Delaware State's Pedro Swann was among the nation's leading hitters with a .424 average. His .856 slugging average ranked fourth in the country, he scored an average of 1.37 runs per game, ranking seventh, and Swann struck out only four times in 38 games, which ranked fourth in the country.

*1995 Coppin State University*
*Mid-Eastern Athletic Conference Champions*

Coppin State won its only MEAC baseball title in 1995, with a roster of 14 team members, after finishing second during the regular season in the North Division. The Eagles' leading hitter, Travis Thornton, was also the conference's top hitter with a .410 batting average. The next four leading hitters for Coppin State, E. J. Fitzgerald, Jamal Davis, Ruffin Bell, and Brian Pisani, along with Travis Thornton, constituted the top five pitchers for the Eagles. The year before, Coppin State finished with a 7-34 record. However, Eagle junior first baseman Adrian Price led the country in hitting with a .474 batting average and was the MEAC Player of the Year. Two years later, Brian Pisani claimed the 1996 MEAC Player of the Year award while leading Coppin State to a first-place finish in the regular season North Division and runner-up

in the MEAC tournament. The Eagles were coached all three years by Coppin State alum Jason Booker, who in 1986 led the country by stealing 49 of 51 bases for an average of 1.23 steals per game.

Of the last four Mid-Eastern Athletic Conference crowns in the 1990s, the Bethune-Cookman College Wildcats won three, and Howard University claimed its last in 1998. The

*Bethune-Cookman's Milt Anderson*
*(left) displays his award as the 1995*
*NCAA National Statistical Stolen*
*Base Leader and Coach Brian Rhees*
*(right) displays the team award.*

following year, Howard University announced it was terminating its baseball program. On the Bethune-Cookman team of 1996 were two who became successful HBCU coaches in senior infielder Mervyl Melendez and junior pitcher Kerrick Jackson. Melendez took over the head coaching position at Bethune-Cookman in 2000 after serving as head coach Richard Skeel's assistant from 1997 through 1999. As the Wildcats' head coach, Mervyl Melendez led the team to an overall record of 379-319 over his 12 seasons there. During that time, 11 of his Bethune-Cookman squads played in the postseason NCAA regional tournament.

Kerrick Jackson accepted the Southern University head coaching job in 2018 after serving as an assistant at several college programs, including a five-year stop at the University of Missouri. In 2019, Coach Jackson turned around the fortunes of Southern University, going from a 9-33 record in 2018 to 32-24 and a

*Mervyl Melendez (above) and Karrick Jackson (right) were teammates at Bethune-Cookman in 1996.*

Southwestern Athletic Conference championship in 2019. His Jaguars ball club competed in the NCAA Division I Starkville Regional Tournament and was named *blackcollegenines.com* "large school" HBCU National Champions.

***

While Tuskegee dominated the Southern Intercollegiate Athletic Conference in the decade of the eighties, it was Savannah State that claimed the most SIAC titles in the nineties. The Tigers won conference championships in 1992 and a stretch of five straight from 1995-1999. Paine College won the SIAC crown in 1990, and Albany State did likewise in both 1991 and 1994. The other league title was claimed by Alabama A&M in 1993 under former Stillman College standout Thomas Wesley. Paine College and

Albany State are currently members of the SIAC; however Alabama A&M, which had been a member of the conference since 1947, and Savannah State, which joined the SIAC in 1969, left the conference by the start of the twenty-first century as they each transitioned from Division II to Division I status.

During Savannah State's run of conference titles, the Tigers' success was built on speed. Each year, the ball club ranked among the nation's NCAA Division II leaders in team stolen bases. In 1995, its average of 4.19 steals per game led the country. In 1996, Savannah State ranked third with a 3.80 average. Fellow SIAC member Miles College led the nation in the number of steals (with 171) and steals per game (with an average of 5.18). The following year, averaging 4.23 steals per game, Savannah State finished second in the country and trailed only Miles College, which repeated as the nation's best with an average of 5.00 steals per game in 1997. That same year, the Golden Bears of Miles College set the current Division II team batting record by averaging an even .400 for the season.

Savannah State's record of 39-9 in 1998 equated to the nation's third-highest winning percentage (.806) in the NCAA Division II classification that year, and it earned them a trip to the postseason regional tournament. Once again, team speed played a significant factor in its success. As a team, the Tigers sat atop the statistical leaders in both stolen bases (with 193) and stolen bases per game (with an average of 3.94 thefts). Junior shortstop Willie Melendez not only led the country with 16 triples, but also set the current NCAA Division II record for triples in a season. With the addition of double-digit triples by teammates Deyano Martin (12) and Brandon Jackson (10), Savannah State set the current national record of 58 team triples in a season.

\*\*\*

Before leaving the Central Intercollegiate Athletic Association for the Mid-Eastern Athletic Conference after the 1996-1997 school year, Norfolk State advanced its grip on CIAA baseball, winning five of the first six titles in the nineties. Its 1993 league crown made seven straight for the Spartans and 13 of the previous 14. Shaw University interrupted Norfolk State's run of titles, winning the championship in 1994 before the Spartans re-claimed its last CIAA crown in 1995. Bowie State had a mini-run of two titles, winning in 1996 and 1997, followed by Virginia State's title in 1998 and a Saint Augustine's College title in 1999.

There were many team and individual superlatives in the CIAA during the decade. Seven Spartans from Norfolk State were drafted in the 1990s, led by Terry Bradshaw, who was drafted by the Saint Louis Cardinals in the ninth round of the 1990 MLB Draft. Teammate Andre Johnson was not only a 12th-round draft pick of the Atlanta Braves in 1991, but was also an American Baseball Coaches Association All-American that year.

Saint Augustine's Ricky Sanders had the highest slugging percentage in the NCAA Division II (an even 1.000) in 1990 and ranked sixth in hitting (.474). Teammate Juan Pratt averaged 1.02 stolen bases per game to lead the country. As a team, the Saint Augustine's College Falcons ranked third in the nation in both hitting (.371) and slugging percentage (.594). The coach of the Falcons that year and also coach of the 1999 CIAA champions was Dr. Henry E. White. Coach White spent 19 years at Saint Augustine's and had a 346-317-2 record there before leaving for North Carolina Central University, tasked with resurrecting its baseball program after a 32-year hiatus.

In 1991, Bowie State's Mike Motta had the highest batting average in the country (.494), and for the next two seasons, Stacey Green of Shaw University was the national leader in stolen bases per game, averaging .97 steals per game in 1992 and nearly doubling that in 1993, averaging 1.74 per game. His 54 steals also was the most in NCAA Division II that year. Shaw University was crowned 1994 CIAA champion, and its 24-7 record produced the nation's 12th best winning percentage of .774. One of Stacey Green's teammates on the '94 Bears squad was Mike Boyd, who, with his 68 runs batted in, led the country by recording an average of 2.19 RBIs per game... a current NCAA Division II national record.

The Bowie State University CIAA championship teams of 1996 and 1997 were led by second baseman Ckori Jones. As a sophomore in 1996, Jones led the Bulldogs in hitting with an average of .393; the following year, his team-leading .459 batting average was the 11th best in the country. Besides his hitting, Ckori Jones had skills on the base paths. His 38 stolen bases in 38 games, for an average of one stolen base per game, ranked fourth highest in Division II and he scored an average of 1.61 runs per game, which was the most in the country.

***

Of the baseball programs not affiliated with any of the four HBCU-designated conferences (SWAC, MEAC, SIAC, and CIAA), the one with probably the most success during the nineties was West Virginia State University. In the decade, the Yellow Jackets produced West Virginia Intercollegiate Athletic Conference championships in 1993, 1994, 1997, and in 1999 when the team finished third in the College World Series. Eight ballplayers were drafted in the '90s, including 1995 NAIA All-American Barry Shelton, who was selected that year in the Major League Draft by the Chicago White Sox. The 36-11 squad of 1999 finished 10th in NCAA Division II hitting with a .351 batting average, and 10th in pitching, with a 3.57 earned run average. West Virginia State also finished second in the

*Justin Graham*
*West Virginia State University*

*Keith Fout*
*West Virginia State University*

country in team home runs, averaging almost two home runs per game. Four Yellow Jackets accounted for ten or more of the team's 88 "round-trippers", led by Justin Graham with 16, Wil Sowers with 14, Keith Fout with 13, and Joe Payne with 12.

***

With over one hundred years of black college baseball under its collective belt, more outstanding team and individual performances lay ahead as HBCU baseball entered the twenty-first century.

As the Southwestern Athletic Conference tournament expanded from a four-team playoff to six teams in the year 2000, and then growing to eight teams by the end of the decade, more schools were afforded an opportunity to capture SWAC crowns than ever before. One such school was Texas Southern University, which had not claimed a league title from the time it initially entered the conference in 1954 until it won its first in 2004. Prairie View A&M, an original member of the SWAC in 1920, claimed its first baseball title in 2006, then repeated in 2007.

The Texas Southern Tigers' championship of 2004 and its repeat title in 2008 were spearheaded by Coach Candy Robinson. In the first round of the 2004 NCAA Division I postseason Houston Regional Tournament, his underdog Tigers pulled off one of the biggest upsets in NCAA baseball tournament history, defeating the defending NCAA World Series Champion Rice University Owls.[14] Coach Robinson's second SWAC championship in 2008 came at the expense of two-time defending champion Prairie View A&M and its head coach, Michael Robertson. Ironically, following Candy Robinson's retirement that year, Texas Southern University turned to rival SWAC head coach Michael Robertson as Robinson's successor. The selection of Michael Robertson proved to be the perfect choice as he led the Tigers of Texas Southern to three additional titles in the following decade.

Before Coach Michael Robertson assumed his position at Texas Southern, his Prairie View A&M Panthers were crowned SWAC champions twice in the twenty-first century's first decade. In his second year at the helm of Prairie View baseball, Robertson's Panthers improved from 10-45 in 2003 to 30-26 in 2004. For his effort, Michael Robertson was named HBCU Coach of the Year by the website *blackcollegebaseball.com*. The site also voted Prairie View A&M ninth in its season-ending HBCU Top 10 poll that year, then bumped the Panthers up to No. 4 in 2005. In 2006, Prairie View A&M was named HBCU baseball's national champion. During its rise to the top, Prairie View was led by brothers Michael and Myrio Richard. Older brother Michael was named the SWAC Player of the Year in 2007, and Myrio claimed the same title in 2008. Michael Richard was named a third-team All-American by *Collegiate Baseball Newspaper* in 2007.

Alcorn State produced two student-athletes who each won SWAC Player-of-the-Year and National Collegiate Baseball Writers Association All-American honors. Dario Rosa accomplished the feat in 2000, finishing third in the country with a .452 batting average, while Corey Wimberley duplicated the laurels in 2005 after leading the nation in hitting with a .462 batting average. Fellow Panther Marcus Davis was named Alcorn State's

*Corey Wimberley*
*Alcorn State*

third NCBWA All-American in the decade, winning his honor in 2007. Davis topped the nation's NCAA Division I leaders in runs batted in with an average of 1.49 per game in 2006 and followed up in 2007, finishing second in the country.

Though Jackson State claimed its only SWAC crown of the decade in 2000, two of its brightest stars earned numerous individual accolades. In 2004, outfielder Bryant Lange was named the Southwestern Athletic Conference Player of the Year and *blackcollegebaseball.com's* Position Player of the Year. His .439 average was the fourth highest in all of NCAA Division I batting. Likewise, but two years later, infielder Joaquin Rodriguez claimed the same two awards and added a third major honor when he was named an All-American by *Collegiate Baseball Newspaper*.

While two never-before SWAC champions accounted for four titles in the decade, perennial champion Southern University claimed five of its own between the years of 2000 and 2009. In a run from 2001 through 2003, Southern University fielded three of the most prolific teams in HBCU baseball history. During that stretch, the Southern University Jaguar baseball team had an overall record of 132-29, yielding a winning percentage of .820, and a conference record of 88-8, for an even higher .917 percentage. In 2003, the National Collegiate Baseball Writers Association ranked Southern University 27th best in its final poll (out of 287 DI baseball-playing schools), which remains the highest ever by an HBCU NCAA Division I program. The website *blackcollegebaseball.com* selected Southern as its HBCU National Champion. As a team, the Jaguars led the country in hitting in both 2002 and 2003, averaging .377 and .351, respectively. Southern also led the nation both years in three additional categories, those being scoring, slugging percentage, and team winning percentage. In 2001, Southern University ranked in the top ten nationally in each of the previously referenced categories and also led the country in triples with 38 and triples per game, averaging over two triples every three games.

*2003 Southern University*

In that three-year period of 2001 through 2003, Southern had many highly ranked individual performances as well. In 2001, Michael Woods Jr., whose father of the same name once recorded the longest hitting streak in NCAA Division II history (45 straight games with Southern University in 1978), finished third in the country with a .453 batting average. His slugging percentage of .918 ranked second in the country, as did his average of .57 doubles per game. *Baseball America* magazine named Woods an All-American in 2001, and in June of that year, the Detroit Tigers made Michael Woods Jr. its first-round draft pick in the Major League Baseball Draft (32nd overall selection).

Eighteen Southern University ballplayers were selected in Major League Baseball annual drafts from Jaguar teams that played between the years 2001 through 2003. Besides Michael Woods Jr., three of them were Fred Lewis, a second-round selection of the San Francisco Giants in 2002, Antoin Gray, a 25$^{th}$-round selection of the Chicago White Sox in 2003 and Andrew Toussaint, a 13$^{th}$-round pick of the Anaheim Angles in 2004. Fred Lewis hit .407 in his only year at Southern and then went on to a seven-year Major League Baseball career and one additional year playing professional baseball in Japan. Though Fred Lewis topped the coveted .400 mark, Antoin Gray hit an even higher .449 in 2002, which ranked fourth in the country in NCAA Division I individual hitting. His 18 doubles and 19 home runs equated to a slugging percentage of .834, which placed Gray fifth highest in the country. Additionally, he scored 88 runs for an average of 1.63 runs per game, which led the nation. At the conclusion of the 2002 college baseball season, Antoin Gray, whose father Robert was a three-time All-SWAC infielder at Mississippi Valley State University in the mid-1970s, was named a *Collegiate Baseball Newspaper* All-American. Two years later, *Collegiate Baseball Newspaper* also selected Andrew Toussaint as an All-American.

Even with the abundance of talent produced at Southern University during its dynamic run in 2001-2003, it was overshadowed by a rare gem in teammate Rickie Weeks. In fact, most informed observers consider Weeks one of the all-time greats in HBCU baseball.

Rickie Weeks' list of accomplishments started accumulating as a freshman in 2001, during a season in which he hit .422, ranking in the top 20 nationally. His 12 triples for an average of .218 per game led the country, and his .849 slugging percentage ranked fourth. Besides the number of SWAC honors he received, Rickie Weeks was named a third-team *Baseball America* All-American. After his freshman season, Weeks was selected to the USA Baseball Collegiate National Team.

As a sophomore in 2002, Rickie Weeks led the country in batting average (.495), slugging percentage (.995), runs batted in (96), and triples (12). The

American Baseball Coaches Association, *Collegiate Baseball Newspaper*, National Collegiate Baseball Writers Association, and *Baseball America* each named Weeks an NCAA Division I first-team All-American. Once again, Rickie Weeks was tabbed to represent the country on its USA Collegiate Baseball National Team.

*Rickie Weeks*
*Southern University*

Going into his junior season, and final one at Southern University, Rickie Weeks was listed on everyone's pre-season All-American team. He was a household name in college baseball circles and in virtually all Major League Baseball scouts' minds. Weeks went on to defend both his national batting and slugging titles. In doing so, he became only the second NCAA Division I collegian to collect back-to-back national hitting titles and the first to record two straight slugging crowns. Rickie Weeks currently holds NCAA Division I career records for having the highest batting average (.465) and slugging percentage (.927) of those who played a minimum of two years with at least 225 total at-bats.

By the end of Weeks' junior season, he was again named to everyone's All-America teams. But the accolades did not stop there. Rickie Weeks was selected the NCAA Division I College Player of the Year by *Baseball America*, *Collegiate Baseball Newspaper*, and the American Baseball Coaches Association. He was the National Collegiate Baseball Writers Association Dick Howser Award recipient, the unofficial equivalent of college football's Heisman Trophy, and the Golden Spikes Award recipient, given annually by USA Baseball to the nation's best amateur baseball player. Not only is Rickie Weeks one of the most honored HBCU baseball players ever, but early in 2020,

*Baseball America* selected him as its eighth most decorated college All-American of the last 40 years (the period of time in which the magazine has been selecting All-Americans).[15] The Milwaukee Brewers selected Rickie Weeks second overall in the 2003 Major League Draft, and he then played 14 seasons in the Major Leagues.

*In 2003, Southern University's entire infield was drafted into professional baseball. The group included first baseman Kevin Vital (top row far left), second baseman Rickie Weeks (top row second from left), third baseman Antoin Gray (bottom row second from left) and shortstop Fernando Puebla (top row second from right). Other draftees included pitchers Dewon Day (top row center) and Damian Ursin (bottom row far right). Also pictured are Jamar Lewis (bottom row far left) and Brandon Mason (bottom row second from right).*

\*\*\*

In the Mid-Eastern Athletic Conference, after claiming three of the final four conference titles in the decade of the nineties, Bethune-Cookman dominated the next decade, winning all but one crown from 2000 through 2010. During the 2002 season, the Wildcats advanced to the Gainesville Regional and became the first MEAC team to win a game in the NCAA Tournament with a 7-4 victory over Florida International. The website *blackcollegebaseball.com* voted Bethune-Cookman as its national HBCU champion in 2002, did so again in 2004, and then from 2007 through 2009. Five times, Wildcats were named MEAC Players of the Year. Infielder Wes Timmons won the title in 2002, pitcher John Gragg won his crown in 2003, outfielder Sebastien Boucher claimed the title in 2004, outfielder Nabil Sagbini was tabbed Player of the Year in 2006, and the last one was won by infielder Jose Lozada in 2008. Wes Timmons was selected to the *Collegiate Baseball Newspaper* All-American team in 2002, and in 2006 *blackcollegebaseball.com* picked Francisco Rodriguez as its Pitcher of the Year. Rodriguez was also named Mid-Eastern Athletic Conference Pitcher of the Year in 2007, and teammate Hiram Burgos duplicated that honor the following year when he finished the season with the nation's fourth lowest earned run average of 1.58. Fifteen Bethune-Cookman Wildcats were drafted during the decade, including Mike Woodyard, a fourth-round selection in the 2000 Major League Baseball Draft, and Hiram Burgos, a sixth-round pick in 2009. Both Woodyard and Burgos would pitch in the Majors.

Interrupting Bethune-Cookman's run of MEAC titles was North Carolina A&T in 2005. That particular Aggies team featured teammates who became conference most valuable players in Jeremy Jones (2005) and Charlie Gamble (2007). Jones and his teammate, Michael Hauff, were selected Player of the Year and Pitcher of the Year, respectively, by *blackcollegebaseball.com* in 2005, and North Carolina A&T shared the title of HBCU National Champions that year with Southern University. Two years later, Charlie Gamble earned All-American honors from *Collegiate Baseball Newspaper*. The 2007 MEAC Rookie of the Year and current conference single-season record holder in doubles with 25 in 2009, NCA&T's C. J. Beatty, was named first-team All-MEAC for three straight seasons.

Though Bethune-Cookman University dominated conference championships in the decade, during the first five seasons of the 2000s, Delaware State had the best overall conference record, going 67-8 for a .893 winning percentage. Standouts on those Hornet teams included third baseman/outfielder Scott Martin, first baseman Bret Underwood, and pitcher Shawn Phillips. Scott Martin, who played at Delaware State during the seasons of 2000 to 2003, was named an American Baseball Coaches Association All-American in 2001 after the sophomore finished 11th in the country in hitting with an average of .432, third in slugging with a .870 average and led the country in runs batted in with an average of 1.75 RBIs per game. Bret Underwood, a Hornet from 2001 through 2004, was a three-time All-MEAC performer with a career batting average of .354, and 2004 *blackcollegebaseball.com* Pitcher of the Year Shawn Phillips had a 2.77 career earned run average from 2002 to 2004.

In 2001, Delaware State's 37-10 won-loss record for a .787 winning percentage was the third-best in the country. The Hornets' .345 team batting average was the fourth-highest nationally, they led the country in scoring by averaging 10.38 runs per game, and the pitching staff's 2.99 earned run average was the lowest in the nation. Individually, John Sterling's 2.08 ERA ranked 14th in the country, Tim Vaillancourt's 2.27 ERA ranked 19th, and Joe Brzeczek's 2.51 ERA ranked 33rd.

*Scott Martin*
*Delaware State University*

*Malkum King, Scott Martin, Dave Gordon, Tim Vaillancourt, Mike August and Phil Sullinger (l to r) display Delaware State's 2001 individual and team national statistical leader awards*

*Bret Underwood*
*Delaware State University*

On the campus of Florida A&M, the idiom "speed merchant" could apply to a number of the school's athletes, both past and present. World record-holding Olympic track champion Robert "Bullet Bob" Hayes was undoubtedly one of the most famous. Rattler baseball's base-stealing champion Vince Coleman in the 1980s was another. Following in the literal footsteps of Coleman was Dwaine Bacon, who topped the country's best base thieves in 2000 with 74 stolen bases, averaging 1.54 steals per game. Teammate Alex Smith finished third nationally, stealing on average 1.02 bases per game. Smith also led the country in walks averaging 1.07 per game. As a team, Florida A&M led the nation in base stealing, averaging 4.06 thefts per outing.

*Rust College head coach Avery Mason (l) with 2002 national stolen base leader James Hymon (r)*

Another school baseball program that regularly displayed its proficiency on the base paths throughout the decade was Rust College. The Bearcats, led by head coach Avery Mason, established a national record for NCAA Division III schools in 2006 averaging 6.06 stolen bases per game. The following year Rust College duplicated its national team stolen base title stealing on average 6.00 bases per game. Individually, in 2002 James Hymon, an 18th-round MLB Draft pick of the Seattle Mariners in 2003, topped the nation's Division III schools, stealing 56 bases for an average of 1.37 per game. The following year, now a senior, Hymon finished second in the country to his freshman teammate Carlos Hardaway, who claimed the national stolen base crown with 50 steals, averaging 1.52 thefts per game. Hardaway repeated in 2006, increasing his national best to 57 steals for an average of 1.78 per game. And once again, a Rust College Bearcat finished runner-up to a teammate, with freshman Justin Kelly collecting 54 stolen bases for an average of 1.64 steals per game. Carlos Hardaway just missed claiming his third national stolen base title when in 2007, teammate Vashun Jackson edged Hardaway for the crown 1.38 stolen bases per game to 1.35 (both in 26 games).

\*\*\*

In NCAA Division II HBCU baseball, Southern Intercollegiate Athletic Conference titles were dominated by three different schools winning the ten championships of the 2000s; Albany State with five crowns, including a run of four straight from 2001 through 2004, Stillman College with three titles, and Paine College with two. Paine's 2000 title-winning team was guided by its head coach Stanley Stubbs, who in unprecedented fashion led in-state rival Albany State to the following year's title of 2001. In the SIAC's Division II counterpart, the Central Intercollegiate Athletic Association, Virginia State University was an even more dominant force, winning seven of the decade's conference titles. Shaw University claimed two, and Elizabeth City State

University won its first and only CIAA title in 2005.

Instrumental in Albany State University's run of SIAC titles were outfielder Tyren Millner, who led the Golden Rams in 2002 hitting .386 with 14 doubles while claiming conference tournament MVP honors, and catcher Dedrick Murphy, who from 2001 through 2003 hit .374 with 29 home runs. In 2003, pitcher Tyrell Miller was the NCAA Division II leader in total strikeouts with 126. He averaged 12.8 strikeouts per nine innings and upped it in 2004 to an average of 13.3, both of which led the nation.

Plenty of other names from the SIAC and CIAA dotted the national Division II leaderboards throughout the decade. Milton Reed, from Shaw University's 2002 conference title-winning squad, finished among the top five in home runs per game, runs batted in per game, and slugging percentage. Reed returned for the 2003 season and led the country in runs batted in per game, while finishing ranked in the top six in batting average, slugging percentage, and runs scored per game. Antoine Tucker, an outfielder from Elizabeth City State, who in 2003 finished sixth nationally in stolen bases, claimed the stolen base crown in 2004. Tucker also led the country in runs scored that year, and, two years later, his Vikings teammate, Carlos Gutierrez, led the county in hitting with a .548 average. Gutierrez added a second individual title in 2006, leading the country with a 1.078 slugging percentage edging DeShaun Brooks of Benedict College. Brooks and Gutierrez battled each other in two other categories for the nation's best; runs batted in and home runs, with DeShaun Brooks claiming both crowns.

For the first time in Division II baseball history, three HBCU programs qualified for the postseason regional tournament in 2007. Joining Stillman College from the SIAC and Virginia State from the CIAA was West Virginia State University, representing the West Virginia Intercollegiate Athletic Conference.

Possibly the strongest HBCU Division II baseball program in the decade of the 2000s, West Virginia State, qualified for the NCAA postseason tournament each year except in 2003 and finished in fifth place at the 2005

College World Series. The teams of 2005 and 2006 each led the country in hitting, and the latter's .827 winning percentage was the second best in the nation. During those 10 years, 13 Yellow Jackets were named All-Americans, led by infielders Ryan Taylor, selected in 2005 and 2006, and Jeff Miller, selected in 2006 and 2007. In 2007, Daktronics Inc., the manufacturer of scoreboards and video displays, began sponsoring an NCAA Division II All-American team. In that initial year, teammates Josh Miller and Brandon Halstead were named first-team and second-team selections, respectively. Four members of WVSU teams were selected in MLB drafts, including 2000 Pittsburgh Pirates pick Shannon Cabell, who that year was nationally ranked individually both in offensive statistical categories as a designated hitter and in pitching statistical categories as a starting pitcher. Though undrafted, 2002 West Virginia Intercollegiate Athletic Conference Pitcher of the Year, Scott Patterson was the only Yellow Jacket to see Major League action, though

*Jeff Miller (l) and Bo Darby (r)*
*West Virginia State University*

briefly, with the New York Yankees. And finally, in the last season of the decade, outfielder Bo Darby established an impressive Division II national record that still currently remains on the books by hitting home runs in five consecutive at-bats (over two games, including four in one contest).[16]

Playing as an independent Division II team in 2000, preparing to move to Division I, Savannah State University had perhaps the most monumental single season of the decade, and maybe for the ages. The Tigers, led by head coach Jamie Rigdon, opened the season on February 2nd with a 15-0 victory over Edward Waters College and did not lose a contest until its forty-seventh game of the season. When Savannah State reached 35 straight, it officially broke the all-division record set by the University of Texas Longhorns in 1977 and tied in 1999 by Florida Atlantic University. However, the celebration was cut short upon learning that Marrieta College in Ohio claimed to have won 40 consecutive games the year prior, but had failed to notify the NCAA's official record keepers. The short-lived controversy ended when Savannah State made Claflin University victim number 41 and then added five more victories, increasing its win streak to a currently recognized season record of 46 consecutive wins. The next game of the 2000 season featured a match with crosstown rival Savannah College of Art and Design, coached by former 19-year Major League pitching great Luis Tiant, Jr. The long winning streak ended at 46 with SCAD's 3-1 victory over Savannah State.

*Savannah State University*
*Brett Higgins, Marcus Johnson, Darron Street, Isiah Brown*
*and Torrie Pinkins (l to r)*

The Tigers' win streak made national news and might have overshadowed individual successes. Nonetheless, that record was achieved with a great blend of both hitting and pitching. Offensively, Savannah State led the country in hitting with a .380 batting average, slugging percentage with an average of .629, and runs scored averaging 12.59 per game (an NCAA Division II record still in existence). Additionally, the Tigers ranked fourth in stolen bases, with five of the regulars stealing 20 or more.

The leading batsman was its hard-hitting catcher Brett Higgins, who led the team and the country in batting with an average of .513 (Michael Reeves, from fellow Georgia HBCU Paine College, was a close second with a .509 batting average). Higgins claimed nine other individual national statistical titles; most total hits (98), doubles (32), doubles per game (.65), runs batted in (93), runs batted in per game (1.90), runs scored (87), runs scored per game (1.78), total bases (193), and slugging percentage (1.010).

Equally impressive, Savannah State University's pitching staff ranked atop the nation with an overall team earned run average of 2.30. Its starting rotation, which included freshman Ricardo Castillo (with a 2.30 ERA), junior Guy Thigpen (with a 2.13 ERA), and junior Chris Cesario (with a 2.06 ERA), accounted for all but two of the pitching staff's 49 starts. Castillo, with 18 wins and Cesario with 16, ranked numbers one and two in the country in pitching victories and the Tigers winning percentage of .939 topped the nation and remains the highest in Division II history.

\*\*\*

The first national media outlet dedicated solely to the coverage of HBCU baseball surfaced in 2002 when "black college baseball aficionado" Ruffin Bell, a former baseball captain at

Coppin State in the mid-1990s, created the internet website *blackcollegebaseball.com*. Bell created the site so that fans could have a centralized media outlet for all their HBCU baseball news and to aid in the promotion of black college baseball. For its first two years, coverage was almost entirely dedicated to baseball programs at HBCU Division I schools. Then beginning in 2005, *blackcollegebaseball.com* expanded coverage to include news on Division II, Division III, NAIA, and independent HBCU baseball programs. From the beginning, Rufin Bell took great care to run a weekly top 10 poll and name a national champion at season's end. Individual stars were recognized with selection onto his "elite" teams, and players and coaches of the year were also honored.

A sister website covering the historical aspect of HBCU baseball made its internet debut in 2009 with the creation of *blackcollegenines.com*. Like fellow black college baseball fan Ruffin Bell wanted to do, giving attention to HBCU baseball, Jay Sokol aimed to do the same, bringing to light the history of HBCU baseball. When duties, including serving as athletic director at Cheney State, became too time-consuming for Bell, the task of covering both current and past black college baseball was assumed by Sokol on his *blackcollegenines.com* website. The dual-purpose site continues to this day, with former Edward Waters College ballplayer Michael Coker's assistance covering both large and small school HBCU baseball, running top 10 polls, and naming all-elite teams.

***

After 45 years of Southwestern Athletic Conference domination by Grambling State University, Jackson State University, and Southern University, there was a shift towards parity in the first decade of the twenty-first century, which followed form into the 2010s. Seven different schools won SWAC titles. Texas Southern led the way with three, and in the decade, both Alcorn State and Alabama State won first-ever conference crowns. Grambling State University claimed the SWAC title in 2010, its first since a three-year run from 1983 through 1985, while Jackson State, Prairie View A&M, and Southern University were the other schools earning championships.

*Jose De Leon (l) and Frazier Hall (r) of Southern University wearing Negro League tribute game throwback uniforms.*

From 2010 through 2019, 29 ballplayers from the SWAC were drafted by Major League Baseball, with Grambling and Alabama State leading the way with seven each. Southern University ranked just below with six draftees, and of those six Jaguars, pitchers Cody Hall and Jose De Leon reached the Major League level. Hall, drafted in 2010, made his MLB debut in 2015 with the San Francisco Giants and De Leon, drafted in 2013, made his debut in 2016 with the Los Angeles Dodgers.

Frazier Hall, the two-time SWAC Player of the Year in 2010 and 2011 representing Southern University, was named an All-American first baseman by *Collegiate Baseball Newspaper* in 2011 and was then drafted by Los Angeles Angles in the sixteenth round of the MLB draft. Jackson State infielder Melvin Rodriguez earned the conference player of the year award in 2015 and was named an All-American by the National Collegiate Baseball Writers Association and *College Baseball Newspaper*. Following the season, Rodriguez was selected by the Washington Nationals in the 18th round of the Major

League Draft. A year after Melvin Rodriguez was recognized as one of the nation's best, pitcher Joseph Camacho of Alabama State received similar accolades in 2016 as the SWAC Pitcher of the Year (which he also won in 2014 and 2015), National Collegiate Baseball Writers Association All-American and a *Collegiate Baseball Newspaper* All-American. Camacho was also voted *blackcollegenines.com* postseason Most Valuable Pitcher in the website's initial foray into recognizing HBCUs' best ballplayers and then signed a free agent contract with the Oakland Athletics.

The mainstays of Texas Southern University's 2018 SWAC title team were conference Pitcher of the Year Aron Solis and Player of the Year Kamren Dukes. Each was a Black College Nines' All-Elite, and Dukes was selected the organization's Player of the Year, as well as a *Collegiate Baseball Newspaper* All-American.

After leading Mid-Eastern Athletic Conference Bethune-Cookman University to 11 conference titles in his 12 years as head coach, Mervyl Melendez took over the same position at Alabama State University in 2012 and then led the Hornets to *blackcollegenines.com* HBCU national championships in 2015 and 2016. Earlier in the decade, before he left Bethune-Cookman University for Alabama State, Coach Melendez led the Wildcats to HBCU baseball titles in 2010 and 2011.

\*\*\*

Parity in the MEAC was less prevalent than that found in the SWAC during the 10-year period from 2010 through 2019. Bethune-Cookman University won six of the first eight titles in the decade, Florida A&M won two, while Savannah State and North Carolina A&T won solo crowns. In 2017, Bethune-Cookman was tapped HBCU Large School National Champion by *blackcollegenines.com*, its fourth title of the decade. While competing in the Gainesville Regional Tournament that year, Bethune-Cookman was one win from being the first HBCU to qualify for an NCAA Division I Super Regional tournament. The following year, North Carolina A&T was the MEAC conference tournament champion and claimed Black College Nines' 2018

HBCU national crown in its "large school" division.

*Bethune-Cookman teammates Juan Perez (l) and Peter O'Brien (r) were both MLB draft selections of the Colorado Rockies*

During this decade, MEAC schools produced 25 Major League Draft selections, including ten from Bethune-Cookman. Of them, Peter O'Brien and Montana Durapau, both of Bethune-Cookman, and Kyle McGowin of Savannah State, reached the Majors. All three received the conference's highest honors, with O'Brien being named Player of the Year in 2010 and McGowin and Durapau winning Pitcher of the Year in 2013 and 2014, respectively. Peter O'Brien was selected an All-American catcher in 2010 by *Collegiate Baseball Newspaper,* and in 2013, Kyle McGowin was named an All-American pitcher by the National Collegiate Baseball Writers Association.

Norfolk State University's Matt Outman was picked the MEAC's top pitcher in 2015 and 2016 and teammate Devin Hemmerich, winner of the same conference MVP award in 2017, became the most decorated Spartan since Norfolk State began playing NCAA Division I baseball in 1998.[17] In addition to his MEAC Pitcher of the Year selection, Hemmerich was named an All-American by the American Baseball Coaches Association, the National Collegiate Baseball Writers Association and *Collegiate Baseball Newspaper*, all in 2017. Black College Nines also named Devin Hemmerich a first-team All-Elite and its Pitcher of the Year.

\*\*\*

Stillman College won the final three Southern Intercollegiate Athletic Conference titles of the 2000s. After Albany State claimed the first crown of the next decade, the Tigers of Stillman recorded a string of four straight titles from 2011 through 2014. In 2016, Claflin University won its only baseball title during the school's ten-year stint in the conference, and Miles College won its first and only title in 2017 after joining the SIAC in 1927. Besides its 2010 championship, the Albany State Golden Rams claimed titles in 2015 and 2018. The final conference baseball championship of the decade was claimed by Spring Hill College, which joined the SIAC in 2014 as its first non-HBCU designated university.

The National Collegiate Baseball Writers Association selected four NCAA Division II All-Americans from HBCU schools in the SIAC during this decade, including Brandon Gipson and Lydell Moseby (son of former major leaguer Lloyd Moseby), both of Benedict College, as well as Albany State University's Jacob Campbell and Darrell Langston of Claflin University. Likewise, Jarius Brown of Stillman College was named a Division II All-American by the American Baseball Coaches Association in 2012. Black College Nines picked Benedict College's David White Jr. as its Small School Player of the Year in 2017. In 2019, the website named SIAC's Gerardic Dobbs of Claflin University and Roman Oliu of Albany State its Player of the Year and Pitcher of the Year, respectively.

In May 2011, *Collegiate Baseball Newspaper* titled its lead story "Amazing Base Stealing Machine", referencing Benedict College swiping 739 bases over the previous three seasons. By decade's end, Selwyn Young coached Tiger teams had accumulated 2,147 stolen bases over ten years. In the interim, Benedict's "greatest show on dirt" racked up several NCAA Division II team base-stealing records as well as annual individual national statistical leaders.

National NCAA Division II team records that were set by Benedict College in the decade of the 2010s that still stand include most stolen bases in a game (24 in 2012), most stolen bases for a season (334 in 2013), most stolen bases per game (8.15 in 2013) and most stolen base attempts for a season (403 in 2013). Individual national statistical leaders in Division II during the decade from Benedict College include Michael Jordan (most stolen bases with 66 in 2012 and highest stolen base average per game of 1.83 in 2012), Kevin Davis (most stolen bases with 58 in 2013 and highest stolen base average per game of 1.57 in 2013 and 1.26 in 2014) and Bradon O'Connor (highest stolen base average per game of 1.38 in 2019).

***

When the decade opened in the Central Intercollegiate Athletic Association, of the 13 schools in the conference, eight played a baseball schedule in 2010, with those being Chowan University (admitted in 2009 as the conference's first non-HBCU school), Elizabeth City State University, Lincoln University of Pennsylvania, Saint Augustine's College (now Saint Augustine's University), Saint Paul's College (which terminated athletics in 2011 and then closed in 2013), Shaw University, Virginia State University and Winston-Salem State University. By the end of the 2018-2019 school year, of the CIAA's 12 members, only three HBCUs played baseball, Claflin University (which moved from the SIAC to the CIAA in 2018), Lincoln University, and Virginia State. Because of minimal participation, the CIAA did not support a conference tournament after the 2017 season.

In 2010, Saint Augustine's College, which terminated baseball just before the 2019 season, won its fourth and final league crown. Chowan University won the conference title in 2017 and then in 2019 joined Conference Carolinas for baseball and most other sports. Other than these two schools, the decade's other six CIAA titles were claimed by Winston-Salem State University, which had pulled out of the conference after the 2005-2006 school year (in a short-lived attempt to move to Division I status and join the MEAC) and then re-joined again in 2010.

During its reign over the CIAA, Winston-Salem State University baseball, coached by Kevin Ritsche, was named "small school" national champions by Black College Nines on its website *blackcollegenines.com* in 2015, 2017, and for a final time in 2019. In 2017, playing in the NCAA Division II Atlantic Regional, the Rams lost in the finals to eventual national champion West Chester University of Pennsylvania. Two years later, on its way to fashioning a 35-16 record while playing an independent schedule, it was announced on March 15th that Winston-Salem State University would realign its athletic program and replace baseball with golf. Besides Winston-Salem State and the other CIAA schools previously mentioned that terminated baseball programs in the decade of the 2010s, Elizabeth City State University suspended baseball after the 2013-2014 school year, and Shaw University announced it would terminate baseball that same year.

*Rashad Ingram*
*Saint Augustine's College*

While participation in the CIAA was on the decline, individual stars who shined during this time included infielder Rashad Ingram of Saint Augustine's College. He was named the CIAA Player of the Year in 2011 and a Daktronics third-team All-American. Ingram, who led the NCAA Division II with 80 stolen bases and the highest stolen base average per game of 1.48 (he also led the country in 2009 with an average of 1.30 steals per game), was drafted by the San Diego Padres in the 2011 Major League Draft.

In 2013, Winston-Salem State University produced two All-Americans. Outfielder Travis Moore and designated hitter Tyler Hickernell were both honored by the National Collegiate Baseball Writers Association. Travis Moore, who led the country in triples with eight in 2013, was selected a Daktronics All-American that year. Winston-Salem State's Randy Norris finished fourth nationally in hitting with a batting average of .437 and first in stolen bases with 47 in 2018. Then, after the season, Norris was the first HBCU ballplayer taken in the 2018 Major League Baseball Draft when he was selected in the 19th round by the San Francisco Giants. The following year, the Houston Astros selected E. P. Reese, also from Winston-Salem State, in the

25<sup>th</sup> round of the 2019 MLB Draft.

***

As it did in the previous two decades, West Virginia State continued to flourish in the decade of the 2010s. The Yellow Jackets twice competed in the NCAA Division II postseason tournament (2010 and 2015). In 2010, *blackcollegebaseball.com* named West Virginia State its HBCU National Champion, and *blackcollegenines.com* did likewise in 2016. The NCAA Division II College Sports Information Directors of America, the selection committee for Daktronics, named designated hitter Jack Hudson an All-American in 2013, and pitcher Joshua Falbo was also selected a Daktronics All-American in 2015. The following year, Falbo earned the honor of Black College Nines "small school" Pitcher of the Year.

***

Of the HBCU programs affiliated with either the National Intercollegiate Athletic Association (NAIA), United States Collegiate Athletic Association (USCAA), or National Christian College Athletic Association (NCCAA), in the decade from 2010 through 2019, Edward Waters University, Talladega College, Jarvis Christian College, and Selma University were the most successful baseball programs... at least according to HBCU polls.

During the decade, between the eight small school polls run by the websites *blackcollegebaseball.com* and *blackcollegenines.com*, both Edward Waters and Talladega were included in the top 10, five times each. Black College Baseball named the Tigers of Edward Waters University its national poll champion in 2011, and Black College Nines named the Tigers number three in 2015 and number two in 2016. Talladega College's best finish in the small school poll (including NCAA Division II teams and those in the NAIA, USCAA, and NCCAA) was second in 2017. Jarvis Christian and Selma University each appeared in the top 10 polls four times, with Selma's third-place finish in 2016 being the highest of the two baseball programs.

In 2009, the NAIA revamped its postseason tournament format by adding an opening round. In the decade of the 2010s, Talladega College appeared four times in the first round (in 2014 and 2017 through 2019). Both Edward Waters University (in 2011) and Jarvis Christian College (in 2019) also competed in the tournament's opening round.

On August 28th of 2019, Selma University, a school that averaged less than 500 full-time students a year in the decade, confirmed it was discontinuing athletics in order to downsize. The news came literally out of left field for a baseball program that had competed in its ninth straight postseason tournament only months before. As a member of the USCAA, the Bulldogs participated in the association's tournament in 2011 through 2014 and then again in 2018 and 2019. For the years of 2015 through 2017, Selma University's athletic programs were affiliated with the NCCAA, and the baseball team competed in that association's postseason regional tournament each year.

In these 10 years, Selma University produced All-Americans six times, twice by second baseman C. J. Lindsey (in 2010 and 2011), first baseman Tashland Robinson and outfielder Eddie Waters (both in 2011), first baseman Marcus Hardy (in 2018), and Ricky Butts (in 2019).

Six of those postseason tournaments came during the tenure of Adrian Holloway. The former Alabama State Hornet served as Selma's head coach from 2014 through the dissolution of baseball in 2019. When that termination announcement was made in late August, the headline declaring the reinstatement of baseball at Xavier University of

*In 2018, Selma University's Marcus Hardy (l) led the USCAA in home runs with 11 and in 2019, teammate Ricky Butts (r) finished sixth in the USCAA, hitting .472.*

Louisiana, after a near sixty-year absence, was only four days old. Before the end of the year, the wheels were already in motion to name Adrian Holloway as Xavier's new head coach, with varsity play to begin in the 2020-2021 school year.

The two strongest HBCU baseball programs in the Gulf Coast Athletic

Conference during the decade were rivals Talladega College and Edward Waters University, with the Tornadoes of Talladega besting the Tigers of Edward Waters in 30 of their 49 contests during the 2010s. However, with five 30-plus winning seasons in the decade, Edward Waters had one more than Talladega's four during that time.

In 2015, Edward Waters went 33-22 for the season and featured NAIA All-American catcher Jesse Baker, who finished in the top five nationally in runs batted in, home runs, slugging percentage, and ninth in hitting with a batting average of .430. One year later, Coach Reginald Johnson was selected as Black College Nines' Small School Coach of the Year.

Talladega's best record came in 2014 when the Tornadoes finished with a record of 39-20. The team led the NAIA in hitting with a batting average of .362 and finished in the top five in slugging percentage, runs scored, and triples. Three years later, the 36-win Tornadoes were led by All-American Kyle Chavez, who led the NAIA with 13 individual pitching victories. Chavez capped the season garnering Black College Nines' Small School Pitcher of the Year honors.

JAVION RANDLE
JARVIS CHRISTIAN COLLEGE
2016
"SMALL SCHOOL"
PLAYER OF THE YEAR

BLACK COLLEGE NINES
ELITES

Another NAIA-level school that had a run of five, 30-plus winning seasons in the 2010s was Jarvis Christian College of Hawkins, Texas. And in 2016, the Bulldogs produced its second national NAIA hitting leader in outfielder Javion Randle, who hit .480 for the season. Like his 1974 national hitting-crown counterpart Nate Chapman did, Javion Randle was selected as an NAIA All-American. He was also picked the Black College Nines' 2016 Small School Position Player of the Year.

---

[1] "Title IX and Sex Discrimination." U.S. Department of Education. Last modified April 2015. https://www2.ed.gov/about/offices/list/ocr/docs/tix_dis.html.

[2] "College Division Records." In *Collegiate Baseballl Recordbook*, 1985 ed., 26. Charlotte, NC:

National Collegiate Baseball Writers Association, 1985.

[3] Hawkins, James E. *History of the Southern Intercollegiate Athletic Conference, 1913-1990*, 444. Butler, GA: Benns Printing Co., 1994.

[4] Ibid., 445.

[5] Ibid.

[6] Streamline Technologies | Nashville, TN. "100 Moments: TSU Baseball Wins 30 Games." TSUTigers.com. Last modified October 16, 2012. http://www.tsutigers.com/news/articles/2012-13/5094/100-moments-tsu-baseball-wins-30-games/.

[7] Russell, Dan. "Aluminum and Composite Bats: Performance Standards in College Baseball." Penn State Engineering: Graduate Program in Acoustics. Last modified October 6, 2017. https://www.acs.psu.edu/drussell/bats/NCAA-stats.html.

[8] Peterson, Armand. "Stan Jefferson." *Society for American Baseball Research | Society for American Baseball Research*, 2016, sabr.org/bioproj/person/50c3b293.

[9] *Baseball America's 1984 College Baseball Annual*, edited by Allan Simpson, 126. Durham, NC: American Sports Publishing, 1984.

[10] Ibid., 126.

[11] Perry, Randall. "Dodgers Pick Tigers' Howell." *Montgomery Advertiser* (Montgomery, AL), June 10, 1982.

[12] Brown, Rich. "Former Baseball Pro Tries to Lift Kathleen High's Game." *The Lakeland Ledger*. Last modified December 27, 2010. https://www.theledger.com/news/20101226/former-baseball-pro-tries-to-lift-kathleen-highs-game.

[13] "Central State Announces 2015 Hall of Fame Inductees." Xenia's Word on the Street. Last modified July 14, 2015.https://xeniaword.com/2015/07/14/central-state-announces-2015-hall-of-fame-inductees/.

[14] Murphy, Michael. "TSU pulls a miracle with upset of Rice." *Houston Chronicle*, June 5, 2004. https://www.chron.com/sports/college/article/TSU-pulls-a-miracle-with-upset-of-Rice-1966843.php.

[15] Eddy, Matt. "The 12 Most Decorated College All-Americans Of The Last 40 Years." College Baseball, MLB Draft, Prospects - Baseball America. Last modified February 4, 2020. https://www.baseballamerica.com/stories/the-12-most-decorated-college-all-americans-of-the-last-40-years/.

[16] "West Virginia State Player Hits 5 Straight HRs." ESPN.com. Last modified April 28, 2009. https://www.espn.com/college-sports/news/story?id=4108447.

[17] "Devin Hemmerich - Baseball - Norfolk State University Athletics." Norfolk State University Athletics. Accessed September 25, 2021. https://nsuspartans.com/sports/baseball/roster/devin-hemmerich/4268.

# CHAPTER 9

# The Impact of HBCU Baseball on the Negro Leagues

The first Negro baseball league is historically recognized as the Negro National League, founded by Andrew "Rube" Foster in 1920, and its 100th anniversary will be celebrated nationwide throughout the year 2020. Yet, at least two black baseball playing leagues came to mind that pre-date the NNL. Historically Black College and University (HBCU) baseball programs faced off against each other as early as 1887, and in 1896, the first formal black college baseball league was formed when in the state of Georgia, Atlanta-based schools Atlanta Baptist College, Atlanta University, Clark University, and Morris Brown College created the Atlanta Negro Intercollegiate Baseball League. Then in 1909, Nashville, Tennessee area schools Fisk University, Roger Williams University, and Walden University (along with Pearl High School) formed the Intercollegiate Baseball League of Nashville.

Beginning with the onset of professional Negro baseball leagues, HBCU baseball has played a large part in its success. The segregated Major Leagues had its Minor League system, a creation attributed to Branch Rickey, to develop young ballplayers. Without those same resources in the Negro Leagues, black college baseball programs often functioned as feeders into the professional ranks of Negro League Baseball. Even during the lean years of the 1930s, when HBCUs didn't sponsor baseball as an intercollegiate sport, Negro League Baseball sought talented athletes off their campuses. Bob Kendrick, director of the Negro Leagues Museum in Kansas City, Kansas, has estimated that around 40% of all Negro leaguers had at least some college education.[1]

Three of the best Negro leaguers who played sports other than baseball at their HBCU institutions were Newark Eagles teammates Monte Irwin from Lincoln University of Pennsylvania and Larry Doby of Virginia Union College, as well as Morgan State's Joe Black of the Baltimore Elite Giants. Some of the best to play Negro League Baseball who previously played HBCU baseball include "Doc" Sykes, Buck O'Neil, Dave Malarcher, Hilton Smith, Bill Foster,

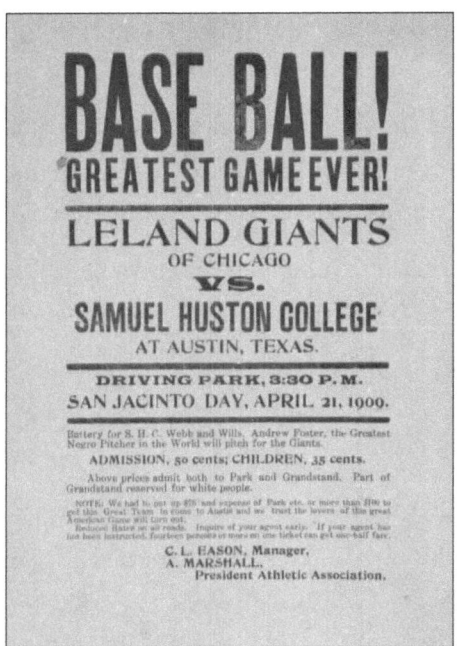

and Willie Wells... just to name a very few.

Besides providing a pool of talented college athletes, HBCUs often served as spring training grounds for black professional teams. Many exhibition games were played, both pre-season and during the regular season, pitting pro black teams versus HBCU teams. Newspapers like the *Chicago Defender* and *Pittsburgh Courier* were dotted with scores and recaps of such games.

In 1910, the barnstorming Chicago Leland Giants went on an estimated 22,000-mile tour of the south and faced black colleges Hampton Institute, Atlanta University, Tuskegee Institute, and Claflin University.[2] The Giants featured manager/pitcher Rube Foster, who ten years later would form the first professional Negro League organization, and also included Pete Hill, Grant Johnson, and several other

Negro all-time greats

The *New York Age* of May 5, 1915 reported on a three-game series between the professional Lincoln Stars and Howard University. The Stars, winner of all three games, featured well-known pros John Henry Lloyd, Spottswood Poles, Dick Redding, and Louis Santop. Both Lloyd and Santop have since been inducted into the Major League Baseball Hall of Fame. In that series of games, Howard University countered with future Negro League greats Frank "Doc" Sykes and Wabishaw "Doc" Wiley.[3] As reported in the *Chicago Defender* of April 19, 1924, Andrew "Rube" Foster's Chicago American Giants bested Wiley College 6-5. Among the stars of the American Giants were former black college ballplayers "Jelly" Gardner, Dave Malarcher, and Bobby Williams, while Wiley College was led by future Negro leaguers Grady Orange, William Ware, John Hines, and John Shackleford.[4]

On April 28, 1928, the *Pittsburgh Courier* reported on the Eastern Colored League's Hilldale Daisies defeat of the North Carolina A&T by the score of 16-1. Of its many stars, the Daisies roster included three future Major League Baseball Hall of Famers in Judy Johnson, Oscar Charleston, and Raleigh "Biz" Mackey.[5]

The *Chicago Defender*, on May 5, 1934, reported on an interesting ballgame between the Chicago American Giants and Alcorn College, played in Alcorn, Mississippi. William Foster returned home and faced off against his alma mater on what was dubbed "Bill Foster Day". Two other Alcornites, Melvin "Putt" Powell and Percy Bailey, played for the American Giants team, which barely bested Alcorn 12-11.[6]

Even after the integration of Major League Baseball, black college teams scheduled games with Negro League teams in their waning years of existence. In April 1949, Grambling College lost a close ballgame to the Kansas City Monarchs by the score of 5-4 and then two weeks later defeated the Chicago American Giants 8-6.[7] The following month, Grambling swamped the Oklahoma City Braves of the short-lived Negro Texas League by the score of 27-0.[8] In an interview years later, Grambling pitcher William Rutledge revealed that during summer months, head coach Ralph Waldo Emerson Jones, the school's president, would often pitch exhibition games for the Grambling team of ballplayers who remained on campus.[9]

The relationship between black college baseball programs and Negro League Baseball flourished throughout the first half of the twentieth century. With lax collegiate eligibility rules in the earlier years of that relationship, Negro League teams provided summer employment, adding student ballplayers to their rosters. Longtime Negro National League umpire Bert Gholston wrote in the Pittsburgh Courier on March 27, 1926, "For years, good college players have been given opportunities to play in summer on different teams in the Negro National and Eastern Colored Leagues. It is encouraging to know that any boy or young man who shows any ability of a 'Class A' player is given a chance to earn money for playing professional ball in either of the above named leagues." He added, "The work is more dignified than dishwashing, hotel work, dining car and Pullman porter services."

*Southern University's Darren Clark (l) and Mario Spann (r) With Buck O'Neil at 2005 throwback game*

With the integration of Major League Baseball came the eventual demise of the Negro Leagues. Years later, few remember or know of the relationship between HBCU baseball programs and the Negro Leagues. One who recognized this relationship and kept those memories alive is now-retired former Southern University baseball coach Roger Cador who came up with the idea of organizing a Negro Leagues "throwback" jersey game during the 1999-2000 school year. The first game was played in 2002 against rival Grambling State University, and in every year but one, versus Texas Southern, Southern University has hosted Grambling. The throwback weekend grew to include vendors, exhibits, and visits from the likes of the legendary Negro Leaguer, Buck O'Neil.

"The throwback jerseys are always a special weekend," Roger Cador said. "Negro leaguers played a special role in baseball history because they were able to tear down barriers with their baseball ability. We wanted to do what we could do to inform and enhance the awareness of Negro League ball," said Cador.[10]

Fred Lewis, who wore similar throwback uniforms at both Southern University and as a San Francisco Giant versus the Kansas City Royals, admitted he did not know many details about the Negro Leagues but said, "I appreciate what they did for us. I didn't know much about what they went through back then. I've read some stuff and seen video clips of what happened. It meant a lot to put on the uniforms of the teams they played for." And the throwback uniform he wore at Southern University in 2002... that of the Kansas City Monarchs.[11]

Not only is the throwback game appreciated by Southern University ballplayers, but also by the opponents. Former Grambling State University outfielder Jeremy Shelby, son of former major leaguer John Shelby, said that the game gave him a better appreciation for the Negro Leagues and that it was an honor to be part of the affair, including the throwback uniforms.[12]

Former Southern University ballplayer and Milwaukee Brewers great Rickie Weeks is one ballplayer who previously had an understanding and appreciation of Negro League Baseball before playing in his first throwback game. "I was told at an early age about the struggles and times these players went through."

In his two Southern University throwback games, Weeks wore uniforms of the Memphis Red Sox in 2002 and the Homestead Grays in 2003. However, Weeks confessed his favorite uniform probably was that of the Newark Eagles. And why might that be? For the same reason he probably had a better understanding of the Negro Leagues than most... his grandfather Victor had a short stint with the Newark Eagles, a team that featured future Major League Hall of Famers Larry Doby and Monte Irvin.[13]

[1] Arnett, Autumn A., and Cmaadmin (EDU). "Experts: HBCUs Powered Baseball's Negro Leagues." Diverse: Issues in Higher Education. Last modified April 1, 2015. https://www.diverseeducation.com/sports/article/15096225/experts-hbcus-powered-baseballs-negro-leagues.

[2] *The Chicago Defender.* "The Chicago Giants Base Ball Club." January 22, 1910, 1.

[3] Chalk, Ocania. *Black College Sport*, 51. New York: Dodd Mead, 1976.

[4] Ibid., 56.

[5] *Baltimore Afro-American.* "Hilldale Unbeaten on Southern Jaunt." April 28, 1928, 13.

[6] *The Chicago Defender.* "College Lads Give Giants of Chicago a Real Scare, 12-11." May 5, 1934, A5

[7] *The Pittsburgh Courier.* "Grambling College Collegians Whip Pro Team, 8-6." April 23, 1949, 23.

[8] *The Chicago Defender.* "Grambling Tigers Swamp Pro Baseball Nine, 27-0." May 29, 1949, 15

[9] Rutledge, William. Phone interview. Grambling, Louisiana June 7, 2011.

[10] Sokol, Jay. "Southern University's "Throwback Game" Weekend." Black College Nines – Current and Historical HBCU Baseball News. Last modified April 7, 2010. https://blackcollegenines.com/southern-universitys-throwback-game-weekend/.

[11] Lewis, Fred. Email Interview. July 30, 2009.

[12] Shelby, Jeremy. Personal interview. July 30, 2009.

[13] Weeks, Rickie. Email interview. July 22, 2009.

# Anatomy of a Championship Season
# 1959 Southern University

On the historical timeline of HBCU baseball firsts and most prominent events, one that deservedly captures attention is Southern University's 1959 National Association of Intercollegiate Athletics baseball championship. It was the first sanctioned baseball championship won by a Historically Black College and University school and, to date, the only HBCU to win a baseball title offered by any of the governing bodies of college athletics, such as the NCAA and NAIA.

The National Association of Intercollegiate Athletics began sponsoring a college world series in 1957, nearly five years after the organization's groundbreaking decision to admit Historically Black Colleges and Universities into its membership. Initially, the tournament was an invitational competition leading to a crown. In 1958, Maryland State College (now known as the University of Maryland Eastern Shore) was the first HBCU to be invited. However, because of distance and final examinations, it was unable to make the trip to Alpine, Texas, the initial home of the series. This gave Southern University of Baton Rouge, Louisiana, the distinction of being the first HBCU program to play in an NAIA World Series when it represented the association's District 6/Area 7 in the eight-team tournament of 1959.

Though the 1958 Jaguars of Southern University failed to duplicate its 1957 SWAC crown and lost two seniors to professional baseball in shortstop Robert Davidson (to the Chicago Cubs) and catcher John Griffin (to the Baltimore Orioles), the prospect for a successful 1959 season was recognized by most followers of Southwestern Athletic Conference baseball.

The "Jags" welcomed back a pitching staff with some experience and several of freshmen from the '58 team, now with a year of grooming under their collective belts. Adding to the mix were quite a few freshmen who would ultimately become regulars in the starting lineup on the 1959 squad.

Southern University's lineup during the bulk of the season included four freshmen (catcher Roy McGriff, center fielder Wiley McMillan, shortstop Alvin Woods, and first baseman Herman Rhodes), first-year sophomore third baseman Henry Triplett, and three sophomores (left fielder Robert "Speedy" Williams, right fielder L.C. "Lou" Brock and second baseman Harry Levy). Of the returnees to the 1959 squad, Harry Levy's .375 batting average topped the group in 1958, followed by Speedy Williams at .282.

On the mound, returning for the 1959 season were now-junior Fred Jackson, who was 5-0 in 1958, sophomores McVea Griffin, Herman James, and Irving Sams, as well as Larry Spencer, the lone senior on the roster in 1959.

In its first series of the season, the Jaguars won two of its three games against Texas Southern (losing the season opener 3-2) and in its final regular season series versus Mississippi Vocational College (now known as Mississippi Valley State University), the Jags likewise won two of the three (losing the regular season finale 4-3). Those two series bookended a fine mid-season run winning 15 of 16, losing only to rival Grambling, and bringing its season record to 19-3. Southern's 15-2 conference record placed the team atop the standings and earned the Jaguars a league crown. Pitchers McVea Griffin and Larry Spencer, as well as Lou Brock, Robert Williams, Roy McGriff, Herman Rhodes, and Harry Levy, were named to the SWAC All-Conference team.

Heading into the NAIA tournament, Lou Brock was hitting a resounding .524 with eight doubles, six triples, and five home runs. Robert Williams had a batting average of .394, was second on the team with 21 runs batted in, and was tied with Brock for the team lead in doubles with eight. Harry Levy led the Jaguars and the Southwestern Athletic Conference with 27 stolen bases while hitting .365, and Herman Rhodes had a batting average of .361. Southern University's formidable pitching staff was led by southpaw McVea Griffin who had a 7-0 record with an earned run average of 1.35, five shutouts, and 58 strikeouts in 61 innings pitched. Herman James and Irving Sams had won-loss records of 3-0 and 2-0, respectively, while Fred Jackson was 4-2 and Larry Spencer was 3-1. At the helm of the Southern University nine were future NAIA Hall of Fame coach Bob Lee and his assistant, Emory Hines, who would succeed Lee as head coach in 1961.

At the 1959 NAIA World Series, besides Southern University, the field of eight also included the 18-0 University of Omaha (now known as the University of Nebraska at Omaha) and 17-1 Patterson State College (now known as William Paterson University). Two other institutions, Rollins College, which came into the tournament as the consensus favorite to win, and host school Sul Ross State College, each had previous world series experience. During the regular season, tournament teams had beaten the likes of Ohio State University, Wake Forest, the University of Florida and Michigan State.

The series opened with lopsided wins by the University of Omaha and Rollins College before Southern University faced its first opponent, host school Sul Ross State College. In the game, Southern took a two-run lead before falling behind in the fifth inning by the score of 3-2. In the sixth inning, the Jaguars tied the game at three, followed by a go-ahead sacrifice fly by ace pitcher McVea Griffin, who no-hit Sul Ross the rest of the way, for the opening round 4-3 victory.

Southern University next faced Western Washington College (now Western Washington University), which featured Roger Repoz, who was named the tournament's MVP and later became a Major League ballplayer. As in its first game, the Jaguars had an early lead before the Vikings of Western Washington plated four runs in the third inning to turn a 3-0 deficit into a 4-3 lead. With single runs in the bottom of the third and fifth innings, the Jaguars would tie the score and then take the lead. Western Washington responded by scoring a tying run in the sixth inning and a go-ahead run in the eighth. Falling behind 6-5 going into the bottom of the ninth inning, the underdog Southern University "Jags" faced its first loss of the tournament. Lou Brock started a rally as he reached first base on an error and advanced to second on a walk issued to Herman Rhodes. Third baseman Henry Triplett doubled to score Brock, and with one out, center fielder Wiley McMillan squeezed Rhodes home for the 7-6, come from behind victory.

In the twelfth game of the series, Southern had an easier time, eliminating Rollins College from competition by the score of 8-3. Meanwhile, coming back from an opening-round loss to Rollins College, the University of Omaha stormed back to win three straight and force a must-win contest with the already 3-0 Southern University Jaguars.

Because of weather delays, including wind, rain, and hail, and an upcoming previously arranged field commitment, for the University of Omaha to win the national title, the Mavericks would have had to play and win five games in a 32-hour span. After eliminating Southern Illinois University, Western Washington, and Rollins College, in the first championship round matchup with Southern University on June 5th, the University of Omaha was on the road to doing just that, winning by the score of 17-9. The victory set up a winner take all rematch with Southern 30 minutes later.

Though the University of Omaha had already played two more games than the Jaguar ball club, the Mavericks went late into the evening battling Southern for the first six innings of the NAIA World Series championship game. In the top of the seventh inning, with the score knotted at two, Lou Brock, who had not been much of a factor in the tournament to that point, connected for a three-run home run as Southern University collected a total of four runs to take a 6-2 lead. From that point on, the deflated and overworked Omaha Mavericks were held in check as Southern scored four more runs to win the game 10-2. When the last out was recorded in the bottom of the ninth inning to give Southern University the 1959 NAIA National Baseball Championship, it was already after midnight and now June 6th.

At the awards ceremony, Lou Brock was named to the NAIA All-Tournament team. Six Jaguars hit over .300 for the series, led by Robert Williams' .455, Henry Triplett's .389, Alvin Woods and Harry Levy with averages of .333, catcher Roy McGriff at .316, and Lou Brock's .304. Pitcher Larry Spencer recorded two of the team's four wins. At season's end, *Collegiate Baseball Newspaper*, originator of the nation's oldest college baseball poll earlier that year, ranked Southern University the 19th best team in the country.

In October 2015, the 1959 team was inducted into the Southern University Sports Hall of Fame. The team's Henry Triplett told *The Advocate* of Baton Rouge, Louisiana, that winning the baseball national title was an outstanding feeling. Still, it took some time before the team realized the significance of their success. "We didn't think about that. We just played ball and tried to win the game."

Aside from what the title meant to the Diamond Jaguars and its university, ever since that late spring gameday when the championship trophy was awarded in the wee hours of the morning, the significance of Southern University's NAIA baseball crown has grown immeasurably within the HBCU community and beyond.

# NCAA Division I National Record Holders and Annual Statistical Leaders

(Historically Black Colleges and Universities only)

*Official NCAA Division I baseball records began with the 1957 season and are based on information submitted to the NCAA statistics service by institutions participating in the statistics rankings. Career records of players include only those years in which they competed in Division I.*

## National Record Holders

**Batting Average – For a Career (Individual)**
.465 Rickie Weeks, Southern University 2001-2003

**Batting Average – For a Season (Team)**
.396 Delaware State University 1989

**Slugging Percentage – For a Career (Individual)**
.927 Rickie Weeks, Southern University 2001-2003

**Stolen Bases – Total For a Game (Individual)**
8 King Lewis, Bethune-Cookman 1994

**Stolen Bases – Average Per Game (Individual)**
1.93 Lawrence Smith, Bethune-Cookman 1988

**Stolen Bases – Average Per Game (Team)**
5.47 Howard University 1974

**Hit By Pitch – Total For a Season (Individual)**
37 Scott Davis, Delaware State University 2012

**Hit By Pitch – Total For a Season (Team)**
152 Delaware State University 2012

## Annual Individual Hitting Statistical Leaders

**Batting Average – For a Season**
1974 Artis Stanfield, North Carolina A&T .500
1983 Greg Daniels, Alcorn State .545
1989 Ira Smith, Maryland Eastern Shore .488
1990 Ira Smith, Maryland Eastern Shore .519
1994 Adrian Price, Coppin State .474
2002 Rickie Weeks, Southern University .495
2003 Rickie Weeks, Southern University .479
2005 Corey Wimberley, Alcorn State .462

**Runs Scored – Average Per Game**
1988 Marquis Grissom, Florida A&M 1.62
1989 Elmore Briggs, Delaware State University 1.74
2002 Antoin Gray, Southern University, 1.63
2003 Rickie Weeks, Southern University, 1.62
2005 Shundell Russaw, Jackson State, 1.53

**Triples – Average Per Game**
1979 Anthony Taylor, Alcorn State 0.29
1981 Terry Blocker, Tennessee State 0.34
1988 Rodney Bullard, Bethune-Cookman 0.29
1998 David Jones, Florida A&M 0.24
2000 Nikki Moses, Southern University 0.18
2001 Rickie Weeks, Southern University 0.22
2002 Rickie Weeks, Southern University 0.22
2004 Joshua LeBlanc, Southern University 0.19

2006 Marcus Davis, Alcorn State 0.28
2007 LaDale Hayes, Alabama A&M 0.21
2011 Bryan Chaikowsky, Maryland Eastern Shore 0.20

**Triples – Total For a Season**
1981 Terry Blocker, Tennessee State 11
1988 Marquis Grissom, Florida A&M 10
2001 Rickie Weeks, Southern University 12
2002 Rickie Weeks, Southern University 12
2006 Marcus Davis, Alcorn State 12

**Runs Batted In – Average Per Game**
2000 Chris Cottonham, Grambling University 1.74
2001 Scott Martin, Delaware State University 1.75
2002 Rickie Weeks, Southern University 1.75
2006 Marcus Davis, Alcorn State 1.49
2018 Rafael Ramirez, Grambling State University, 1.40

**Runs Batted In – Total For a Season**
2002 Rickie Weeks, Southern University 96

**Slugging Percentage – For a Season**
1993 Miguel Cruz, North Carolina A&T .886
2002 Rickie Weeks, Southern University .995
2003 Rickie Weeks, Southern University .933
2005 Gerald Smith, Savannah State University .785

**On Base Percentage – For a Season**
2014 Aaron Nardone, Delaware State University .521

**Stolen Bases – Average Per Game**
1974 Artis Stanfield, North Carolina A&T 1.32
1982 Vince Coleman, Florida A&M 1.56
1983 Prince Cousinard, Texas Southern 1.63
1986 Jason Booker, Coppin State 1.23
1988 Lawrence Smith, Bethune Cookman 1.93
1993 Ricky Farley, Maryland Eastern Shore 1.21
1994 King Lewis, Bethune Cookman 1.30
1995 Milton Anderson, Bethune Cookman 1.21
2000 Dwaine Bacon, Florida A&M 1.54
2002 Bartowski Cowan, Alabama State 1.08
2004 Carl Lipsey, Jackson State 1.04
2006 Calvin Lester, Prairie View A&M 1.04
2009 Jeff Squier, Mississippi Valley State 0.82
2010 Willie Wesley, Jackson State 0.98

**Stolen Bases – Total For a Season**
1981 Vince Coleman, Florida A&M 65
1983 Stan Jefferson, Bethune Cookman 67
1994 King Lewis, Bethune Cookman 57
2004 Carl Lipsey, Jackson State 49
2006 Calvin Lester, Prairie View A&M 56
　　　Zach Penprase, Mississippi Valley State 56

**Base On Balls – Average Per Game**
1991 Scott Pokorny, Delaware State University 1.18
1994 Brent Mollohan, Delaware State University 1.27
2000 Alex Smith, Florida A&M 1.07

**Toughest To Strike Out**
1986 Gregory Perkins, Florida A&M 1 *(in 115 ABs)*
1992 Kevin Nalls, Grambling University 2 *(in 180 ABs)*
1999 Gilbert Lanoix, Grambling University 4 *(in 168 ABs)*
2011 Marquis Riley, North Carolina A&T 4 *(in 207 ABs)*
2016 J.T. O'Reel, Alabama A&M 6 *(in 205 ABs)*

**Hit By Pitch – Average Per Game**
2004 Brad Frick, Bethune-Cookman 0.53
2010 Cortez Cole, Jackson State 0.58
2012 Scott Davis, Delaware State University 0.64
2015 PJ Biocic, Alabama State 0.51
2016 Ashanti Wheatley, Southern University 0.49

**Hit By Pitch – Total For a Season**
2012 Scott Davis, Delaware State University 37

## Annual Individual Pitching Statistical Leaders

**Lowest Earned Run Average – For a Season**
1974 Al Holland, North Carolina A&T 0.26

**Strikeouts Per Nine Innings – For a Season**
1974 Al Holland, North Carolina A&T 14.3
1975 Al Holland, North Carolina A&T 15.4
1979 Melvin Gilliam, Florida A&M 12.5

## Annual Team Hitting Statistical Leaders

**Batting Average – For a Season**
1989 Delaware State University .396
2002 Southern University .377
2003 Southern University .351
2006 Jackson State .349

**Runs Scored – Average Per Game**
1989 Delaware State University 10.26
2001 Delaware State University 10.38
2002 Southern University 11.13
2003 Southern University 10.18
2004 Southern University 10.07
2005 Jackson State 10.53
2006 Jackson State 9.44
2016 Alabama State 8.58

**Triples – Average Per Game**
1988 Florida A&M 0.79
1996 Grambling University 0.73
1998 Grambling University 0.70
1999 Bethune Cookman 0.55
2001 Southern University 0.69
2011 Grambling University 0.73

**Triples – For a Season**
2001 Southern University 38
2008 Jackson State 38
2011 Grambling University 36

**Slugging Percentage – For a Season**
2001 Southern University .690
2011 Grambling University .730
1989 Delaware State University .594
2002 Southern University .643
2003 Southern University .572
2004 Southern University .568

**Stolen Bases – Average Per Game**
1976 Howard University 5.47
1979 Tennessee State 4.21
1983 Texas Southern 3.97
1986 Coppin State 4.27
1988 Bethune Cookman 5.03

1990 Jackson State 4.82
1991 Florida A&M 2.98
1995 Bethune Cookman 3.41
1997 Alcorn State 3.58
1998 Grambling University 3.19
2000 Florida A&M 4.06
2002 Alabama State 3.28
2003 Jackson State 3.25
2004 Jackson State 4.08
2005 Jackson State 3.62
2006 Prairie View A&M 3.96
2007 Prarie View A&M 2.64
2009 Savannah State 3.31
2010 Jackson State 4.08
2011 Savannah State 3.06
2013 Delaware State University 3.02
2015 Texas Southern 2.72
2016 Texas Southern 3.32
2017 Jackson State 2.52

**Stolen Bases – Total For a Season**
1990 Jackson State 241
2004 Jackson State 200
2005 Jackson State 170
2006 Prairie View A&M 218
2007 Prarie View A&M 156
2009 Savannah State 169
2010 Jackson State 216
2011 Savannah State 159
2017 Jackson State 141

**Hit By Pitch – Total For a Season**
2012 Delaware State University 152

## Annual Team Pitching Statistical Leaders

**Lowest Earned Run Average – For a Season**
2012 Delaware State University 2.99

## Annual Team Miscellaneous Statistical Leaders

**Winning Percentage – For a Season**
2002 Southern University (45-10) .818
2003 Southern University (44-7) .863

**Most Improved – From Previous Season**
2004 Prairie View A&M 19½ games
2013 Coppin State 18½ games
2014 Florida A&M 20 games

# NCAA Division II National Record Holders and Annual Statistical Leaders

(Historically Black Colleges and Universities only)

*Official NCAA Division II baseball records began with the 1963 season and are based on information submitted to the NCAA statistics service by institutions participating in the statistics rankings. Career records of players include only those years in which they competed in Division II.*

## National Record Holders

**Batting Average – For a Season (Individual)**
.582 Ralph Garr, Grambling State University 1967

**Batting Average – For a Season (Team)**
.400 Miles College 1997

**Runs Scored – Average Per Game (Team)**
12.59 Savannah State University 2000

**Triples – For a Season (Individual)**
16 Willie Melendez, Savannah State University 1998

**Triples – For a Season (Team)**
58 Savannah State University 1998

**Triples – Average Per Game (Individual)**
0.53 Larry Crowe, Texas Southern University 1970

**Triples – Average Per Game (Individual)**
1.18 Savannah State University 1998

**Home Runs – Consecutive (Individual)**
5 Bo Darby, West Virginia State 2009

**Home Runs – In an Inning (Team)**
6 Tuskegee University 2017

**Runs Batted In – Average Per Game (Individual)**
2.19 Mike Boyd, Shaw University 1994

**Base On Balls – Average Per Game (Individual)**
1.38 Ralph Davis, Miles College 1993

**Stolen Bases – Total For a Game (Individual)**
9 Clarence Williamson, North Carolina A&T 1968

**Stolen Bases – Total For a Game (Team)**
24 Benedict College 2012

**Stolen Bases – Total For a Season (Team)**
334 Benedict College 2013

**Stolen Bases – Average Per Game (Individual)**
2.73 Charles Stukes, Maryland State 1967

**Stolen Bases – Average Per Game (Team)**
8.15 Benedict College 2013

**Stolen Base Percentage – For a Career (Individual)**
.958 Andrew Dixon, Norfolk State 1983-1986

**Stolen Base Attempts – For a Season (Team)**
403 Benedict College 2013

**Hit By Pitch – Total For a Game (Individual)**
4 Ryan Green, Tuskegee University 2017 (twice)

**Relief Pitching Appearances – For a Season**
43 Jhonattan Schloeter, Bluefield State 2004

**Consecutive Victories – Total For a Season (Team)**
46 Savannah State University 2000

**Winning Percentage – Average for a season (Team)**
.939 Savannah State University 2000

## Annual Individual Hitting Statistical Leaders

**Batting Average – For a Season**
1963 James Morrow, Stillman College .544
1964 Frank Smith, Hampton University .526
1967 Ralph Garr, Grambling University .582
1968 Walter Thompson, Alcorn State .508
1969 Arthur Jones, Shaw University .580
1974 Tyrone Phinnessee, Tuskegee University .482
1976 Willie Powell, Mississippi Valley State .563
1982 Eddie White, Saint Augustine's .516
1983 Terry Edwards, Central State .514
1984 Sammy Ruiz, Central State .509
1991 Mike Motta, Bowie State .494
2000 Brett Higgins, Savannah State University .513
2006 Carlos Gutierrez, Elizabeth City State .548
2013 Joe Fields, LeMoyne-Owen .455

**Runs Scored – Average Per Game**
1997 Ckori Jones, Bowie State 1.61
2000 Brett Higgins, Savannah State 1.78
2004 Antoine Tucker, Elizabeth City State 1.65
2006 Ryan Taylor, West Virginia State 1.58
2008 Jeffrey Cannon, Shaw University 1.65
2013 Kevin Davis, Benedict College 1.43

**Runs Scored – Total For a Season**
2000 Brett Higgins, Savannah State 87
2005 Ryan Taylor, West Virginia State 85
2006 Ryan Taylor, West Virginia State 84

**Doubles – Average Per Game**
1968 Marty Miller, Norfolk State 0.56
1999 Shawn Stokes, Saint Augustine's 0.60
2000 Brett Higgins, Savannah State 0.65
2007 Meshaw Taylor, Elizabeth City State 0.56
2019 Jahleel Sewer, Virginia State 0.58

**Doubles – Total For a Season**
1975 Tyrone Phinnessee, Tuskegee University 18
2000 Brett Higgins, Savannah State 32

**Triples – Average Per Game**
1964 Lewis Crockett, Prairie View A&M 0.41
1965 John Walker, Wiley College 0.50
1969 Clarence Williamson, North Carolina A&T 0.29
1970 Larry Crowe, Texas Southern 0.53
1971 Robert Edmond, Fort Valley State 0.44
1972 Joe Graham, Winston-Salem State 0.29
1978 Frank Williams, Saint Augustine's 0.26
1983 Julius Rawlings, Norfolk State 0.25
1991 Denton Higgins, Kentucky State 0.30
1993 Derric Taylor, Morehouse University 0.19
1996 Brad Gardner, Alabama A&M 0.21
1998 Willie Melendez, Savannah State 0.33
1999 Ashref Elshazli, Bowie State 0.21
2003 Brandon Stancil, Tuskegee University 0.30
2004 Starling Odoms, Paine College 0.23
2005 Azor Cloud, Saint Augustine's 0.26

2006 Sean Blair, Stillman College 0.25
2008 William Watkins, Clark Atlanta University 0.22
2017 Andrew McCoy, Benedict College 0.23

**Triples – Total For a Season**
1986 Steve Williams, Kentucky State 10
1991 Denton Higgins, Kentucky State 10
1998 Willie Melendez, Savannah State 16
2003 Brandon Stancil, Tuskegee University 9
2005 Michael Meredith, Tuskegee University 9
2006 Sean Blair, Stillman College 13
2013 Travis Moore, Winston-Salem State University 8

**Home Runs – Average Per Game**
1967 Leon Taylor, Univ. of Arkansas at Pine Bluff .33
1970 Dennis Bailey, South Carolina State .41
2006 DeShaun Brooks, Benedict College .49

**Runs Batted In – Average Per Game**
1966 Charles Stukes, Maryland State 2.67
1967 Pete Barnes, Southern University 1.72
1989 Melvin Wearing, Norfolk State 1.65
1993 Wayne Fajerski, Bowie State 1.64
1994 Mike Boyd, Shaw University 2.19
2000 Brett Higgins, Savannah State University 1.90
2003 Milton Redd, Shaw University 1.74
2005 Troy Nunnally, Tuskegee University 1.68
2006 DeShaun Brooks, Benedict College 2.19
2012 Dave Weber, Benedict College 1.49

**Runs Batted In – Total For a Season**
2000 Brett Higgins, Savannah State University 93

**Slugging Percentage – For a Season**
1967 Ronald Woods, Knoxville College .957
1990 Ricky Sanders, Saint Augustine's 1.000
2000 Brett Higgins, Savannah State 1.010
2002 Milton Redd, Shaw University .911
2006 Carlos Gutierrez, Elizabeth City State 1.078

**Total Bases – Total For a Season**
2000 Brett Higgins, Savannah State University 193

**On Base Percentage – For a Season**
2008 Brandon Heard, Miles College .584
2009 Clay Scott, Benedict College .616
2013 David Weber, Benedict College .625

**Stolen Bases – Average Per Game**
1966 Charles Stukes, Maryland State 1.67
1967 Charles Stukes, Maryland State 2.73
1968 Clarence Williamson, North Carolina A&T 1.75
1970 Jimmy Johnson, Bethune Cookman 2.00
1971 Charles Meachum, Savannah State 1.88
1972 William Parks, North Carolina A&T 1.95
1973 Calvin Jones, Delaware State 1.95
1974 Cliff Marshall, Jackson State 1.43
1977 Greg Hall, Lincoln (Mo.) University 1.27
1978 Eli Aldridge, Prairie View A&M 1.29
1980 Preston Terry, Central State 1.29
1988 Van Williams, Savannah State 1.14
1990 Julian Pratt, Saint Augustine's 1.02
1992 Stacey Green, Shaw University 0.97
1993 Stacey Green, Shaw University 1.74

1994 Vernorris Dodson, Albany State 1.26
1996 Rico DeGraffenreid, Shaw University 1.43
2004 Antoine Tucker, Elizabeth City State 1.74
2009 Rashad Ingram, Saint Augustine's 1.30
2011 Rashad Ingram, Saint Augustine's 1.48
2012 Michael Jordan, Benedict College 1.83
2013 Kevin Davis, Benedict College 1.57
2014 Kevin Davis, Benedict College 1.26
2019 Bradon O'Connor, Benedict College 1.38

**Stolen Bases – Total For a Season**
1970 Cliff Hayes, Jackson State 45
1972 William Parks, North Carolina A&T 37
   Smith Atwater, Tuskegee University 37
1973 Richard Shaw, Tuskegee University 42
1974 Cliff Marshall, Jackson State 50
1993 Stacey Green, Shaw University 54
1994 Vernorris Dodson, Albany State 49
2004 Antoine Tucker, Elizabeth City State 59
2009 Sean Blair, Stillman College 52
2011 Rashad Ingram, Saint Augustine's 80
2012 Michael Jordan, Benedict College 66
2013 Kevin Davis, Benedict College 58
2017 Randy Norris, Winston-Salem State University 47
2019 Bradon O'Connor, Benedict College 47

**Base On Balls – Average Per Game**
1993 Ralph Davis, Miles College 1.38
1996 Adrian Harris, Norfolk State 1.13
2000 Darryl Dixon, Shaw University 1.36
2002 Gregory Lee, LeMoyne-Owen 1.02
2003 Warren Tyson, Shaw University 1.10
2004 Jermaine Rogers, Shaw University 1.06
2005 Chad Tittle, Miles College 1.03
2006 Jeffrey Cannon, Shaw University 1.12
2008 Jeffrey Cannon, Shaw University 1.38
2013 David Weber, Benedict College, 1.32

**Base On Balls – Total For a Season**
2013 David Weber, Benedict College, 54

**Toughest To Strike Out – Total For a Season**
1995 Alan Henry, Norfolk State 1 *(in 103 ABs)*
1998 Keith Fout, West Virginia State 2 *(in 157 ABs)*
2014 Anthony Payne, West Virginia State 4 *(in 180 ABs)*

## Annual Individual Pitching Statistical Leaders
**Lowest Earned Run Average – For a Season**
1970 Herbert Allen, Stillman College 0.35
1972 Al Holland, North Carolina A&T 0.54
1974 Anthony Roberson, Kentucky State 0.81
1984 Greg Watkins, Shaw University 0.81

**Strikeout Ratio – For a Season** *(strikeouts per nine innings)*
1965 Alex Pero, Grambling University 18.5
1972 Al Holland, North Carolina A&T 15.5
1973 Steve Barlow, Morehouse College 16.5
2003 Tyrell Moore, Albany State 13.2
2004 Tyrell Moore, Albany State 12.8

**Strikeout – Total For a Season**
1972 Al Holland, North Carolina A&T 143

*Strikeouts-total for a season (continued)*
1975 Roy Lee Jackson, Tuskegee University 160
2003 Tyrell Moore, Albany State 126

**Victories – Total For a Season**
2000 Ricardo Castillo, Savannah State University 18

## Annual Team Hitting Statistical Leaders

**Batting Average – For a Season**
1965 Shaw University .360
1966 Maryland State .377
1967 Shaw University .349
1968 South Carolina State .362
1972 Southern University .334
1974 Kentucky State .331
1976 Mississippi Valley State .370
1993 Shaw University .356
1996 LeMoyne-Owen .375
1997 Miles College .400
2000 Savannah State .380
2005 West Virginia State .366
2006 West Virginia State .380
2012 Stillman College .356

**Runs Scored – Average Per Game**
1994 Shaw University 10.29
1995 Shaw University 10.32
1999 Savannah State 10.52
2000 Savannah State 12.59
2003 Shaw University 10.31
2004 Elizabeth City State 11.08
2005 Shaw University 10.03
2006 West Virginia State 10.47
2008 Shaw University 10.92
2011 Benedict College 8.93
2013 Benedict College 10.15
2017 Benedict College 9.76

**Runs Scored – Total For a Season**
1996 LeMoyne-Owen 525
2000 Savannah State University 617

**Doubles – Average Per Game**
2003 Shaw University 2.83

**Triples – Average Per Game**
1991 Bowie State 0.67
1992 Alabama A&M 0.73
1994 Norfolk State 0.63
1998 Savannah State University 1.18
1999 Saint Augustine's 0.94
2000 Saint Augustine's 0.62
2003 Saint Augustine's 1.14
2004 Saint Augustine's 0.70
2006 Tuskegee University 0.69
2008 Shaw University 0.65
2011 Tuskegee University 0.80

**Triples – Totals For a Season**
1998 Savannah State University 58
1999 Saint Augustine's 34
2003 Saint Augustine's 40

**Home Runs – Average Per Game**
2006 West Virginia State 1.95

**Home Runs – Totals For a Season**
2006 West Virginia State 107

**Slugging Percentage – For a Season**
2000 Savannah State University .627
2003 Shaw University .579
2006 West Virginia State .628

**Stolen Bases – Average Per Game**
1992 Bowie State 3.61
1995 Savannah State University 4.19
1996 Miles College 5.18
1997 Miles College 5.00
1998 Savannah State University 3.94
2001 Savannah State University 3.62
2002 LeMoyne-Owen 4.40
2003 Shaw University 4.54
2004 Elizabeth City State 5.00
2007 North Carolina Central 4.64
2008 Shaw University 3.03
2009 Benedict College 6.06
2010 Benedict College 5.96
2011 Benedict College 6.07
2012 Benedict College 7.19
2013 Benedict College 8.15
2014 Benedict College 4.93
2018 Benedict College 4.19
2019 Benedict College 5.21

**Stolen Bases – Total For a Season**
1996 Miles College 171
1997 Savannah State University 203
1998 Savannah State University 193
2001 Savannah State University 181
2002 LeMoyne-Owen 185
2004 Elizabeth City State 170
2007 North Carolina Central 209
2009 Benedict College 194
2010 Benedict College 316
2011 Benedict College 261
2012 Benedict College 266
2013 Benedict College 334
2014 Benedict College 207
2019 Benedict College 177

## Annual Team Pitching Statistical Leaders

**Lowest Earned Run Average – For a Season**
1972 North Carolina A&T 0.97
1976 Mississippi Valley State 1.79
2000 Savannah State University 2.30

**Strikeout Ratio – For a Season** *(strikeouts per nine innings)*
2006 Miles College 9.65

## Annual Team Miscellaneous Statistical Leaders

**Winning Percentage – For a Season**
2000 Savannah State (46-3) .939

# NCAA Division III National Record Holders and Annual Statistical Leaders

(Historically Black Colleges and Universities only)

*Official NCAA Division II baseball records began with the 1974 season and are based on information submitted to the NCAA statistics service by institutions participating in the statistics rankings. Career records of players include only those years in which they competed in Division III.*

## National Record Holders

**Stolen Bases – Average Per Game (Team)**
6.06 Rust College 2006

**Lowest Earned Run Average – For a Season (Team)**
1.28 Miles College 1974

## Annual Individual Hitting Statistical Leaders

**Batting Average – For a Season**
1976 Billy Richmond, LeMoyne-Owen .535
1977 Anthony Johnson, LeMoyne-Owen .574

**Triples – Average Per Game**
1980 Thomas Wesley, Stillman College 0.28
1986 Reggie Zinn, Rust College 0.24

**Triples – Total For a Season**
1976 Willie Dawson, Stillman College 9
       Lacy Curry, Bishop College 9
1980 Thomas Wesley, Stillman College 11
1986 Reggie Zinn, Rust College 10

**Home Runs – Average Per Game**
1977 Anthony Johnson, LeMoyne-Owen 0.41

**Slugging Percentage – For a Season**
1977 Anthony Johnson, LeMoyne-Owen 1.096

**Stolen Bases – Average Per Game**
1974 Theophalus Gregory, Savannah State 1.92
1986 Reggie Zinn, Rust College 1.38
2002 James Hymon, Rust College 1.37
2003 Carlos Hardaway, Rust College 1.52
2006 Carlos Hardaway, Rust College 1.78
2007 Vashun Jackson, Rust College 1.38

**Stolen Bases – Total For a Season**
1975 Joe Pierce, Bishop College 34
1976 Lacy Curry, Bishop College 47
1977 Charles Grove, LeMoyne-Owen 35
1986 Reggie Zinn, Rust College 58
2002 James Hymon, Rust College 56
2006 Carlos Hardaway, Rust College 57

## Annual Individual Pitching Statistical Leaders

**Strikeout Ratio – For a Season** *(strikeouts per nine innings)*
1980 Reggie Jackson, Fisk University 15.4

**Strikeouts – Total For a Season**
1980 Reggie Jackson, Fisk University 144

## Annual Team Hitting Statistical Leaders

**Batting Average – For a Season**
1987 Stillman College .387

**Triples – Average Per Game**
2001 Stillman College 1.04

**Stolen Bases – Average Per Game**
2006 Rust College 6.06
2007 Rust College 6.00

## Annual Team Pitching Statistical Leaders

**Lowest Earned Run Average – For a Season**
1974 Miles College 1.28

**Strikeout Ratio – For a Season** *(strikeouts per nine innings)*
2006 Lincoln (PA) University 9.1

---

# NCAA Small College Division Annual Statistical Leaders

(Historically Black Colleges and Universities only)

*During the years from 1957 through 1962, after which time the NCAA established a Division II statistical classification, records were classified as either "university division" (major colleges) or "college division" (small schools). The statistical leaders below are ones officially recognized by the NCAA during that time period, but since 1963 are no longer recognized.*

## Annual Individual Hitting Statistical Leaders

**Batting Average – For a Season**
1962 Jerry Smith, West Virginia State .538

**Home Runs – Average Per Game**
1957 James Purce, Howard University .60

**Slugging Percentage – For a Season**
1957 James Purce, Howard University .984
1960 Harold Gray, Maryland State 1.000

**Stolen Bases – Average Per Game**
1962 Robert Williams, Mississippi Valley State 1.75
       Cornell Gordon, North Carolina A&T 1.75
       Sim Bowden, North Carolina A&T 1.75

## Annual Team Hitting Statistical Leaders

**Runs Scored – Average Per Game**
1957 Central State 10.80
1959 North Carolina A&T 11.40
1960 North Carolina A&T 14.15
1962 North Carolina A&T 12.30

**Doubles – Average Per Game**
1958 Florida A&M 2.42
1959 North Carolina A&T 2.62

**Stolen Bases – Average Per Game**
1958 Maryland State 5.70
1959 North Carolina A&T 4.30
1960 North Carolina A&T 4.69
1962 North Carolina A&T 7.25

# NAIA National Record Holders and Annual Statistical Leaders

(Historically Black Colleges and Universities only)

*The National Association of Intercollegiate Athletics officially began compiling statistics and maintaining a record database in 1960. Prior to that, the only recognition of statistical leaders for NAIA level schools was published in the Official NCAA Baseball Guide, under the classification of "small schools". It was first published in 1958 and contained statistics from the previous collegiate baseball season.*

## National Record Holders

**Triples – Total For a Game (Individual)**
3 Matt McEuen, Texas College 2011

**Home Runs – Consecutive (Team)**
4 West Virginia State 1987

**Fielding – Assists For a Game (Individual)**
12 Oswaldo Calderon, Talladega College 2019

**Stolen Bases – For a Career (Individual)**
186, Kevin Gamblin Texas College 1985-1988

**Stolen Bases – Total For a Season (Team)**
328 Texas College 1987

**Hit By Pitch – Total For a Game (Team)**
13 Texas College 2012

**Fewest Runs Allowed – Total For a Season (Team)**
34 Norfolk State 1975

**Fewest Earned Runs Allowed – Total For a Season (Team)**
16 Norfolk State 1975

**Fewest Walks Allowed – Total For a Season (Team)**
29 Norfolk State 1975

**Fewest Hits Allowed – Total For a Season (Team)**
55 Norfolk State 1975

**Lowest Earned Run Average – For a Season (Team)**
1.07 Grambling University 1967

## Annual Individual Hitting Statistical Leaders

**Batting Average – For a Season**
1967 Ralph Garr, Grambling University .582
1974 Nathan Chapman, Jarvis Christian College .551
1976 Willie Powell, Mississippi Valley State .563
1977 Anthony Johnson, LeMoyne-Owen .574*
1981 Toney Howell, Central State .524
1988 Earl Carter, Paul Quinn College .562
2016 Javion Randle, Jarvis Christian College .480

**Doubles – Total For a Season**
1977 Don Wilcher, Fort Valley State 11**
2013 Neiro Barreto, Talladega College 29

**Doubles – Average Per Game**
1965 Lawrence Williams, Allen University 0.83
1989 Trevor Nance, Florida Memorial 0.61
2014 Jared Holloman, Morris College 0.65

**Triples – Total For a Season**
1961 Perry McGee, Grambling University 6
1963 Euna Edwards, Hampton University 6
1990 George Lowery, Texas College 15

**Triples – Average Per Game**
1972 Alphana Hobbs, Fayetteville Stats 0.29
    Hank Gates, Grambling University 0.29
1990 George Lowery, Texas College 0.47
1994 Edward Bady, Talladega College 0.21

**Home Runs – Total For a Season**
1977 Anthony Johnson, LeMoyne-Owen 12**

**Home Runs – Average Per Game**
1966 Pete Barnes, Southern University 0.36
1967 Pete Barnes, Southern University 0.32
1994 William Patton, Morris College 0.45

**Runs Batted In – Total For a Season**
1967 Pete Barnes, Southern University 43

**Runs Batted In – Average Per Game**
1966 Charles Stukes, Maryland State 2.67
1967 Pete Barnes, Southern University 1.72
1995 Barry Shelton, West Virginia State 1.57

**On Base Percentage – For a Season**
2013 Travonne Fuller, Edward Waters College .550

**Stolen Bases – Average Per Game**
2015 Seth Eakin, Voorhees 1.08

**Stolen Bases – Total For a Season**
1960 Robert Williams, Grambling 23
1970 Cliff Hayes, Jackson State 45
1974 Cliff Marshall, Jackson State 50
1977 Anthony Johnson, LeMoyne-Owen 32**
1983 Calvin Green, Texas College 46

**Stolen Bases Percentage – For a Season**
1982 Richard Hannah, Norfolk State 1.000
1983 Reginald Cuington, Texas College 1.000
1988 Mike Foster, Paul Quinn College 1.000

## Annual Individual Pitching Statistical Leaders

**Earned Run Average – For a Season**
1960 Charles Gray, Southern University 0.56
1961 Clyde Parquet, Grambling University 0.66
1962 Hillary Bossier, Grambling University 0.53
1963 Alex Pero, Grambling University 0.00

**Lowest Opponent's Batting Average – For a Season**
2009 John Holbeck, Edward Waters College .091

**Strikeouts – For a Season**
1972 Al Holland, North Carolina A&T 143

**Strikeout Ratio – For a Season** *(strikeouts per nine innings)*
1960 Charles Gray, Southern University 12.3
1979 Lester Strode, Jackson State 14.0
1982 Paul Zeazell, West Virginia State

**Victories – Total For a Season**
2017 Kyle Chavez, Talladega College 13

**Highest Winning Percentage – For a Season**
1965 Alex Pero, Grambling University 1.000 (10-0)

## Annual Team Hitting Statistical Leaders

**Batting Average – For a Season**

1961 Grambling University .362
1963 Grambling University .370
1965 Allen University .368
1967 Grambling University .355
1968 South Carolina State .362
1969 Saint Augustine's College .379
1970 Jackson State .369
1971 Jackson State .389
1972 Fayetteville State .389
1973 Jackson State .371
1975 Kentucky State .375
1976 Mississippi Valley State .370
1995 West Virginia State .371
2014 Talladega College .362

## Annual Team Pitching Statistical Leaders

**Lowest Earned Run Average – For a Season**

1963 Grambling University 0.61
1967 Grambling University 0.88
1972 Fayetteville State 1.43
1976 Mississippi Valley State 1.79

**Lowest Opponent's Batting Average – For a Season**

2009 Edward Waters College .232

**Fewest Earned Runs Allowed – For a Season**

2009 Edward Waters College 36

## Annual Team Fielding Statistical Leaders

**Fielding Average – For a Season**

1961 Grambling University .964
1984 West Virginia State .964

*\* Based on 100 bats or less*
*\*\* Based on 30 games or less*

# All-Americans and Other Nationally Recognized Awards
(Historically Black Colleges and Universities only)

## American Baseball Coaches Association
**NCAA Division I** *(award began in 1949)*
    1986 Earl Sanders, Jackson State (Outfield)
    1987 Kenneth Clark, Southern University (Designated Hitter)
    2001 Scott Martin, Delaware State (Third Base)
    2002 Rickie Weeks, Southern University (Second Base)
    2003 Rickie Weeks, Southern University (Second Base)*
    2014 Charles Sikes, Savannah State (Designated Hitter)
    2017 Devin Hemmerich, Norfolk State (Pitcher)
    * *Player of the Year*

**NCAA Division II** *(award began in 1969)*
    1975 Danny Goodwin, Southern University (Catcher)
    1980 Howard Carter, Tuskegee University (Outfield)
    1989 Melvin Wearing, Norfolk State (Infield)
    1991 Andre Johnson, Norfolk State (Outfield)
    2002 David Smith, West Virginia State (Outfield)
    2005 Ryan Taylor, West Virginia State (Second Base)
    2005 Kevin Goode, West Virginia State (Outfield)
    2005 Zach Baldwin, West Virginia State (Pitcher)
    2006 Jeff Miller, West Virginia State (First Base)
    2006 Ryan Taylor, West Virginia State (Second Base)
    2006 Kyle Jones, West Virginia State (Designated Hitter)
    2006 Brandon Halstead, West Virginia State (Outfield)
    2007 Josh Miller, West Virginia State (Outfield)
    2012 Jarius Brown, Stillman College (Infield)

**NCAA Division III** *(award began in 1976)*
    1977 Don Wilcher, Fort Valley State (First Base)
    1977 Anthony Johnson, LeMoyne-Owen College (Outfield)
    1987 John Eckfert, Stillman College (Outfield)

**NAIA** *(award began in 1969)*
    1970 Lee Richard, Southern University (Shortstop)
    1972 Danny Goodwin, Southern University (Catcher)
    1973 Danny Goodwin, Southern University (Catcher)
    1976 Jerome Williams, Kentucky State (Infield)
    1982 Eugene Hawkins, Norfolk State (Catcher)
    1982 Jim Trimble, West Virginia State (Catcher)
    1982 Carl Hollins, Stillman College (Infield)
    1982 Terry Edwards, Central State (Outfield)
    1982 Vernon Holstine, West Virginia State (Pitcher)
    1994 Edward Bady, Talladega College (Outfield)
    1995 Barry Shelton, West Virginia (Third Base)
    2005 Jerry Hodges, Harris Stowe College (Third Base)
    2015 Jesse Baker, Edward Waters College (Catcher)
    2016 Javion Randle, Jarvis Christian College (Outfield)
    2017 Kyle Chavez, Talladega College (Pitcher)

## Sporting News *(selected from 1964-1992)*
    1970 Lee Richard, Southern University (Shortstop)
    1975 Danny Goodwin, Southern University (Catcher)*
    1983 Dave Clark, Jackson State (Outfield)
    1983 Stanley Jefferson, Bethune-Cookman University (Outfield)
    * *Player of the Year*

## National Collegiate Baseball Writers Association

**NCAA Division I** *(since 2000)*

2000 Dario Rosa, Alcorn State (Utility)
2002 Rickie Weeks, Southern University (Second Base)
2003 Rickie Weeks, Southern University (Second Base)*
2003 John Gragg, Bethune-Cookman University (Utility)
2005 Corey Wimberley, Alcorn State (Second Base)
2006 Zach Penprase, Mississippi Valley State (Shortstop)
2007 Marcus Davis, Alcorn State (Outfield)
2013 Kyle McGowin, Savannah State (Pitcher)
2015 Melvin Rodriguez, Jackson State (Second Base)
2016 Joseph Camacho, Alabama State (Pitcher)
2017 Drew Hemmerich, Norfolk State (Pitcher)
* *Player of the Year*

**NCAA Division II** *(since 2002)*

2005 Kevin Goode, West Virginia State (Outfield)
2005 Zach Baldwin, West Virginia State (Pitcher)
2005 Ryan Taylor, West Virginia State (Second Base)
2005 Jon McDowell, West Virginia State (Catcher)
2006 Carlos Gutierrez, Elizabeth City State (Outfield)
2006 Brandon Halstead, West Virginia State (Outfield)
2006 DeShaun Brooks, Benedict College (Third Base)
2006 Ryan Taylor, West Virginia State (Second Base)
2006 Kyle Jones, West Virginia State (Utility)
2006 Jeff Miller, West Virginia State (Second Base)
2007 Jeff Miller, West Virginia State (Second Base)
2007 Josh Miller, West Virginia State (Outfield)
2009 Eric Workman, West Virginia State (Outfied)
2011 Brandon Gipson, Benedict College (Designated Hitter/Utility)
2013 Tyler Hickernell, Winston-Salem State (Designated Hitter)
2013 Travis Moore, Winston-Salem State (Outfield)
2013 Lydell Moseby, Benedict College (Shortstop)
2015 Jacob Campbell, Albany State (Outfield)
2018 Darrell Langston, Claflin College (Outfield)

## Collegiate Baseball Newspaper *(since 1991)*

2001 Michael Woods, Southern University (Second Base)
2002 Antoin Gray, Southen University (Third Base)
2002 Wes Timmons, Bethune-Cookman University (Shortstop)
2002 Rickie Weeks, Southern University (Second Base)
2003 Rickie Weeks, Southern University (Second Base)*
2003 John Gragg, Bethune-Cookman University (Utility)
2004 Andrew Toussaint, Southern University (Third Base)
2005 Corey Wimberley, Alcon State (Second Base)
2006 Joaquin Rodriguez, Jackson State (Shortstop)
2007 Charlie Gamble, North Carolina A&T (First Base)
2007 Michael Richard, Prairie View A&M (Shortstop)
2010 Peter O'Brien, Bethune-Cookman University (Catcher)
2011 Frazier Hall, Southern University (First Base)
2013 Kevin Freeman, North Carolina A&T (First Base)
2013 Luke Tendler, North Carolina A&T (Shortstop)
2015 Melvin Rodriguez, Jackson State (Second Base)
2016 Joseph Camacho, Alabama State (Pitcher)
2017 Devin Hemmerich, Norfolk State (Pitcher)

   2018 Kamren Dukes, Texas Southern (Outfield)
   2019 Tyler LaPorte, Southern University (Third Base)
   * *Player of the Year*

## Baseball America
**NCAA Division I** *(since 1981)*
   1983 Stanley Jefferson, Bethune-Cookman University (Outfield)
   1986 Earl Sanders, Jackson State (Designated Hitter)
   1987 Adell Davenport, Southern University (First Base)
   1989 Greg Rideau, Grambling State University (Outfield)
   2001 Michael Woods, Southern University (Second Base)
   2001 Rickie Weeks, Southern University (Outfield)
   2002 Rickie Weeks, Southern University (Designated Hitter)
   2003 Rickie Weeks, Southern University (Second Base)*
   * *Player of the Year*

## NAIA Baseball Coaches Association *(award began in 1961)*
   1961 Tommie Agee, Grambling State University (Outfield)
   1961 McVea Griffin Southern University (Pitcher)
   1961 Harry Levy Southern University (Second Base)
   1961 Clyde Parquet Grambling State University (Pitcher)
   1962 Hillary Bossier Grambling State University (Pitcher)
   1963 Frank Garnet Grambling State University (Infield)
   1963 James Morrow Stillman College (Outfield)
   1963 Don Welch Grambling University (Catcher)
   1964 Candy Robinson Grambling State University (Pitcher)
   1964 John Wyatt Grambling State University (Outfield)
   1965 Alex Pero Grambling State University (pitcher)
   1966 Pete Barnes Southern University (Outfield)
   1966 Jophrey Brown Grambling State University (Pitcher)
   1967 Pete Barnes Southern University (Outfield)
   1967 Ralph Garr Grambling State University (Infield)
   1967 Jimmie Jackson Grambling StateUniversity (Pitcher)
   1970 Lee Richard Southern University (Infield)
   1970 Barry Steele Central State (Catcher)
   1972 Danny Goodwin Southern University
   1972 Al Holland North Carolina A&T (Pitcher)
   1972 Ben Samuels South Carolina State (Catcher)
   1973 Danny Goodwin Southern University (Catcher)
   1975 Nate Chapman Jarvis Christian College (Outfield)
   1976 Jerome Williams Kentucky State (Infield)
   1981 Eugene Hawkins Norfolk State (Catcher)
   1982 Terry Edwards Central State (Outfield)
   1982 Eugene Hawkins Norfolk State (Catcher)
   1982 Carl Hollis Stillman College (Infield)
   1982 Vernon Holstine West Virginia State (Pitcher)
   1982 Jim Tribble West Virginia State (Catcher)
   1994 Edward Bady Talladega College (Outfield)
   1995 Barry Shelton West Virginia State (Third Base)
   2005 Jerry Hodges Harris-Stowe State (Third Base)
   2015 Jesse Baker Edward Waters College (Catcher)
   2016 Javion Randle Jarvis Christian College (Outfield)
   2017 Kyle Chavez Talladega College (Pitcher)

## Daktronics NCAA Division II *(since 2007)*
   2007 Josh Miller, West Virginia State University (Outfield)

2007 Brandon Halstead, West Virginia State (Shortstop)
2008 Nathan Goggins, Albany State University (Designated Hitter)
2009 Eric Workman, West Virginia State (Outfield)
2011 Brandon Gipson, Benedict College (Utility)
2011 Rashad Ingram, Saint Augustine's University (Shortstop)
2012 Michael Jordan, Benedict College (Utility)
2013 Travis Moore, Winston-Salem State University (Outfield)
2013 Jack Hudson, West Virginia State University (Designated Hitter)
2015 Joshua Falbo, West Virginia State University (Pitcher)

## United States Christian Athletic Association *(since 2008)*

2002 Fred Bryant, Concordia College of Alabama (Outfield)
2002 Jason Foster, Concordia College of Alabama (Pitcher)
2003 LaDarrell Banks, Concordia College of Alabama (Utility)
2010 C.J. Lindsey, Selma University (Second Base)
2011 C.J. Lindsey, Selma University (Second Base)
2011 Tashland Robinson, Selma University (First Base)
2011 Eddie Waters, Selma University (Outfield)
2018 Peyton Durham, Bluefield State College (Infield)
2018 Marcus Hardy, Selma University (First Base)
2018 Tanner Brandon, Bluefield State College (Utility)
2019 Ricky Butts, Selma University (Shortstop)

## College Sports Information Directors Academic All-Americans

*(began in 1970 – NCAA selections only)*
1977 Roger Claypool, Lincoln (MO) University
1980 Jerry Davis, Howard University
1985 Robert Williams, Prairie View A&M
1987 Elijah Moore, Alcorn State
1990 John Choinski, Coppin State
1990 Harry Brown, Grambling State University
1998 Cecil Christwell, Coppin State
1999 Mark Circo, Delaware Sate
2013 Gavin Guarrera, North Carolina Central
2016 James Day, North Carolina Central
2017 Brian Beard, Norfolk State
2018 Andrew Valichka, North Carolina Central
2018 Rafael Ramirez, Grambling State University
2018 Hunter Phillips, Alabama State
2019 Caleb Ward, Norfolk State

## National College Baseball Hall of Fame

2011 Dr. Ralph W.E.Jones, Grambling State University (Coach)
2011 Danny Goodwin, Southern University (Player)
2012 Lou Brock, Southern University (Player)
2013 Ralph Garr, Grambling State University (Player)
2014 William C. Matthews, Tuskegee (Player)
2015 Al Holland, North Carolina A&T (Player)
2016 Robert Braddy, Jackson State (Coach)
2019 Andre Dawson, Florida A&M (Player)

## Black College Baseball Player of the Year *(began in 2004)*

2004 Bryant Lange, Jackson State (Position Player)
    Shawn Phillips, Delaware State (Pitcher)
    Michael Robertson, Prairie View A&M (Coach of the Year)
2005 Jeremy Jones, North Carolina A&T (Position Player)

Michael Hauff, North Carolina A&T (Pitcher)
Keith Shumate, North Carolina A&T (Coach of the Year)
2006 Jaquin Rodriguez, Jackson State (Position Player)
*Black College Baseball Player of the Year (continued)*
Francisco Rodriguez, Bethune-Cookman University (Pitcher)
Mervyl Melendez, Bethune-Cookman University (Co-Coach of the Year)
Michael Robertson, Prairie View A&M (Co-Coach of the Year)
2007 Michael Richard, Prairie View A&M (Position Player)
Luke Foss, Norfolk State (Pitcher)
Mervyl Melendez, Bethune-Cookman University (Coach of the Year)

## Black College Nines Player of the Year *(began in 2016)*

2016 Jesus Santana, Jackson State (Position Player- Large School)
Joseph Camacho, Alabama State University (Pitcher- Large School)
Mervyl Melendez, Alabama State (Coach of the Year- Large School)
Javion Randle, Jarvis Christian College (Position Player-Small School)
Joshua Falbo, West Virginia State (Pitcher-Small School)
Reginald Johnson, Edward Waters (Coach of the Year-Small School)
2017 Marshawn Taylor, Grambling State University (Position Player-Large School)
Devin Hemmerich, Norfolk State (Pitcher- Large School)
Cage Cox, Alabama State (Freshman of the Year-Large School)
Ben Hall, North Carolina A&T (Coach of the Year- Large School)
David White Jr., Benedict College (Position Player-Small School)
Kyle Chavez, Talladega College (Pitcher-Small School)
Darius England, Voorhees College (Freshman of the Year-Small School)
Marcos Domingues, Talladege College (Coach of the Year-Small School)
2018 Kamren Dukes, Texas Southern (Position Player-Large School)
Darrius Wright, Alabama State (Pitcher- Large School)
Marcos Castillo, Coppin State (Freshman of the Year-Large School)
Michael Robertson, Texas Southern (Coach of the Year- Large School)
Sergio Chil, Florida Memorial (Position Player-Small School)
Steven Wells, Harris-Stowe State (Pitcher-Small School)
Kelin Washington, Edward Waters (Freshman of the Year-Small School)
Florentino Burgos, Florida Memorial (Coach of the Year-Small School)
2019 Tyler LaPorte, Southern University (Position Player-Large School)
Jeremiah McCollum, Florida A&M (Pitcher- Large School)
Alex Martinez, Prairie View A&M (Freshman of the Year-Large School)
Kerrick Jackson, Southern University (Coach of the Year- Large School)
Gerardic Dobbs, Claflin University (Position Player-Small School)
Roman Oliu, Albany State (Pitcher-Small School)
Roman Sorrell, Wiley College (Freshman of the Year-Small School)
Rob Henry, Kentucky State (Coach of the Year-Small School)

## Golden Spikes Player of the Year

*(awarded annually to the country's best amateur player by the United States Baseball Federation)*
2003 Rickie Weeks, Southern University

## NAIA Hall of Fame *(baseball only)*

1961 George Altman, Tennessee State (Player)
1964 Dr. Ralph W.E. Jones, Grambling State University (Coach)
1966 Donn Clendenon, Morehouse College (Player)
1967 Robert Lee, Southern University (Coach)

## Black College Baseball National Champions *(named from 2002-2011)*

2002 Bethune-Cookman University
2003 Southern University

2004 Bethune-Cookman University
2005 North Carolina A&T University/Southern University *(co-champions)*
2006 Prairie View A&M University
2007 Bethune-Cookman University
2008 Bethune-Cookman University
2009 Bethune-Cookman University
2010 Bethune-Cookman University (Large School)
    West Virginia State University (Small School)
2011 Bethune-Cookman University (Large School)
    Edward Waters College (Small School)
2012 Bethune-Cookman University (Large School)
2012 Stillman College (Small School)

**Black College Nines National Champions** *(named from 2015 - present)*
2015 Alabama State University (Large School)
    Winston-Salem State University (Small School)
2016 Alabama State University (Large School)
    West Virginia State University (Small School)
2017 Bethune-Cookman University (Large School)
    Winston-Salem State University (Small School)
2018 North Carolina A&T University (Small School)
    Albany State University (Small School)
2019 Southern University (Large School)
    Winston-Salem State University (Small School)

**Black College National Champions** *(Black College Baseball and Black College Nines combined)*

| | |
|---|---|
| Bethune-Cookman University | 9 (2002, 2004, 2007, 2008 2009, 2010, 2011, 2012, 2017) |
| Southern University | 3 (2003, 2005*, 2019) |
| Winston-Salem State University | 3 (2015, 2017, 2019) |
| Alabama State University | 2 (2015, 2016) |
| North Carolina A&T University | 2 (2005*, 2018) |
| West Virginia State University | 2 (2010, 2016) |
| Albany State University | 1 (2018) |
| Edward Waters College | 1 (2011) |
| Prairie View A&M University | 1 (2006) |
| Stillman College | 1 (2012) |

* *(co-champions)*

# Major League Annual Amateur Baseball Draft
(Historically Black Colleges and Universities only)

*In 1965, Major League Baseball established its annual baseball draft (renamed the First-Year Player Draft in 1998). Prior to 1965, a player was free to sign with any team of his choice that offered a contract. The original draft concept incorporated three separate draft periods, those being in January, June and August. The January and June drafts involved a secondary phase (which was eliminated in 1987) for previously drafted, but unsigned players. Though tweaked through the years, the original concept was to hold a June draft for recent high school graduates and college students who had attained sophomore status or age 21. The January draft was designated for high school and college players who graduated in the winter (this was also eliminated in 1987). The August draft, which was eliminated after just two years, was intended for amateur players who had completed their summer American Legion seasons. Beginning with the consolidation of the remaining drafting periods and phases in 1987, the annual draft in June also incorporated supplemental rounds used as team compensation measures involving the inter-team movement of free agent ballplayers. Those selected immediately between the first and second rounds of the regular draft are typically referenced as first round picks.*

## First Round Draft Selections
*(Year, Name, School, Drafted by, Overall selection, Phase)*

1967 Tommy Campbell, Jackson State – New York Mets, 19th (January Secondary Phase)
1967 Jimmie Jackson, Grambling SUniversity – Saint Louis Cardinals, 10th (June Secondary Phase)
1969 Jake Brown, Southern University - San Francisco Giants, 2nd (June Secondary Phase)
1970 Lee Richard, Southern University – Chicago White Sox, 6th (June Regular Phase)
1970 Greg Gaffey, Lincoln (PA) University – New York Yankees, 16th (June Secondary Phase)
1975 Danny Goodwin, Southern University – California Angles, 1st (June Regular Phase)
1975 Gene Richards, South Carolina State – San Diego Padres, 1st (January Regular Phase)
1975 Willie Aikens, South Carolina State – California Angles, 2nd (January Regular Phase)
1976 William Free, Tuskegee University – Atlanta Braves, 4th (January Secondary Phase)
1976 Nate Puryear, Stillman College – Boston Red Sox, 21st (January Secondary Phase)
1981 Terry Blocker, Tennessee State – New York Mets, 4th (June Regular Phase)
1983 Dave Clark, Jackson State – Cleveland Indians, 11th (June Regular Phase)
1983 Stan Jefferson, Bethune-Cookman University – New York Mets 20th (June Regular Phase)
1986 Earl Sanders, Jackson State – Toronto Blue Jays 26th (June Regular Phase)
--------------------------- *All draft cycles eliminated except June Regular Phase* ---------------------------
2001 Michael Woods Jr., Southern University – Detroit Tigers, 32nd (Supplemental)
2003 Rickie Weeks, Southern University – Milwaukee Brewers, 2nd

## Top 10 Institutions With Most Draft Selections *(1965-2019)*
*(Includes players who were drafted more than once from the same school)*

1. Southern University (92)
2. Jackson State (58)
3. Grambling State University (52)
4. Bethune-Cookman University (36)
5. Florida A&M (27)
6. Norfolk State (20)
6. North Carolina A&T (20)
8. West Virginia State (19)
9. Texas Southern University (16)
9. Prairie View A&M (16)

## Annual MLB Draft Selections *(1965-2019)*
*(Includes players who were drafted more than once from the same school)*
*(Year, Name, School and Position - Drafted by, Round/Overall selection and Phase)*

1965 Peter Barnes, Southern University OF - Los Angeles Dodgers 6/110*
1965 Hal McRae, Florida A&M SS - Cincinnati Reds 6/117*
1965 Johnny Hairston, Southern University C - Chicago Cubs 16/301*
1965 Jophrey Brown, Grambling State University P - Pittsburgh Pirates 21/402*
1965 Nathaniel Perkins, Benedict College SS - Chicago Cubs 27/509*
1965 Elvatous Peters, Southern University OF - Chicago White Sox 27/525*

1965 John Bacot, Alabama A&M OF - Chicago Cubs 29/543*
1965 Cliff Matthews, North Carolina A&T C - Baltimore Orioles 29/557*
1965 Robert Jones, Grambling State University SS - Baltimore Orioles 34/631*
1965 Ray Frank, Southern University OF - Baltimore Orioles 35/643*
1965 Jesse Cleveland, Alabama State OF - St. Louis Cardinals 44/731*
1965 James Watts, Howard University SS - Kansas City Athletics 45/741*
1965 Lionel Jones, Southern University OF - Houston Astros 54/783*
1966 Jophrey Brown, Grambling State University P - Chicago Cubs 2/23**
1966 Jophrey Brown, Grambling State University P - Boston Red Sox 4/60***
1966 Elvatous Peters, Southern University OF - Chicago Cubs 9/225*
1966 Lionel Jones, Southern University OF - Washington Senators 9/102****
1966 Frank Patterson, Grambling State University OF - St. Louis Cardinals 15/287*
1966 Calvin Bailey, West Virginia State P - Pittsburgh Pirates 23/455*
1966 Nathaniel Dixon, Tuskegee University P - Detroit Tigers 26/514*
1966 Tommy Campbell, Jackson State OF - Baltimore Orioles 26/516*
1966 Louis Inman, Mississippi Valley State 3B - Boston Red Sox 28/543*
1966 Jimmy Jackson, Grambling State University P - Atlanta Braves 32/617*
1966 Dicky Shaw, Central State SS - Los Angeles Dodgers 45/769*
1966 Robert Height, Shaw University OF - New York Yankees 47/779*
1967 Jimmie Jackson, Grambling State University P - St. Louis Cardinals 1/10**
1967 Tommy Campbell, Jackson State OF - New York Mets 1/19****
1967 James Herbert, Southern University P - Los Angeles Dodgers 2/36***
1967 Ralph Garr, Grambling State University 2B - Atlanta Braves 3/52*
1967 Frank Patterson, Grambling State University OF - Atlanta Braves 5/83****
1967 Louis Ganious, Southern University 1B - Detroit Tigers 7/136**
1967 Allen Robinson, Tennessee State OF - Chicago Cubs 8/141*
1967 Theodore Taylor, Florida A&M 3B/OF - Pittsburgh Pirates 9/175*
1967 Jon Keirns, Central State OF - Los Angeles Dodgers 9/162**
1967 Willie Garrison, Alabama State P - Chicago White Sox 37/687*
1967 Melvin McNeil, Grambling State University OF - New York Mets 44/787*
1967 Garland Godwin, Alcorn State 1B - Kansas City Athletics 47/824*
1968 Matt Alexander, Grambling State University 3B - Chicago Cubs 2/35*
1968 Charles Jones, Grambling State University P - Baltimore Orioles 2/24**
1968 Paul Johnson, South Carolina State OF - Los Angeles Dodgers 3/45*
1968 Dewayne Chambers, Florida Memorial College OF - Washington Senators 4/62***
1968 Jerry Turk, Fort Valley State P - Cincinnati Reds 6/98***
1968 Lloyd Lightfoot, North Carolina A&T SS - Baltimore Orioles 10/214*
1968 Al Bumbry, Virginia State OF - Baltimore Orioles 11/238*
1968 Benjamin Williams, Grambling State University C/OF - Cincinnati Reds 21/478*
1969 Jake Brown, Southern University C - San Francisco Giants 1/2**
1969 Charles Jones, Grambling State University P - California Angels 3/24**
1969 Lloyd Lightfoot, North Carolina A&T SS - Kansas City Royals 3/214****
1969 Michael Cummings, Grambling State University SS - Boston Red Sox 7/131*
1969 William Robinson, North Carolina A&T OF/P - Pittsburgh Pirates 10/224*
1969 Arthur Gainous, Southern University 1B - Chicago Cubs 17/398*
1969 Cleothus Jackson, Jackson State P - Chicago White Sox 26/601*
1969 Fred Ruben, Delaware State 3B - Philadelphia Phillies 27/627*
1969 Lewis Braddy, Stillman College SS - Chicago White Sox 30/692*
1969 Kenneth Samuels, Stillman College P - Chicago White Sox 31/714*
1970 Lee Richard, Southern University SS - Chicago White Sox 1/6*
1970 Greg Gaffey, Lincoln (PA) University 1B - New York Yankees 1/16**
1970 Henry Baker, Southern University 3B - Chicago White Sox 2/30**
1970 Ulysses Wilson, Florida A&M SS - San Diego Padres 5/97*
1970 Thomas Hallums, South Carolina State 1B - New York Mets 9/215*
1970 Lendon Brookins, Texas Southern 3B - Atlanta Braves 13/309*
1970 Ted Cooper, Morgan State University 2B - Pittsburgh Pirates 13/182***

1970 Jimmy Collins, Southern University P - Chicago White Sox 15/342*
1970 Anthony McLin, Stillman College OF - Boston Red Sox 16/376*
1970 Eric Wharton, Delaware State OF - Philadelphia Phillies 19/437*
1970 Wilson Stallworth, North Carolina A&T P - Atlanta Braves 24/573*
1970 Cliff Hayes, Jackson State OF/IF - Chicago White Sox 25/582*
1970 Jeff Anderson, Jackson State OF - New York Mets 31/718*
1971 Henry Baker, Southern University 3B - Boston Red Sox 3/43**
1971 Henry Baker, Southern University 3B - Philadeliphia Phillies 3/65****
1971 Jimmy Collins, Southern University P - Atlanta Braves 4/89****
1971 Kim Hall, University of Maryland Eastern Shore SS - Baltimore Orioles 20/476*
1971 Robert Edmond, Fort Valley State 2B - Cincinnati Reds 25/586*
1971 Bobby Johnson, Southern University OF/C - Los Angeles Dodgers 27/619*
1971 Oscar Fisher, Southern University OF - California Angels 30/661*
1972 Edward Ricks, Grambling State University P - New York Yankees 6/134*
1972 Gregory Dobson, Bethune Cookman OF/P - New York Mets 21/491*
1972 William Robinson, Delaware State OF - New York Mets 38/753*
1973 Roger Cador, Southern University OF - Atlanta Braves 10/226*
1973 Willie Clark, Jackson State P - Kansas City Royals 11/249*
1973 Steve Barlow, Morehouse University P - Atlanta Braves 17/394*
1973 William Martin, Shaw University P - Cincinnati Reds 34/693*
1973 Richard Shaw, Tuskegee University 3B - St. Louis 50/743*
1974 Arthur Spann, Alcorn State OF - San Francisco Giants 2/43****
1974 Melvin Jackson, LeMoyne Owen College SS - Detroit Tigers 4/88*
1974 Alvin Harper, Southern University SS - Los Angeles Dodgers 5/117*
1974 Steve Henderson, Prairie View A&M SS/3B - Cincinnati Reds 5/119*
1974 Robert Woodland, Howard University OF - Montreal Expos 12/271*
1974 Calvin Jones, Delaware State SS - Detroit Tigers 20/458*
1974 Dale Brock, Southern University OF - Texas Rangers 21/466*
1974 Aaron Randall, Grambling State University 1B - Chicago Cubs 23/507*
1974 Al Holland, North Carolina A&T P - Texas Rangers 30/604*
1975 Danny Goodwin, Southern University C - California Angels 1/1*
1975 Gene Richards, South Carolina State OF - San Diego Padres 1/1****
1975 Willie Aikens, South Carolina State 1B - California Angels 1/2****
1975 Nate Chapman, Jarvis Christian College OF - New York Yankees 3/67*
1975 Dale Brock, Southern University OF - Minnesota Twins 3/67****
1975 Al Holland, North Carolina A&T P - San Diego Padres 4/81****
1975 Joe Pittman, Southern University 3B - Houston Astros 5/110*
1975 Andre Dawson, Florida A&M OF - Montreal Expos 11/250*
1976 William Free, Tuskegee University P - Atlanta Braves 1/4****
1976 Nate Puryear, Stillman College P - Boston Red Sox 1/21****
1976 Nate Puryear, Stillman College P - Cleveland Indians 2/31**
1976 Reggie Baldwin, Grambling State University C - Houston Astros 3/49*
1976 Odie Davis, Prairie View A&M SS - Chicago Cubs 7/151*
1976 Ron Adkins, Grambling State University SS - Baltimore Orioles 7/164*
1976 Michael Brooks, Jackson State P - Montreal Expos 11/249*
1976 Jimmy Giles, Alcorn State OF - Los Angeles Dodgers 12/283*
1976 Eddie Milner, Central State OF - Cincinnati Reds 21/503*
1976 Bobby DuPree, Grambling State University P - San Diego Padres 23/532*
1977 Odie Davis, Prairie View A&M SS - Texas Rangers 7/165*
1977 Carl Spikes, Southern University OF - Chicago Cubs 7/168*
1977 Paul Cooper, Jackson State OF - Houston Astros 9/222*
1977 Eddie Curry, Jackson State P - Houston Astros 12/300*
1977 Joe Mitchell, Prairie View A&M OF - Milwaukee Brewers 14/341*
1977 Calvin King, Southern University SS - Seattle Mariners 22/562*
1977 Jessie Owens, Jackson State C - Pittsburgh Pirates 23/579*
1977 Reggie Walker, Tuskegee University 2B - Cleveland Indians 24/596*

1977 Richard Phillips, Kentucky State OF/1B - Montreal Expos 25/610*
1977 Anthony Johnson, LeMoyne-Owen College OF - Montreal Expos 26/631*
1977 Eric Robertson, Stillman College OF - Chicago Cubs 26/640*
1978 Kelvin Moore, Jackson State 1B - Oakland Athletics 6/134*
1978 Wesley Hair, Albany State OF - Pittsburgh Pirates 14/357*
1978 Ira Turner, Bethune Cookman 1B - Kansas City Royals 14/363*
1978 Razor Shines, St. Augustine's University C - Montreal Expos 18/451*
1978 James McBride, Jackson State P - Cleveland Indians 19/477*
1978 Ken Malone, Prairie View A&M OF - St. Louis Cardinals 19/481*
1978 Keith Shelllings, Southern University P - Texas Rangers 20/509*
1978 Mike Godley, Jackson State OF - Chicago Cubs 24/587*
1978 Alvin Williams, Jackson State 3B - Texas Rangers 41/766*
1979 Huey Gayden, Jackson State OF - New York Yankees 8/207*
1979 Ken Ford, Albany State C - Pittsburgh Pirates 10/250*
1979 Mel Gilliam, Florida A&M P - Texas Rangers 11/277*
1979 Kirk Forbes, Tennessee State 2B - Montreal Expos 13/322*
1979 Michael Woods, Southern University SS - San Francisco Giants 18/460*
1979 Paul Ash, Delaware State OF - San Francisco Giants 20/512*
1979 Maunce Christian, Texas Southern OF - California Angels 21/534*
1979 Homer Moncrief, Jackson State P - Texas Rangers 21/536*
1979 Kevin Hinds, Jackson State 2B - Cincinnati Reds 21/541*
1979 Eli Aldridge, Prairie View A&M OF - California Angels 23/584*
1979 Perry Estep, West Virginia State OF - Cincinnati Reds 23/591*
1979 William Hardy, Alabama State OF - Detroit Tigers 25/630*
1979 Arthur Neal, Morehouse University OF - Atlanta Braves 35/822*
1980 Lester Strode, Kentucky State P - Kansas City Royals 4/94*
1980 Roy Johnson, Tennessee State OF - Montreal Expos 5/125*
1980 Ron Dillard, Norfolk State SS - Baltimore Orioles 5/130*
1980 Jerry Davis, Howard University 3B - San Diego Padres 6/135*
1980 Tom Wesley, Stillman College 1B - Cincinnati Reds 7/175*
1980 Homer Moncrief, Jackson State P - Detroit Tigers 9/226*
1980 Otis Tramble, Southern University SS - New York Mets 10/235*
1980 Greg Smith, Southern University 1B - Los Angeles Dodgers 13/321*
1980 Howard Carter, Tuskegee University OF - Detroit Tigers 16/408*
1980 Dennis Boyd, Jackson State P - Boston Red Sox 16/414*
1980 Don Howard, Norfolk State P - Pittsburgh Pirates 28/697*
1980 Gregg Goodman, Mississippi Valley State P - Chicago Cubs 31/735*
1980 Bill Lucas, Florida A&M SS - Texas Rangers 34/774*
1981 Terry Blocker, Tennessee State OF - New York Mets 1/4*
1981 Curtis Burke, Tennessee State OF - Houston Astros 3/75*
1981 Curt Ford, Jackson State 2B - St. Louis Cardinals 4/85*
1981 Stan Barker, Alcorn State OF - Detroit Tigers 5/119*
1981 Reggie Williams, Southern University OF - St. Louis Cardinals 6/136*
1981 Ken Brown, Grambling State University IF - Pittsburgh Pirates 9/220*
1981 James Randall, Grambling State University 1B - California Angels 10/235*
1981 Charles Epperson, Jackson State OF - Chicago White Sox 11/265*
1981 Charles Hudson, Prairie View A&M P - Philadelphia Phillies 12/304*
1981 Buck Long, Texas Southern P - California Angels 13/313*
1981 Al Jones, Alcorn State P - Chicago White Sox 13/317*
1981 Willie Weston, Mississippi Valley State P - Boston Red Sox 14/355*
1981 Larry McNutt, Jackson State 1B - New York Mets 15/366*
1981 Keith Stafford, Wiley College P - Pittsburgh Pirates 15/376*
1981 Tony Howell, Central State OF/1B - Cincinnati Reds 16/404*
1981 Otis Tramble, Southern University SS - Chicago Cubs 18/442*
1981 Bo Jordan, Mississippi Valley State P - Oakland Athletics 18/455*

1981 Vince Coleman, Florida A&M OF - *Philadelphia Phillies 20/512\**

1981 Charles Dinkins, Southern University P - *Milwaukee Brewers 22/564\**

1981 Wendel Henderson, Grambling State University OF - Chicago Cubs 24/596\*

1981 Adolph Crump, Prairie View A&M OF - Philadelphia Phillies 26/660\*

1981 Tim Richie, Howard University OF - Baltimore Orioles 27/687\*

1981 Ira Lane, Texas Southern OF - Houston Astros 28/708\*

1981 Mike King, Jackson State OF - Montreal Expos 30/745\*

1981 Bill Lucas, Florida A&M 2B/SS - Atlanta Braves 31/758\*

1981 Lary Aaron, Florida A&M OF - Atlanta Braves 32/775\*

1981 Charlie Scott, Jackson State P - Montreal Expos 37/834\*

1982 Ken Howell, Tuskegee University P - Los Angeles Dodgers 3/73\*

1982 Vince Coleman, Florida A&M OF - St. Louis Cardinals 10/257\*

1982 Reggie Williams, Southern University OF - Los Angeles Dodgers 13/332\*

1982 Derrick Smith, Grambling State University 1B - Chicago Cubs 17/418\*

1982 Carl Hollis, Stillman College SS - New York Mets 18/448\*

1982 Eugene Hawkins, Norfolk State OF - New York Mets 23/575\*

1982 Roger Cole, Wiley College P - Philadelphia Phillies 27/682\*

1982 Michael Cain, Jackson State 2B - Baltimore Orioles 29/737\*

1983 Dave Clark, Jackson State OF - Cleveland Indians 1/11\*

1983 Stan Jefferson, Bethune Cookman OF - New York Mets 1/20\*

1983 Terry Edwards, Central State OF - Chicago Cubs 4/86\*

1983 Prince Cousinard, Texas Southern P - Philadelphia Phillies 8/180\*

1983 John Harrington, Alcorn State P - Texas Rangers 8/187\*

1983 Bobby Buchanon, Jackson State 1B/3B - California Angels 11/285\*

1983 Aaron Carlie, Jackson State P - Pittsburgh Pirates 14/352\*

1983 Ray Chadwick, Winston-Salem State P - California Angels 16/415\*

1983 DeMarlo Hale, Southern University 1B - Boston Red Sox 17/437\*

1983 Gerald Adams, Howard University P - Baltimore Orioles 18/469\*

1983 Chris Chapman, Southern University OF - Los Angeles Dodgers 19/487\*

1983 Norland Claxton, Jackson State 3B - Montreal Expos 21/532\*

1983 Jeffrey Smith, Central State 1B - New York Yankees 24/602\*

1983 Tyrone Barnes, Mississippi Valley State P - Detroit Tigers 31/752\*

1983 Stanley Johnson, Texas Southern SS - New York Yankees 33/779\*

1983 Charles Carr, West Virginia State 1B - Pittsburgh Pirates 34/788\*

1983 Wayne Stephens, Texas Southern P - Atlanta Braves 35/799\*

1984 Marvin Freeman, Jackson State P - Philadelphia Phillies 2/49\*

1984 Julius McDougal, Jackson State SS - Chicago Cubs 3/57\*

1984 Rozier Jordan, Howard University OF - Cleveland Indians 8/188\*

1984 John Lewis, Grambling State University OF - Chicago Cubs 18/447\*

1984 Emmett Robinson, St. Augustine's University SS - Pittsburgh Pirates 18/459\*

1984 Tony Bailey, Grambling State University P - Atlanta Braves 21/540\*

1984 Rufus Ellis, Alabama State P - Detroit Tigers 25/638\*

1984 James Starling, Delaware State P - New York Yankees 26/657\*

1984 Herman Boddy, Mississippi Valley State P - Montreal Expos 28/685\*

1984 James Byrd, Florida Memorial College 2B - Chicago White Sox 31/739\*

1984 Ira Tieul, Grambling State University C - New York Yankees 45/828\*

1985 Leonard Kelly, Tennessee State P - Montreal Expos 5/114\*

1985 Tim Watkins, Mississippi Valley State P - Cincinnati Reds 8/188\*

1985 Gary Eave, Grambling State University P - Atlanta Braves 12/302\*

1985 Ron Narcisse, Norfolk State OF - New York Mets 12/308\*

1985 Juan McWilliams, Grambling State University 3B - Pittsburgh Pirates 18/450\*

1985 Samuel Ruiz, Central State 2B - Chicago White Sox 20/501\*

1985 Leonard Webster, Grambling State University OF - Minnesota Twins 21/535\*

1985 Thelanious Prioleau, Central State SS - Detroit Tigers 23/600\*

1985 Rufus Ellis, Alabama State P - Kansas City Royals 24/617\*

1985 Richard Anderson, Florida Memorial College P - Toronto Blue Jays 28/724\*

1986 Earl Sanders, Jackson State P - Toronto Blue Jays 1/26*
1986 Franklin Harris, Jackson State C - Philadelphia Phillies 10/244*
1986 Larry Carter, West Virginia State P - St. Louis Cardinals 10/260*
1986 Robbie Gilbert, Mississippi Valley State P - Oakland Athletics 12/301*
1986 Trent Hubbard, Southern University 2B - Houston Astros 12/302*
1986 Martin Foley, Grambling State University SS - Philadelphia Phillies 16/400*
1986 Andrew Dixon, Norfolk State OF - San Francisco 17/422*
1986 Ernest Radcliffe, Central State 1B/P - Saint Louis Cardinals 20/520*
1986 Olen Parker, Grambling State University 2B - Philadelphia Phillies 23/580*
1986 Glenn Abraham, Howard University OF - Texas Rangers 27/669*
1987 Wes Chamberlain, Jackson State OF - Pittsburgh Pirates 4/86*
1987 Howard Farmer, Jackson State P - Montreal Expos 7/174*
1987 Gerald Williams, Grambling State University OF - New York Yankees 14/366*
1987 Ray Payton, Southern University OF/1B - Chicago White Sox 19/478*
1987 Franklin Harris, Jackson State C - Chicago White Sox 24/608*
1987 Roy Hill, Alcorn State P - Oakland Athletics 24/614*
1987 Lawrence Smith, Bethune Cookman SS - Chicago White Sox 40/1004*
1987 Glenn Abraham, Howard University OF - San Francisco Giants 45/1100*
1987 Floyd Wade, Jackson State 1B - Toronto Blue Jays 46/1117*
1987 Brent McCoy, Howard University SS - New York Yankees 54/1208*
1988 Marquis Grissom, Florida A&M OF/P - Montreal Expos 3/76*
1988 Dennis Walker, Grambling State University 3B/C - Chicago White Sox 11/275*
1988 Cedric Shaw, Grambling State University P - Texas Rangers 12/297*
1988 Rodney Lofton, Grambling State University SS - Baltimore Orioles 13/321*
1988 Mitchell Burke, Florida A&M OF - Pittsburgh Pirates 15/382*
1988 Adell Davenport, Southern University 3B - San Francisco Giants 18/464*
1988 LeWayne Busby, Mississippi Valley State SS - Chicago White Sox 19/483*
1988 Donovan Campbell, Texas Southern OF - Atlanta Braves 22/554*
1988 Lawrence Smith, Bethune Cookman 2B - Cleveland Indians 27/683*
1988 Michael Mungin, Norfolk State P - Oakland Athletics 27/697*
1988 James Garrett, Southern University P - Chicago White Sox 31/795*
1988 Tim Stargell, Southern University 2B - Seattle Mariners 33/851*
1988 Cecil Pettiford, Jackson State P - Cleveland Indians 36/917*
1988 David Booth, West Virginia State OF - San Francisco Giants 37/958*
1988 Edward Fletcher, West Virginia State P - Philadelphia Phillies 40/1029*
1988 Ricardo Cartwright, Florida A&M OF - Montreal Expos 40/1036*
1988 Brian Cornelius, Southern University OF - Baltimore Orioles 41/1047*
1988 Brent McCoy, Howard University SS - Atlanta Braves 51/1255*
1988 Marco Paddy, Southern University OF - Atlanta Braves 56/1322*
1989 Todd Watson, Howard University 3B - Cincinnati Reds 14/368*
1989 Avery Johnson, Texas Southern SS - Cleveland Indians 21/539*
1989 Tyrone Washington, Southern University P - Texas Rangers 23/585*
1989 Mel Wearing, Norfolk State 1B - Baltimore Orioles 25/633*
1989 Henderson Mosley, Central State OF - Baltimore Orioles 27/685*
1989 Rico Coleman, Grambling State University OF - San Diego Padres 36/934*
1989 Horace Gaither, Southern University 2B/SS - Chicago White Sox 39/1003*
1989 Brian Cornelius, Southern University OF - Detroit Tigers 43/1119*
1989 Alvin Rittman, Bethune Cookman SS - Seattle Mariners 48/1217*
1989 Landon Williams, Grambling State University SS - Seattle Mariners 49/1238*
1989 Sidney Gilliam, Florida A&M OF - New York Yankees 61/1426*
1990 Ron Lockett, Jackson State 1B - Phlladelphia Phillies 8/206*
1990 Terry Bradshaw, Norfolk State OF - St. Louis Cardinals 9/242*
1990 Jimmy Davenport, Jackson State OF - St. Louis Cardinals 12/320*
1990 Jerome Edwards, Jackson State OF - Phlladelphia Phillies 13/336*
1990 Jonathan Story, Southern University SS/2B - Chicago White Sox 25/649*

1990 Dan Magee, Jackson State P - Chicago White Sox 29/753*
1990 Roosevelt Smith, Southern University P - Chicago White Sox 30/779*
1990 Ira Smith, University of Maryland Eastern Shore OF/2B - Los Angeles Dodgers 37/965*
1990 Jeffrey Gunn, Grambling State University OF - Philladelphia Phillies 45/1144*
1990 Clemente Gordon, Grambling State University C - Chicago White Sox 51/1258*
1991 Andre Johnson, Norfolk State OF - Atlanta Braves 12/310*
1991 Keiver Campbell, Alcorn State OF - Toronto Blue Jays 12/329*
1991 Kenny Winzer, Southern University P - Seattle Mariners 17/449*
1991 Dan McGee, Jackson State P - Texas Ranger 18/483*
1991 Grady Davidson, Southern University P - Cleveland Indians 22/581*
1991 Pedro Swann, Delaware State OF - Atlanta Braves 26/674*
1991 Wayne Wilkerson, Norfolk State OF - Cincinnatti Reds 26/692*
1991 Howard House, Howard University OF - Milwaukee Brewers 32/833*
1991 Antonio Boone, Norfolk State P - St. Louis Cardinals 33/858*
1991 Carlton Hardy, Grambling State University 3B/P - Philladelphia Phillies 37/968*
1992 Willie Brown, Florida A&M OF - Florida Marlins 4/124*
1992 Morisse Daniels, Florida A&M OF - California Angels 12/328*
1992 Curtis George, Florida A&M SS - Cleveland Indians 18/490*
1992 Derrick Calvin, Southern University P - Atlanta Braves 31/873*
1992 Bobby Gorham, Howard University P - San Francisco Giants 33/915*
1992 Ted Hassan, Jackson State P - Atlanta Braves 48/1349*
1992 Kevin Nails, Grambling State University 3B - Atlanta Braves 49/1377*
1993 Derrick Calvin, Southern University P - Colorado Rockies 21/604*
1993 Ronald Smith, Southern University 1B - Chicago Cubs 27/754*
1993 Bennie Tillman, Jackson State OF - Atlanta Braves 31/880*
1993 Roderick Jackson, Jackson State P - Detroit Tigers 32/893*
1993 Leroy McKinnis, Jackson State C - San Diego Padres 32/898*
1993 Chad Akers, West Virginia State SS - Cincinnatti Reds 34/960*
1993 William Baldwin, Florida Memorial College P - Chicago White Sox 37/1041*
1993 Michael Gibson, Bowie State 2B/OF - Chicago Cubs 57/1515*
1993 Artis Johnson, Florida A&M OF - Chicago Cubs 58/1532*
1993 Pedro Marte, Florida Memorial College 2B/OF - Cleveland Indians 71/1651*
1993 Jamil Cunningham, Bethune Cookman SS - Chicago Cubs 77/1676*
1994 Arthur Jenkins, Texas Southern P - San Diego Padres 31/850*
1994 Courtney Mitchell, Grambling State University P - Philadelphia Phillies 36/1010*
1994 Wilton Person, Florida A&M OF - Atlanta Braves 53/1420*
1994 Clarence Johns, Southern University P - St. Louis Cardinals 55/1450*
1995 Antone Brooks, Norfolk State P - Atlanta Braves 11/309*
1995 Bryan Graves, Southern University OF - California Angels 20/536*
1995 Barry Shelton, West Virginia State 3B - Chicago White Sox 21/588*
1995 Harold Boggs, West Virginia State P - Minnesota Twins 36/996*
1995 John Davis, Bethune Cookman P - Los Angeles Dodgers 41/1143*
1995 Jamel McAdory, Jackson State 1B - Atlanta Braves 53/1429*
1996 Craig Quintal, Southern University P - Detroit Tigers 8/221*
1996 Theo Fefee, Bethune Cookman OF - California Angels 15/445*
1996 Courtney Duncan, Grambling State University P - Chicao Cubs 20/592*
1996 Jason Moore, West Virginia State C/1B - Arizona Diamondbacks 37/1115*
1997 Deon Eaddy, Norfolk State SS - Chicago Cubs 17/514*
1997 Derrick Lewis, Florida A&M P - Atlanta Braves 20/622*
1997 Keith Maxwell, Florida A&M OF/C - Pittsburgh Pirates 21/632*
1997 Robert Averett, Florida A&M P - Cincinnatti Reds 21/638*
1997 Michael Rawls, Bethune Cookman P - Los Angeles Dodgers 24/738*
1997 Cory Lima, North Carolina A&T P - Florida Marlins 25/756*
1997 Wayne Slater, Bethune Cookman OF - Los Angeles Dodgers 31/948*
1997 Paul Shanklin, West Virginia State P - Atlanta Braves 42/1274*

1998 Schuyler Doakes, Jackson State SS - Seattle Mariners 14/425*
1998 Terrance Hill, Southern University P - Boston Red Sox 18/535*
1998 Auntwan Riggins, Texas Southern OF - Toronto Blue Jays 20/591*
1998 Fontella Jones, Mississippi Valley State P - Milwaukee Brewers 24/716*
1998 Jesse Gutierrez, Texas Southern 1B - San Diego Padres 44/1306*
1998 Sonny Garcia, Texas Southern P - Baltimore Orioles 47/1389*
1999 Harold Featherstone, North Carolina A&T P - San Francisco Giants 15/468*
1999 Brandon Jackson, Savannah State OF - Anaheim Angels 16/491*
1999 Justin Graham, West Virginia State CF - Arizona Diamondbacks 20/598*
1999 Chris Warren, Howard University SS - Colorado Rockies 20/610*
1999 Alva Thompson, Southern University C - Atlanta Braves 24/744*
1999 Sherwin Lockridge, Florida A&M SS - Minnesota Twins 29/869*
1999 Christopher Hills, Jackson State CF - Anaheim Angels 32/971*
1999 Trevor Sansom, West Virginia State P - Saint Louis Cardinals 32/972*
1999 Enrique Mendieta, Norfolk State OF - Florida Marlins 35/1046*
1999 Byron Ewing, Howard University 1B - Cleveland Indians 39/1187*
1999 Douglas Sowers, West Virginia State 3B - Baltimore Orioles 44/1319*
1999 Garry Templeton, North Carolina A&T SS - Anaheim Angels 49/1443*
2000 Mark Woodyard, Bethune Cookman P - Detroit Tigers 4/108*
2000 Scott Schneider, Norfolk State P - Anaheim Angels 12/350*
2000 Reginald Grigg, Florida A&M 1B - Philadelphia Phillies 18/535*
2000 Shannon Cabel, West Virginia State P - Pittsburgh Pirates 22/650*
2000 Melvin Anderson, Southern University SS - Philadelphia Phillies 24/715*
2000 Ralph Coleman, Texas Southern LF - Atlanta Braves 26/790*
2000 Quentin Jones, Norfolk State P - Atlanta Braves 30/910*
2000 Elgin Graham, Bethune Cookman P - San Francisco 38/1141*
2000 Eric Crozier, Norfolk State 1B - Cleveland Indians 41/1234*
2001 Michael Woods, Southern University 2B/OF - Detroit Tigers 1/32*
2001 Marcus Chandler, Southern University CF - Kansas City Royals 17/505*
2001 Dewayne Jones, Jackson State C - Atlanta Braves 22/675*
2001 Franco Blackburn, Southern University OF - Florida Marlins 27/812*
2001 Cesar Montes De Oca, Bethune Cookman P - Atlanta Braves 27/825*
2001 Brian Middleton, West Virginia State P - Houston Astros 31/926*
2001 Torik Harrison, Southern University P - Florida Marlins 33/992*
2002 Fred Lewis, Southern University OF - San Francisco Giants 2/66*
2002 Anthony Pearson, Jackson State P - Montreal Expos 5/137*
2002 Michael Goss, Jackson State LF - Boston Red Sox 11/328*
2002 Wes Timmons, Bethune Cookman SS - Atlanta Braves 12/365*
2002 David Smith, West Virginia State OF - Toronto Blue Jays 15/446*
2002 Sherman Primus, Southern University P - Florida Marlins 23/683*
2002 Rusty Moore, Bethune Cookman LF - San Diego Padres 23/685*
2002 Adrian Urquhart, Alabama State RF - Montreal Expos 25/737*
2002 Dewon Day, Southern University P - Toronto Blue Jays 26/776*
2002 Eric Thomas, Southern University P - Milwaukee Brewers 28/829*
2002 Leon Stephens, Virginia State CF - Kansas City Royals 32/948*
2002 Jason Dooley, Bethune Cookman P - Colorado Rockies 42/1251*
2002 David Nelson, North Carolina A&T P - Kansas City Royals 43/1278*
2003 Rickie Weeks, Southern University 2B - Milwaukee Brewers 1/2*
2003 Damian Ursin, Southern University P - Cincinnati Reds 8/231*
2003 John Gragg, Bethune Cookman P - Kansas City Royals 9/252*
2003 Marcus Townsend, Southern University OF - Cincinnati Reds 14/411*
2003 James Hymon, Rust College SS – Seattle Mariners 18/536*
2003 Kevin Vital, Southern University 1B - Houston Astros 18/539*
2003 Temetric Thomas, Mississippi Valley State 2B - St. Louis Cardinals 24/725*
2003 Antoin Gray, Southern University 3B - Chicago White Sox 25/742*

2003 Jefferey Urgelles, Savannah State C - Cincinnati Reds 26/771*
2003 Fernando Puebla, Southern University SS - Tampa Bay Devil Rays 29/848*
2003 Tim Vaillancourt, Delaware State P - Arizona Diamondbacks 31/936*
2003 Scott Martin, Delaware State OF - Chicago White Sox 34/1012*
2003 Clay Cleveland, Savannah State 1B - Cincinnati Reds 39/1161*
2004 Joshua LeBlanc, Southern University 2B - California Angels 6/173*
2004 Jason Quarles, Southern University P - Pittsburgh Pirates 7/202*
2004 Sebastian Boucher, Bethune Cookman OF - Seattle Mariners 7/213*
2004 Duron LeGrande, North Carolina A&T OF - Montreal Expos 10/294*
2004 Eric Carter, Delaware State P - Seattle Mariners 10/303*
2004 Andrew Toussaint, Southern University 3B - California Angels 13/383*
2004 Jermel Lomack, Prairie View A&M 2B - Pittsburgh Pirates 14/412*
2004 Vincent Davis, Southern University P - Arizona Diamondbacks 18/536*
2004 Matthew Paul, Southern University 2B - Los Angeles Dodgers 18/538*
2004 Shawn Phillips, Delaware State P - Texas Rangers 20/591*
2004 Mumba Rivera, Bethune Cookman P - Seattle Mariners 21/633*
2004 Terrance Sparks, Prairie View A&M P - Cincinnati Reds 29/858*
2004 Alfred Ard, Southern University CF - Cleveland Indians 30/887*
2004 Marcus Townsend, Southern University OF - Arizona Diamondbacks 31/926*
2004 James Cooper, Grambling State University OF - Houston Astros 33/994*
2004 Juan Figueroa, Bethune Cookman 1B - Florida Marlins 37/1118*
2004 Gerald Miller, Prairie View A&M OF - Chicago Cubs 50/1494*
2005 Corey Wimberly, Alcorn State 2B - Colorado Rockies 6/177*
2005 Carl Lipsey, Jackson State 2B - Boston Red Sox 23/708*
2005 Brandon Stricklen, Texas Southern P - Houston Astros 42/1270*
2006 Zach Penprase, Mississippi Valley State SS - Philadelphia Phillies 13/397*
2006 Jeremy Jones, North Carolina A&T OF - Colorado Rockies 25/738*
2006 Zachary Baldwin, West Virginia State P - Washington Nationals 31/931*
2006 Bradley Roper-Hubbert, Alcorn State C - New York Mets 32/964*
2006 Sanduan Dubose, Stillman College 3B - Milwaukee Brewers 35/1052*
2006 Donald Green, Texas Southern OF - New York Mets 39/1174*
2007 Baron Short, Southern University P - Los Angeles Angels 7/238*
2007 Michael Richard, Prairie View A&M SS - Oakland Athletics 11/360*
2007 Charlie Gamble, North Carolina A&T 3B - Houston Astros 23/711*
2007 Angel Mercado, Bethune Cookman OF - San Diego Padres 23/717*
2007 James Sims, Jackson State OF - Colorado Rockies 27/822*
2007 Roydrick Merritt, Southern University P - New York Mets 29/903*
2007 Jeffery McCollum, Southern University P - Washington Nationals 33/998*
2007 Calvin Lester , Prairie View A&M OF - Baltimore Orioles 36/1084*
2007 Ernie Banks, Norfolk State 1B - Florida Marlins 44/1307*
2007 Lindon Bond, Texas Southern OF - Arizona Diamondbacks 50/1438*
2008 Calvin Anderson, Southern University 1B - Pittsburgh Pirates 12/354*
2008 Jose Lozada , Bethune Cookman SS - Washington Nationals 17/511*
2008 Joseph Gautier, Bethune Cookman P - Arizona Diamondbacks 19/588*
2008 Pernell Halliman, Jackson State P - Kansas City Royals 40/1195*
2009 Hiram Burgos, Bethune Cookman P - Milwaukee Brewers 6/196*
2009 Myrio Richard, Prairie View A&M OF - Oakland Athletics 9/273*
2009 Charles Thomas, Edward Waters College 3B - Chicago Cubs 10/320*
2009 Michael Thomas, Southern University C - Boston Red Sox 12/378*
2009 Jeff Squier, Mississippi Valley State SS - Colorado Rockies 14/421*
2009 Eric Thomas, Bethune Cookman P - Seattle Mariners 19/563*
2009 C J Beatty, North Carolina A&T OF - St. Louis Cardinals 26/789*
2009 Brandon Whitby, Prairie View A&M C - Colorado Rockies 34/1021*
2009 Andrew Moss, Lincoln (MO) University P - St. Louis Cardinals 35/1059*
2009 Zac Varnell, University of Arkansas - Pine Bluff C - Arizona Diamondbacks 44/1326*
2009 Anthione Shaw, St. Augustine's University OF - Oakland Athletics 45/1353*

2010 Juan Perez, Bethune Cookman P - Colorado Rockies 18/560*
2010 Cody Hall, Southern University P - Detroit Tigers 35/1063*
2010 Jeremy Shelby, Grambling State University OF - Baltimore Orioles 38/1138*
2010 Derrick Shaw, Florida A&M OF - Milwaukee Brewers 41/1239*
2011 Peter O'Brien, Bethune Cookman C - Colorado Rockies 3/107*
2011 Xavier Macklin, North Carolina A&T OF - Oakland Athletics 12/376*
2011 Frazier Hall, Southern University 1B - Los Angeles Angles 16/495*
2011 Cody Hall, Southern University P - San Francisco Giants 19/597*
2011 Rashaad Ingram, St. Augustine's University 2B - San Diego Padres 28/863*
2011 Eldred Barnett, Grambling State University OF - San Francisco Giants 29/897*
2012 Ryan Gonzalez, Bethune Cookman P - Colorado Rockies 21/648*
2012 Christopher Wolfe, Grambling State University SS - Oakland Athletics 30/919*
2012 Donald Smith, Claflin University C - Boston Red Sox 38/1171*
2013 Kyle McGowin, Savannah State P - Los Angeles Angles 5/157*
2013 Angel Rosa, Alcorn State SS - Los Angeles Angles 13/397*
2013 Kelvin Freeman, North Carolina A&T 1B - Chicago Cubs 17/498*
2013 Jose De Leon, Southern University P - Los Angeles Dodgers 24/724*
2013 Cory Jordan, Grambling State University P - Tampa Bay Rays 35/1058*
2014 Emmanuel Marrero, Alabama State SS - Philadelphia Phillies 7/202*
2014 John Sever, Bethune Cookman P - Pittsburgh Pirates 20/611*
2014 B.J. Robinson, Florida A&M 1B - Arizona Diamondbacks 28/840*
2014 Richard Gonzalez, Alabama State C - Houston Astros 29/856*
2014 Luke Tendler, North Carolina A&T OF - Texas Rangers 29/876*
2014 Montana Durapau, Bethune Cookman P - Pittsburgh Pirates 32/971*
2014 Keith Zuniga, Bethune Cookman P - Miami Marlins 35/1037*
2014 Isias Alcantar, University of Arkansas - Pine Bluff C - Tampa Bay Rays 36/1087*
2015 Andre Davis, University of Arkansas - Pine Bluff P - Kansas City Royals 8/249*
2015 Melvin Rodriguez, Jackson State 2B - Washington Nationals 18/554*
2015 Kevin Walsh, University of Arkansas - Pine Bluff P - Philadelphia Phillies 21/624*
2015 Armando Ruiz, Alabama State P - Oakland Athletics 29/878*
2015 Tyler Payne, West Virginia State C - Chicago Cubs 30/893*
2015 Earl Burl III, Alcorn State OF - Toronto Blue Jays 30/902*
2015 Jorge Pantoja, Alabama State P - Washington Nationals 30/914*
2015 Kalik May, Mississippi Valley State OF - Toronto Blue Jays 33/992*
2015 Lance Jones, Southern University OF - Toronto Blue Jays 36/1082*
2015 Edwin Drexler, Grambling State University OF - Los Angeles Dodgers 38/1152*
2016 Michael Cruz, Bethune Cookman C - Chicago Cubs 7/224*
2016 Angel Alicea, Alabama State P - Toronto Blue Jays 20/612*
2016 Clayton Middleton, Bethune Cookman C - Texas Rangers 22/669*
2016 Andrew Vernon, North Carolina Central P - Milwaukee Brewers 28/831*
2017 Demetrius Sims, Bethune Cookman SS - Miami Marlins 14/419*
2017 Bryce Brown, Jackson State OF - Tampa Bay Rays 15/439*
2017 Noah Cutter Dyals, North Carolina A&T P - Atlanta Braves 17/500*
2017 Aubrey McCarty, Florida A&M P - Colorado Rockies 26/776*
2017 Devin Hemmerich, Norfolk State P - Los Angeles Dodgers 26/790*
2017 Alex Mauricio, Norfolk State P - New York Yankees 27/812*
2017 Tanner Raiburn, Grambling State University P - Boston Red Sox 33/1001*
2017 Austin Bizzle, Alabama State P - Minnesota Twins 40/1186*
2018 Randy Norris, Winston-Salem State OF - San Francisco Giants 19/556*
2018 Darrien Williams, Prairie View A&M P - Anaheim Angels 26/781*
2018 Marshawn Taylor, Grambling State University SS - Arizona Diamondbacks 28/849*
2018 Ray Hernandez, Alabama State 3B - Atlanta Braves 29/863*
2019 Anthony Maldonado, Bethune Cookman P - Miami Marlins 11/321*
2019 Corey Joyce, North Carolina Central INF - Detroit Tigers 12/352*
2019 Garrett Lawson, Delaware State P - Los Angeles Angels 19/571*
2019 Javeyan Williams, Southern University OF - San Francisco Giants 22/656*

2019 E.P. Reese, Winston-Salem State OF - Houston Astros 25/766*
2019 Leon Hunter, North Carolina A&T P - Texas Rangers 35/1045*
2019 Justin Washington, Savannah State OF - Los Angeles Dodgers 35/1061*

     *\* June Regular Phase*
   *\*\* June Secondary Phase*
 *\*\*\* January Regular Phase*
*\*\*\*\* January Secondary Phase*

# HBCU Ballplayers in the Major Leagues
(Historically Black Colleges and Universities only)

*Before the integration of organized baseball, historically black colleges and universities' baseball programs were considered as somewhat of a feeder system for the Negro Leagues. Once blacks were able to sign professional contracts with Major League organizations, scouts were frequent visitors to HBCU campuses, especially in the days before the annual MLB Draft was installed in 1965. The below list includes those student-athletes who played college baseball at an HBCU and eventually made their way to the Major Leagues... though some only for a very brief period. Note: this list does not include those Major Leaguers who attended an HBCU, but did not play baseball for their college team.*

**Tommie Agee** – Grambling State University - Mets/White Sox/Astros/Indians/Cardinals 1962-1973
**Willie Aikens** - South Carolina State University - Royals/Angels/Blue Jays 1977-1985
**Matt Alexander** – Grambling State University - Athletics/Pirates/Cubs 1973-1981
**Tom Alston** - North Carolina A&T University - Cardinals 1954-1957
**George Altman** - Tennessee State University - Cubs/Cardinals/Mets 1959-1967
**Reggie Baldwin** – Grambling State University - Astros 1978-1979
**Billy Baldwin** - Southern University - Tigers/Mets 1975-1976
**Terry Blocker** - Tennessee State University - Braves/Mets 1985-1989
**Sam Bowens** - Tennessee State University - Orioles/Senators 1963-1969
**Dennis Boyd** - Jackson State University - Red Sox/Expos/Rangers 1982-1991
**Larry Bradford** - Clark Atlanta University - Braves 1977-1981
**Terry Bradshaw** - Norfolk State University - Cardinals 1995-1996
**Harvey Branch** - Alabama State University - Cardinals 1962
**Lou Brock** - Southern University - Cardinals/Cubs 1961-1979
**Jophery Brown** – Grambling State University - Cubs 1968
**Jake Brown** - Southern University - Giants 1975
**Al Bumbry** - Virginia State University - Orioles/Padres 1972-1985
**Hiram Burgos** - Bethune-Cookman University - Brewers 2013
**Larry Carter** - West Virginia State University - Giants 1992
**Wes Chamberlain** - Jackson State University - Phillies/RedSox 1990-1995
**Dave Clark** - Jackson State University - Pirates/Indians/Cubs/Astros/Dodgers/Royals 1986-1998
**James "Buzz" Clarkson** - Wilberforce University - Braves 1952
**Donn Clendenon** - Tuskegee University - Pirates/Mets/Cardinals/Expos 1961-1972
**Vince Coleman** - Florida A&M University - Cardinals/Mets/Royals/Mariners/Reds/Tigers 1985-1997
**Eric Crozier** - Norfolk State University - Blue Jays 2004
**Jerry Davis** - Howard University - Padres 1983-1985
**Odie Davis** - Prairie View A&M University - Rangers 1980
**Andre Dawson** - Florida A&M University - Expos/Cubs/Red Sox/Marlins 1976-1996
**Dewon Day** - Jackson State University/Southern University - White Sox 2007
**Jose DeLeon** – Southern University – Dodgers/Rays/ 2016-2019
**Courtney Duncan** – Grambling State University - Cubs 2001-2002
**Montana DuRapau** – Bethune-Cookman University – Pirates 2019
**Gary Eave** – Grambling State University - Mariners/Braves 1988-1990
**Howard Farmer** - Jackson State University - Expos 1990
**Mike Farmer** - Jackson State University - Rockies 1996
**Paul Fletcher** - West Virginia State University - Phillies/Athletics 1993-1996
**Curt Ford** - Jackson State University - Cardinals/Phillies 1985-1990
**Marvin Freeman** - Jackson State University - Braves/Rockies/Phillies/White Sox 1986-1996
**Ralph Garr** – Grambling State University - Braves/WhiteSox/Angels 1968-1980
**Danny Goodwin** - Southern University - Twins/Angels/Athletics 1975-1982
**Marquis Grissom** - Florida A&M University - Expos/Brewers/Giants/Braves/Dodgers/Indians 1989-2005
**Johnny Hairston** - Southern University - Cubs 1969
**Cody Hall** - Southern University – Giants/Marlins 2015-2016

**Steve Henderson** - Prairie View A&M University - Mets/Mariners/Cubs/Athletics/Astros 1977-1988
**Chuck Hinton** - Shaw University - Indians/Senators/Angels 1961-1971
**Al Holland** - North Carolina A&T University - Giants/Phillies/Pirates/Yankees/Angels 1977-1987
**Ken Howell** - Tuskegee University - Dodgers/Phillies 1984-1990
**Trenidad Hubbard** - Southern University - Dodgers/Padres/Rockies/Braves/Orioles/Giants/Cubs/Indians/Royals 1994-2003
**Charles Hudson** - Prairie View A&M University - Phillies/Yankees/Tigers 1983-1989
**Roy Jackson** - Tuskegee University - Blue Jays/Mets/Twins/Padres 1977-1986
**Alvin Jackson** - Wiley College - Mets/Cardinals/Reds/Pirates 1959-1969
**Stan Jefferson** - Bethune-Cookman University - Padres/Indians/Orioles/Mets/Reds/Yankees 1986-1991
**Johnny Jeter** – Grambling State University - Padres/Pirates/White Sox/Indians 1969-1974
**Roy Johnson** - Tennessee State University - Expos 1982-1985
**Anthony Johnson** - LeMoyne-Owen College - Blue Jays/Expos 1981-1982
**Al Jones** - Alcorn State University - White Sox 1983-1985
**Fred Lewis** - Southern University - Giants/Blue Jays/Reds/Mets 2006-2012
**Kyle McGowin** – Savannah State University – Nationals 2019
**Hal McRae** - Florida A&M University - Royals/Reds 1968-1987
**Alan Millls** - Tuskegee University - Orioles/Dodgers/Yankees 1990-2001
**Eddie Milner** - Central State University - Reds/Giants 1980-1988
**Kelvin Moore** - Jackson State University - Athletics 1981-1983
**Bubba Morton** - Howard University - Angels/Tigers/Braves 1961-1969
**Peter O'Brien** - Bethune-Cookman University - Diamondbacks 2015
**Scott Patterson** - West Virginia State University -Padres/Yankees 2008
**Joe Pittman** -Southern University - Astros/Padres/Giants 1981-1984
**Dale Polley** - Kentucky State University - Yankees 1996
**Jim Proctor** – University of Maryland Eastern Shore – Tigers 1959
**Sap Randall** – Grambling State University - White Sox 1988
**Clay Rapada** - Virginia State University - Yankees/Tigers/Orioles/Rangers/Indians/Cubs 2007-2013
**Lee Richard** - Southern University - WhiteSox/Cardinals 1971-1976
**Gene Richards** - South Carolina State University - Padres/Giants 1977-1984
**Razor Shines** – Saint Augustine's University – Royals 1983-1987
**Nate Smith** - Tennessee State University - Orioles 1962
**Nate Snell** - Tennessee State University - Orioles/Tigers 1984-1987
**Everett Stull** - Tennessee State University - Brewers/Expos/Braves 1997-2002
**Pedro Swann** - Delaware State University - Blue Jays/Orioles/Braves 2000-2003
**Milt Thompson** - Howard University - Phillies/Cardinals/Astros/Braves/Dodgers/Rockies 1984-1996
**Fred Valentine** - Tennessee State University - Senators/Orioles 1959-1968
**Lenny Webster** – Grambling State University - Orioles/Expos/Twins/Phillies/RedSox 1989-2000
**Rickie Weeks** - Southern University - Brewers/Mariners 2003-2015
**Greg Wells** - Albany State University - Blue Jays/Twins 1981-1982
**Gerald Williams** – Grambling State University - Yankees/Braves/Devil Rays/Brewers/Mets/Marlins 1992-2005
**Reggie Williams** - Southern University - Dodgers/Indians 1985-1988
**Jake Wood** - Delaware State University - Tigers/Reds 1961-1967
**Mark Woodyard** - Bethune-Cookman University - Tigers 2005

## Top 5 Institutions With the Most Major Leaguers
*(Includes players who were drafted more than once from the same school)*

  1. Southern University (14)
  2. Grambling State University (11)
  3. Jackson State University (9)
  4. Tennessee State University (8)
  5. Bethune-Cookman University (5)

# Early Black Integrators of Historically White College Baseball

*The following have been (unofficially in some cases) identified as the first integrating varsity baseball players at their historically white institutions. If not the first know integrators, then at least they must be considered very early integrators. A number of smaller schools are included here, because in the early years of college baseball, they quite often faced what are now considered much larger schools. (This list is not all-inclusive.)*

1881 Oberlin College - Moses Fleetwood Walker
1882 University of Michigan - Moses Fleetwood Walker
1887 Marietta College - John Langston Harrison
1888 Ohio State University – William H. Clark
1888 University of Kansas - Sherman Harvey
1889 Olivet College - Hiram Archer
1889 Western Reserve University - Edward C. Williams
1890 Denison University - Carter Barnett
1892 Colby College - Edward Osborne
1895 Geneva College - Solomon Ford Kingston
1896 Amherst College - James Francis Gregory
1896 Cornell University (NY) - Ralph Victor Cook
1897 Beloit College - Merrill Strothers
1897 Franklin College - Arthur Wilson
1898 Cornell College (IA) - Frank Armstrong
1898 Emporia State - Gaitha Adolphus Paige
1900 University of Wisconsin - Julian V. Ware
1900 University of Wisconsin - Adelbert R. Matthews
1901 Colgate University - George Lewis Hayes
1901 Syracuse University - Marcellus Raymond Atwell
1901 Knox College – Charles Hopkins
1902 College of Wooster - Charles Follis
1902 Harvard University - William Clarence Matthew
1903 Ohio Wesleyan University - Charles Lee Thomas
1903 Washburn University - John Johnson
1904 Northwestern University - Arthur Butler
1904 University of Vermont - George Walter William
1904 University of Minnesota - Bobby Marshall
1904 Wesleyan University - John Davis Smith
1906 Indiana University - Charles Williamson
1909 Bradley University - John R Lynch Conway
1909 Whitworth College - Ernest C Tanner
1911 Williams College - Henry Alexander Williams
1913 South Dakota State University - Cleveland Abbott
1915 Millikin University - Fred Long
1915 Springfield College - William T Kindle
1916 Duquesne University - Cumberland Posey
1916 Rutgers University - Paul Robeson
1916 Western Michigan University - Samuel J. Dunla
1917 Norwich University - Harold Martin
1919 University of Akron – Emmer Lancaster
1920 Drake University - Charles Howard
1920 University of Pennsylvania - Doug Sheffey

1920 University of Washington - John Prim
1922 Boston University - George Crosson
1923 Indiana State University – William S. Holland
1923 New York University - James Washington
1923 University of Southern California - John Riddle
1924 University of Idaho - Bazz Smaulding
1927 Illinois State University - Richard Tate
1927 Western Illinois University - Ernest Page
1934 Northern Illinois University - Elzie Cooper
1934 University of Connecticut - Harrison Fitch
1936 Arizona State University - Joe Island
1937 Butler University - Tom Harding
1937 UCLA - Kenny Washington
1937 University of Toledo - Richard Craig
1938 University of Redlands – Nate Moreland
1939 Boston College - Louis M Montgomery
1939 San Jose State University - John Allen
1939 University of Indianapolis - Ray Crowe
1941 Chapman University – Emmett Ashford
1942 Fresno State University - Jack Kelley
1942 San Diego State University - John Ritchey
1947 Youngstown State - John Lawhorn
1948 Miami University - Brooks Lawrence
1949 Siena College - Billy Harrell
1950 Seton Hall University - Benjamin Veal
1950 University of San Francisco - Gene Jacobs
1951 University of Massachuttes - Wray Gunn
1952 Iowa State University - Grandland Shipp
1952 Kansas State University - Earl Woods
1953 Central Michigan Univesity - Charles Pruitt
1954 Cal Poly - Perry Jeter
1954 University of California - Thelton Henderson
1954 Ithaca College – Grover "Deacon" Jones
1954 University of Chicago - Walter L Walker
1955 College of Idaho - Gary Mays
1955 Creighton University - Bob Gibson
1955 University of Colorado - Jim Liggins
1956 University of Arizona - Hadie Reed
1957 Bowling Green State University - Joseph Bates
1957 Kent State University - Eddie Warner
1957 Marshall University - Hal Greer
1957 Penn State University - Bob Hoover
1958 University of Iowa - Robert Pearl
1959 Pepperdine University - Ray Wrenn
1959 University of Louisville - Ernie Green
1960 Purdue University - Clyde Washington
1961 Oregon State University - Gene Hilliard
1961 Wichita State University - A J Jones
1963 University of Oregon - H D Murphy
1963 University of Texas at El Paso - Nolan Richardson
1963 University of Texas at El Paso - Cletus James
1963 University of Texas at El Paso - John Jimerson
1964 University of Wyoming - Gerry Marion
1965 Ohio University - Mac Wagner
1965 Oklahoma State University - Don Kuykendall
1965 Oklahoma State University - Fred Moulder

1965 Stetson University - Jimmie Johnson
1965 University of Illinois - Trenton Jackson
1965 University of Missouri - Ray Thorpe
1966 University of Cincinnati - Darryl Allen
1966 Santa Clara University - Haywood Coleman
1966 St. John's University - Shane Moore
1966 Tulane University - Steve Martin
1967 East Carolina University - Vincent Colbert
1967 Florida State University - Ed Harris
1967 Long Beach State University - Phil Johnson
1967 Old Dominion University - Arthur Speakes
1967 Rollins University - Eddie Campbell
1967 Yale - Carl Crew Jr
1968 Southern Illinois University - Jerry Bond
1968 Western Kentucky University - Harry Jones
1969 Oral Roberts University - Greg Davis
1969 Washington State University - Fred Moore
1969 University of Texas-Pan American - Andre Rabouin
1970 Florida Southern - Reggie Ardis
1970 Florida Southern - Atlas Jones
1970 Louisiana State University - Henry LeBoyd*
1970 Middle Tennessee State University - Chester Brown
1970 Missouri State University - David Shipps
1970 Southern Methodist University - James Lee Robinson
1970 University of South Carolina - Ansel (Jackie) Brown
1971 The Citadel - W. D. Jennings
1971 University of Kentucky - Derek Bryant
1971 University of North Carolina - Mickey Hickerson
1972 Air Force Academy - Clarence D Smith
1972 David Lipscomb University - Jacob Robinson
1972 David Lipscomb University - Ted Jamison
1972 Jacksonville State - Ralph Clayton
1972 Jacksonville State - Ralph Scott
1972 James Madison University - Vinnie Jefferson
1972 Texas A&M University - Michael Frazier
1972 University of Tennessee - Condredge Holloway
1973 Georgia Southern - Carl Person
1973 High Point - Otis Foster
1973 University of Miami - Clarence Poitier
1974 Liberty University - Willard DeShavor
1974 Notre Dame University - Ronald Goodman
1974 Stanford University - Ray Anderson
1974 Texas Tech University - Michael Pace**
1974 University of Alabama - Edwin Smith
1974 University of South Alabama - Michael Walker
1974 Vanderbilt University - Steve Chandler
1974 Virginia Tech University - Paul Adams
1975 Baylor University - Leonard Woods
1975 Clemson University - Ellis Meredith
1975 Western Carolina University - Jerry Gaines
1976 Auburn University - J. B. Brown
1976 Duke University - Larry Doby Jr.
1976 University of Arkansas - Arvis Harper
1976 University of Arkansas - Hank Thompson
1976 University of Maryland - Billy Gardner
1976 University of Memphis - Earl (E.C.) Cody

1976 University of Mississippi - Roy Coleman
1976 University of Virginia - Columbus Duncan
1976 Wake Forest University - Vic Elliott
1976 West Virginia University - Bruce Clinton
1976 University of Texas – Gralyn Wyatt***
1977 University of Oklahoma - Michael Pace
1977 University of Oklahoma - Joe Oliver
1977 US Military Academy - Patrick Landry
1977 US Naval Academy - Warren Lewis
1978 Brigham Young University - Stan Younger
1978 University of Florida - Jim Watkins
1978 University of Houston - Alvin Ruben
1979 North Carolina State University - Chuckie Canady
1979 University of Alabama, Birmingham - Earl Robinson
1979 University of Central Florida - Wayne Gardner
1980 University of Southern Mississippi - Curt Washington
1980 Mississippi State University - Harold Myles
1980 Mississippi State University - Glen Young
1980 University of Georgia - Guy Stargell
1982 University of North Carolina at Charlotte - Tony Koger
1982 University of North Carolina at Charlotte - James Dickerson
1984 Florida Atlantic University - Jeff Forney
1985 Georgia Tech University - Derrick (K.G.) White
1985 Georgia Tech University – Riccardo Ingram
1988 Rice University - Merritt Robinson
1991 University of North Carolina at Greensboro - John Garris

*Henry LeBoyd pitched one inning with the varsity in 1970. Don Newman was next, playing an entire varsity season for Louisiana State University in 1976.*

** *Michael Pace appeared in one game with the varsity in 1974. Mitchell Jones was next, playing an entire varsity season for Texas Tech in 1983.*

*** *Gralyn Wyatt pitched one inning with the varsity in 1976. Andre Robertson was next, playing an entire varsity season for the University of Texas in 1977.*

## Central Intercollegiate Athletic Association (CIAA)

*The Central Intercollegiate Athletic Association (originally called the Colored Intercollegiate Athletic Association) was founded in 1912.*

| | |
|---|---|
| 1921 Virginia State | 1977 Norfolk State |
| 1922 Virginia Union | 1978 Norfolk State |
| 1923 Virginia State | 1979 St Augustine's U |
| 1924 Virginia State | 1980 Norfolk State |
| 1925 Virginia Union | 1981 Norfolk State |
| 1926 Virginia State | 1982 Norfolk State |
| 1927 Virginia State | 1983 Shaw University |
| 1928 Virginia State | 1984 Norfolk State |
| 1929 Virginia State | 1985 Norfolk State |
| 1930 Lincoln University | 1986 St Augustine's U |
| 1931 Virginia State | 1987 Norfolk State |
| 1932 Virginia State | 1988 Norfolk State |
| 1933 Virginia State | 1989 Norfolk State |
| 1934-1947 * | 1990 Norfolk State |
| 1947 North Carolina A&T | 1991 Norfolk State |
| 1948 Shaw University | 1992 Norfolk State |
| 1949 Howard University | 1993 Norfolk State |
| 1950 North Carolina A&T | 1994 Shaw University |
| 1951 North Carolina A&T | 1995 Norfolk State |
| 1952 North Carolina A&T | 1996 Bowie State |
| 1953 North Carolina A&T | 1997 Bowie State |
| 1954 Maryland State | 1998 Virginia State |
| 1955 North Carolina A&T | 1999 St Augustine's U |
| 1956 Maryland State | 2000 Virginia State |
| 1957 Maryland State | 2001 Virginia State |
| 1958 Maryland State | 2002 Shaw University |
| 1959 North Carolina A&T | 2003 Virginia State |
| 1960 North Carolina A&T | 2004 Virginia State |
| 1961 North Carolina A&T | 2005 Elizabeth City St |
| 1962 Delaware State | 2006 Shaw University |
| 1963 Maryland St/Delaware St | 2007 Virginia State |
| 1964 Shaw University | 2008 Virginia State |
| 1965 Shaw University | 2009 Virginia State |
| 1966 Maryland State | 2010 St Augustine's U |
| 1967 Maryland State | 2011 Winston-Salem St |
| 1968 North Carolina A&T | 2012 Winston-Salem St |
| 1969 North Carolina A&T | 2013 Winston-Salem St |
| 1970 NC A&T/Shaw Univ+ | 2014 Winston-Salem St |
| 1971 Del St/NCA&T/VSU++ | 2015 Winston-Salem St |
| 1972 Hampton University | 2016 Chowan Univ^ |
| 1973 Virginia State | 2017 Winston-Salem St |
| 1974 Norfolk State | 2018 * |
| 1975 Norfolk State | 2019 * |
| 1976 Virginia State+++ | |

\*     *conference baseball not supported*

+     *tie-no playoff due to lateness of season*

++    *tie-no playoff due to weather*

+++   *unofficial- conference participation below required number of schools*

^     *not an HBCU institution*

## Southern Intercollegiate Athletic Conference (SIAC)

*The Southern Intercollegiate Athletic Conference (originally called the Southeastern Intercollegiate Athletic Conference) was founded in 1913.*

| | |
|---|---|
| 1915 Morris Brown College | 1974 Bethune-Cookman |
| 1916 Morris Brown College | 1975 Fisk University |
| 1917 Morehouse College | 1976 Bethune-Cookman |
| 1918 Morehouse College | 1977 Bethune-Cookman |
| 1919 Talladega College | 1978 Florida A&M |
| 1920 Morehouse College | 1979 Tuskegee Institute |
| 1921 Atlanta University | 1980 Tuskegee Institute |
| 1922 Atlanta University | 1981 Tuskegee Institute |
| 1923 Morehouse College | 1982 Tuskegee Institute |
| 1924 Morehouse College | 1983 Tuskegee Institute |
| 1925 Morehouse College | 1984 Tuskegee Institute |
| 1926 Morehouse College | 1985 Tuskegee Institute |
| 1927 Alabama State | 1986 Tuskegee Institute |
| 1928 Alabama State | 1987 Tuskegee Institute |
| 1929 Clark University | 1988 Benedict College |
| 1930 Morris Brown College | 1989 Tuskegee Institute |
| 1931 Morris Brown College | 1990 Paine College |
| 1932 Morris Brown College | 1991 Albany State |
| 1933 Morris Brown College | 1992 Savannah State |
| 1934-1946 * | 1993 Alabama A&M |
| 1947 Alabama State | 1994 Albany State |
| 1948 Tuskegee Institute | 1995 Savannah State |
| 1949 Morris Brown College | 1996 Savannah State |
| 1950 Morris Brown College | 1997 Savannah State |
| 1951 Florida A&M | 1998 Savannah State |
| 1952 Alabama State | 1999 Savannah State |
| 1953 Florida A&M | 2000 Paine College |
| 1954 Florida A&M | 2001 Albany State |
| 1955 Florida A&M | 2002 Albany State |
| 1956 Florida A&M | 2003 Albany State |
| 1957 Alabama State | 2004 Albany State |
| 1958 Alabama State | 2005 Paine College |
| 1959 Florida A&M | 2006 Albany State |
| 1960 Allen University | 2007 Stillman College |
| 1961 Florida A&M | 2008 Stillman College |
| 1962 Florida A&M | 2009 Stillman College |
| 1963 Florida A&M | 2010 Albany State |
| 1964 Florida A&M | 2011 Stillman College |
| 1965 Florida A&M | 2012 Stillman College |
| 1966 Florida A&M | 2013 Stillman College |
| 1967 Fisk University | 2014 Stillman College |
| 1968 South Carolina State | 2015 Albany State |
| 1969 Tuskegee Institute | 2016 Claflin University |
| 1970 Alabama A&M | 2017 Miles College |
| 1971 South Carolina State | 2018 Albany State |
| 1972 Alabama State | 2019 Spring Hill College^ |
| 1973 Tuskegee Institute | |

\*     *conference baseball not supported*

^     *not an HBCU institution*

## Southwestern Athletic Conference (SWAC)

*The Southwestern Athletic Conference (originally called the Southern Athletic Conference) was founded in 1920.*

| | |
|---|---|
| 1923 Wiley College | 1979 Southern University |
| 1924 Unknown | 1980 Jackson State |
| 1925 Prairie View | 1981 Southern University |
| 1926 Prairie View | 1982 Jackson State |
| 1927 Texas College | 1983 Grambling University |
| 1928 Texas College | 1984 Grambling University |
| 1929 Texas College | 1985 Grambling University |
| 1930 Wiley College | 1986 Jackson State |
| 1931 Wiley College | 1987 Southern University |
| 1932 Texas College | 1988 Southern University |
| 1933-1948* | 1989 Jackson State |
| 1949 Bishop College | 1990 Jackson State |
| 1950 Southern University | 1991 Southern University |
| 1951 Texas College | 1992 Southern University |
| 1952 Southern University | 1993 Jackson St/Southern+ |
| 1953 Southern University | 1994 Jackson State |
| 1954 Wiley/Southern U | 1995 Jackson State |
| 1955 Southern University | 1996 Southern University |
| 1956 Wiley College | 1997 Southern University |
| 1957 Southern University | 1998 Southern University |
| 1958 Wiley College | 1999 Southern University |
| —*The above are unofficial*— | 2000 Jackson State |
| 1959 Southern University | 2001 Southern University |
| 1960 Southern University | 2002 Southern University |
| 1961 Grambling University | 2003 Southern University |
| 1962 Grambling University | 2004 Texas Southern Univ |
| 1963 Grambling University | 2005 Southern University |
| 1964 Grambling University | 2006 Prairie View A&M |
| 1965 Southern University | 2007 Prairie View A&M |
| 1966 Southern University | 2008 Texas Southern Univ |
| 1967 Grambling University | 2009 Southern University |
| 1968 Jackson State | 2010 Grambling University |
| 1969 Southern University | 2011 Alcorn State |
| 1970 Southern University | 2012 Prairie View A&M |
| 1971 Jackson State | 2013 Jackson State |
| 1972 Southern University | 2014 Jackson State |
| 1973 Jackson State | 2015 Texas Southern Univ |
| 1974 Southern University | 2016 Alabama State |
| 1975 Southern University | 2017 Texas Southern Univ |
| 1976 Southern University | 2018 Texas Southern Univ |
| 1977 Jackson State | 2019 Southern University |
| 1978 Jackson State | |

\* *conference baseball not supported*
\+ *tie-no tournament final due to weather*

## Mid-Eastern Athletic Conference (MEAC)

*The Mid-Eastern Athletic Conference was founded in 1970.*

| | |
|---|---|
| 1972 Howard University | 1999 Bethune-Cookman |
| 1973 South Carolina State | 2000 Bethune-Cookman |
| 1974 North Carolina A&T | 2001 Bethune-Cookman |
| 1975 Howard University | 2002 Bethune-Cookman |
| 1976 Howard University | 2003 Bethune-Cookman |
| 1977 Howard University | 2004 Bethune-Cookman |
| 1978-1983* | 2005 North Carolina A&T |
| 1984 Howard University | 2006 Bethune-Cookman |
| 1985 Bethune-Cookman | 2007 Bethune-Cookman |
| 1986 Howard University | 2008 Bethune-Cookman |
| 1987 Florida A&M | 2009 Bethune-Cookman |
| 1988 Florida A&M | 2010 Bethune-Cookman |
| 1989 Delaware State | 2011 Bethune-Cookman |
| 1990 Florida A&M | 2012 Bethune-Cookman |
| 1991 Florida A&M | 2013 Savannah State |
| 1992 Florida A&M | 2014 Bethune-Cookman |
| 1993 North Carolina A&T | 2015 Florida A&M |
| 1994 Florida A&M | 2016 Bethune-Cookman |
| 1995 Coppin State | 2017 Bethune-Cookman |
| 1996 Bethune-Cookman | 2018 North Carolina A&T |
| 1997 Bethune-Cookman | 2019 Florida A&M |
| 1998 Howard University | |

\* *conference baseball not supported*

## Defunct HBCU Baseball Playing Conferences

Eastern Intercollegiate Conference 1939-1966
Eastern Intercollegiate Athletic Conference (EIAC) 1983-2005
Middle Atlantic Athletic Association (MAAA) 1931-?
Midwestern Athletic Association (MWAA) 1926-1966
South Atlantic Athletic Conference (SAAC) 1925-1968
South Central Athletic Conference (SCAC) 1923-1962
Southeastern Athletic Conference (SEAC) 1929-1961

# Postseason National Tournament Participation

(Historically Black Colleges and Universities only)

*The NCAA Division I tournament was first played in 1947. In 1999, the NCAA began awarding automatic postseason bids to the Mid-Eastern Athletic Conference (MEAC) and Southwestern Athletic Conference (SWAC). The NCAA added a Division II tournament in 1968 and in 1976 added a postseason tournament for Division III. The National Association Intercollegiate Athletics (NAIA) began playing its first tournament in 1957.*

## NCAA Division I Tournament Participants

Alcorn State (2011)
Alabama State (2016)
Bethune-Cookman (1999-2000-01-02-03-04-06-07-08-09-10-11-12-14-16-17)
Florida A&M (2015-19)
Grambling University (1983-84-85-2010)
Jackson State (1982-86-89-2000-13-14)
North Carolina A&T (2005-18)
Prairie View A&M (2006-07-12)
Savannah State University (2013)
Southern University (1987-88-99-2001-02-03-05-09-19)
Texas Southern (2004-08-15-17-18)

## NCAA Division II Tournament Participants

Alabama State (1974)
Albany State (1978-2006-10-15-18)
Claflin University (2016)
Miles College (2017)
Norfolk State (1988-89-90)
Savannah State (1999)
Southern University (1975)
Stillman College (2007-08-09-11-12-13-14)
Tuskegee University (1969-72-73)
Virginia State (2007)
West Virginia State (1998-99-2000-01-02-04-05-06-07-08-09-10-15)
Winston-Salem (2011-12-13-14-15-17)

## NCAA Division III Tournament Participants

Stillman College (1978-79)

## NAIA Tournament Participants

Edward Waters College (2011)
Florida A&M University (1962)
Grambling University (1961-63-64-67)
Jarvis Christian College (2019)
Kentucky State University (1976)
Southern University (1959-60-65-66)
Talladega College (2014-17-18-19)

## USCAA Tournament Participants

Bluefield State (2017-18-19)
Concordia College of Alabama (2001-2004)
Selma University (2011-2012-2013-2014-2018-2019)

*The only HBCU school to win a national collegiate baseball title occurred in 1959 when Southern University of Baton Rouge, Louisiana won the NAIA national crown. The team featured future Major League Hall of Famer, Lou Brock who led the Jaguars with a .524 batting average*

*Two other teams reached the championship game of the NAIA national tournament only to finish as runners-up each time. The Grambling University Tigers of 1963 and 1964 each came up one run short of garnering titles.*

*No HBCU team has ever played for a national title in any of the NCAA's three divisions.*

*Southern University – 1959 NAIA National Champions*

# Photo Credits

*Unless noted, all photos used are within the public domain, with permission of the institutions' athletic department, from the subject's personal collection or from the author's personal collection.*

*National Baseball Hall of Fame and Museum* (page 3)

*Illustration created by author* (page 4)

*Amherst College Archives and Special Collections* (pages 7,49)

*Beinecke Rare Book & Manuscript Library at Yale University* (page 12)

*Montages and other images created by author* (pages 14,32,34,39,77,78,83)

*Collection of Dourest Robinson* (page 18)

*Collection of the family of William Wallace* (page 19)

*Fisk University Franklin Library Special Collections* (page 20)

*Virginia State University Special Collections and Archives* (pages 21,31)

*Anacostia Community Library, Smithsonian Institution* (page 22)

*Alcorn State University Athletic Department* (pages 35,162))

*Inez Moore Parker Archives and Research Center at Johnson C. Smith University* (page 38)

*Oberlin College Library Special Collections* (pages 44,45)

*Berea College Hutchins Library Special Collections and Archives* (page 48)

*Special Collections, College of Wooster Libraries* (page 53)

*South Dakota State University Archives* (page 57)

*Special Collections and University Archives, Rutgers University Libraries* (page 58)

*Millikin University Archives* (page 60)

*UCLA Student Media, a division of Associated Students UCLA* (page 63)

*Special Collections and Archives, Leatherby Libraries at Chapman University* (page 64)

*Special Collections and Archives, San Diego State University* (page 64)

*Collection of William Rutledge* (page 70)

*Collection of Paul S. Dixon* (page 71,111)

*F.D. Bluford Library Archives, North Carolina A&T University* (74,113,116)

*Florida A&M Athletic Department* (pages 75,76,105,131,132,144,145,146)

*University of Maryland Eastern Shore Frederick Douglas Library* (pages 80,81,107)

*National Association of Intercollegiate Athletics* (pages 82,227)

*Archives, Manuscripts and Rare Books Department, John B. Cade Library, Southern University and A&M College, Baton Rouge, Louisiana* (pages 83 on far left and far right,101)

*Siena College Archives* (page 87)

*Morse Department of Special Collections, Kansas State University Libraries* (page 88)

*U-M Library Digital Collections Bentley Image Bank, Bentley Historical Library* (page 89)

*Creighton University Athletic Department* (pages 90,118)

*Marshall University Libraries Archives and Special Collections* (page 92)

*Tulane University Athletic Department* (page 94)

*Grambling State University Athletic Department* (pages 98,99,103,141,142)

Tuskegee University Archives, Tuskegee University (pages 114, 115, 126)

*University of Washington Athletic Department* (page 108)

*College World Series of Omaha, Inc.* (page 120)

*Lou Pavlovich, Collegiate Baseball* (page 123)

*Collection of Dr. John Winters* (page 123)

*Jarvis Christian College Athletic Department* (pages 126,183)

*Jackson State University Athletic Department* (pages 129,137,138)

*Kentucky State University* (page 134)

*Tennessee State University* (page 135)

*Southern University Athletic Department* (pages 139,163,166)

*Delaware State University Athletic Department* (pages 147,168)

*Collection of Solomon Knight* (page 148)

*Norfolk State University Athletic Department* (page 151)

*Central State University Athletic Department* (page 152)

*Coppin State University Athletic Department* (page 156)

*Bethune Cookman University Athletic Department* (page 157)

*West Virginia State University Athletic Department* (pages 160, 171)

*The Baton Rouge Advocate* (page 165)

*Rust College Athletic Department* (page 169)

*Collection of Juan Perez* (page 176)

*Benedict College Athletic Department* (page 178)

*Saint Augustine's College Athletic Department* (page 179)

*Selma Times-Journal* (page 182)

# Selected Bibliography

### Books

Ashe, Arthur R. Jr. *A Hard Road to Glory: A History of the African-American Athlete 1619-1918*, New York, NY: Amistad Press, Inc., 1988.

Bacote, Clarence A. *The story of Atlanta University: a century of service, 1865-1965*, Princeton, NJ: Princeton University Press, 1969.

Bond, Gregory. "Jim Crow at Play: Race, Manliness, and the Color Line in American Sports, 1876-1916." PhD diss., University of Wisconsin-Madison, 2008.

Brawley, Benjamin. *History of Morehouse College*, Atlanta: Morehouse College, 1917.

Brawley, James P. *The Clark College Legacy: An Interpretive History of Relevant Education 1869-1975*, Princeton, NJ: Princeton University Press, 1977.

Brunson, James E. *Black Baseball, 1858-1900: A Comprehensive Record of the Teams, Players, Managers, Owners and Umpires*, Jefferson, NC: McFarland & Company, 2019.

Cador, Roger. *Against All Odds*, Baton Rouge, LA: Cador & Cador Publishing, 2014.

Chalk, Ocania. *Black College Sport*, New York, NY: Dodd Mead, 1976.

Chambers, Ted. *The History of Athletics and Physical Education at Howard University*. New York, NY: Vantage Press, 1986.

Dixon, Phil, and Patrick J. Hannigan. *The Negro Baseball Leagues, 1867-1955: A Photographic History*, Mattituck, NY: Amereon House, 1992.

Douglass, Frederick. *Narrative of the Life of Frederick Douglass, an American Slave*, Boston, MA: The Anti-Slavery Office, 1849.

Egan, James M. Jr. *Base Ball on the Western Reserve: The Early Game in Cleveland and Northeast Ohio, Year by Year and Town by Town, 1865-1900*, Jefferson, NC: McFarland & Co., 2008.

Fisher, Miles Mark. *Virginia Union University and Some of Her Achievements*, Richmond, VA: Brown Print Shop, 1924.

Forbes, Frank L. *The History of Athletics at Morehouse College, 1896-1966*, Atlanta, Georgia: Morehouse College, 1966.

Gallot, Mildred B. G. *A History of Grambling State University*, Lanham, MD: University Press of America, 1985.

Gibson, Everett D. *A Portrait of Southern University: History, Achievements and Great Football Traditions*, Indianapolis, IN: Dog Ear Publishing, 2013.

Grigsby, Daryl Russell. *Celebrating Ourselves: African-Americans and the Promise of Baseball*, Indianapolis, IN: Dog Ear Publishing, 2010.

Harvey, B. T. *Golden Jubilee 1913-1963*, Atlanta, GA: Southern Intercollegiate Athletic Conference, 1963.

Harvey, Harold M. *Freaknik Lawyer: A Memoir on the Craft of Resistance*,.Atlanta, GA: Cascade Publishing House, 2019.

Hawkins, James E. *History of the Southern Intercollegiate Athletic Conference*, 1913-1990, Butler, GA: Bennis Printing Company, 1994.

Hawkins Billy, Joseph Cooper, Akilah Carter-Francique, J. Kenyatta Cavil. *The Athletic Experience at Historically Black Colleges and Universities: Past, Present, and Persistence*, Lanham, MD: Rowman and Littlefield, 2015.

Henderson, Edwin B. *The Negro in Sports*, Washington, D. C.: The Associated Publishers, Inc., 1949.

Johnson, James W. *Along This Way: The Autobiography of James Weldon Johnson*, Cambridge, MA: Da Capo Press, 2000.

Jones, Edward A. *A Candle in the Dark; a History of Morehouse College*, Valley Forge, PA: Judson Press, 1967.

Jones, Maxine D. And Joe M Richardson *Talladega College: The First Century*, Tuscaloosa, AL: The University of Alabama Press, 1980.

Kirsch, George B. *Baseball in Blue and Gray*, Princeton, NJ: Princeton University Press, 2013.

Lindholm, Karl. *The Cooperstown Symposium on Baseball and American Culture, 1997 (Jackie Robinson)*, Jefferson, NC: McFarland & Company, 2000.

Martin, Charles H. *Benching Jim Crow: The Rise and Fall of the Color Line in Southern College Sports, 1890-1980*, Urbana, IL: University of Illinois Press, 2010.

Mason, Herman Jr. *Black Atlanta in the Roaring Twenties*, Charleston, SC: Arcadia Publishing 1997.

Millen, Patricia E. *From Pastime to Passion: Baseball and the Civil War*. Westminster, MD: Heritage Books, 2001.

Motley, Bob, and Byron Motley. *Ruling Over Monarchs, Giants & Stars: Umpiring in the Negro Leagues & Beyond*, Champaign, IL: Sports Publishing LLC, 2007.

Muller, John. *Frederick Douglass in Washington, D.C.: the Lion of Anacostia*, Charleston SC: The History Press, 2012.

Posey, Josephine McCann. *Against Great Odds: The History of Alcorn State University*, Jackson, MS: University Press of Mississippi, 1994.

Range, Willard. *The Rise and Progress of Negro Colleges in Georgia, 1865-1949*, Athens, GA: University of Georgia Press, 2009.

Rhodes, Lelia Gaston. *Jackson State University: The First Hundred Years, 1877-1977*, Jackson, MS: University Press of Mississippi, 1979.

Riley, James A. *The Biographical Encyclopedia of the Negro Baseball Leagues*, New York, NY: Carroll & Graf Publishers, Inc., 1994.

Ryczek, William J. *Baseball's First Inning: A History of the National Pastime Through the Civil War*. Jefferson, NC: McFarland, 2009.

Seymour, Harold. *Baseball: The Early Years*, New York, NY: Oxford University Press, 1960.

Seymour, Harold. *Baseball: The Peoples Game*, New York, NY: Oxford University Press, 1990.

Swanson, Ryan A. *When Baseball Went White: Reconstruction, Reconciliation, and Dreams of a National Pastime*, Lincoln, NE: University of Nebraska Press, 2014.

Thorn, John. *Baseball in the Garden of Eden*, New York, NY: Simon and Schuster Paperbacks, 2011.

Tygiel, Jules. *Past Time: Baseball as History*, New York, NY: Oxford University Press, USA, 2000.

Whitfield, A. B. *Pictorial history of the CIAA professionals, 1950-1984*, Brooklyn, NY: A.B. Whitfield, 1985.

Zoss, Joel, John Bowman, and John S. Bowman *Diamonds in the Rough: The Untold History of Baseball*. Lincoln, NE: University of Nebraska Press, 2004.

## Annuals

*Baseball America Almanac*, Durham, NC: American Sports Publishing Inc., editions 1988 through 2020

*Baseball America's College Baseball Annual*, Durham, NC: American Sports Publishing, Inc., editions 1984 through 1986

*Baseball America's Statistical Report*, Durham, NC: American Sports Publishing, Inc., editions 1981, 1983 through 1987

*Bulletin of the Colored Intercollegiate Athletic Association*, Hampton, Virginia: Hampton Institute Press, editions 1939, 1942, 1945, 1947, 1948 1951, 1952, 1953

*Official Handbook, Interscholastic Athletic Association of Middle Atlantic States*, New York: American Sports Publishing Company, editions 1910 through 1913.

*Official NCAA Baseball Guide*, New York: The National Collegiate Athletic Bureau, editions 1958 through 1982

*Spalding's Official College Base Ball Annual*, New York: American Sports Publishing Company, editions 1911 through 1914

## Internet Websites

Agate Type: Reconstructing Negro League & Latin American Baseball History - https://agatetype.typepad.com/

Center for Negro League Baseball Research - http://www.cnlbr.org/

Protoball Project - http://protoball.org

Society for American Baseball Research - https://sabr.org/

The Online Books Page (The Crisis) - http://onlinebooks.library.upenn.edu/webbin/serial?id=crisisnaacp

The Seamheads Negro Leagues Database - https://www.seamheads.com/NegroLgs/index.php

NCAA Baseball Statistics - https://www.ncaa.org/sports/2013/11/21/baseball-statistics.aspx

Baseball Reference - https://www.baseball-reference.com/register/league.cgi

The Baseball Cube - https://www.thebaseballcube.com/content/college/

E-Yearbook - https://www.e-yearbook.com

Newspaper Archive - https://newspaperarchive.com

Newspapers by Ancestry - https://www.newspapers.com

## Newspapers and Periodicals

*Atlanta Daily World*
*Atlanta, Independent*
*Baltimore Afro-American*
*Baseball Digest*
*Baton Rouge Advocate*
*The Chicago Defender*
*Cleveland Call and Post*
*Cleveland Gazette*
*Collegiate Baseball Newspaper*
*The Constitution (Atlanta)*
*Daily Evening Bulletin (San Francisco)*
*Dallas Express*
*Ebony Magazine*
*The Freeman (Indianapolis)*
*Houston Informer*

*Indianapolis Recorder*
*Jet Magazine*
*Los Angeles Sentinel*
*The Nashville Globe*
*The New York Age*
*The New York Amsterdam News*
*Norfolk Journal and Guide*
*The Pittsburgh Courier*
*The Philadelphia Tribune*
*Ruston Daily Leader*
*San Antonio Register*
*The Sporting News*
*Washington Bee*
*Weekly Pelican (New Orleans)*

## School Yearbooks, Baseball Media Guides, Newspapers, Catalogs and Bulletins

Alabama State
Alcorn A&M
Atlanta University
Bethune-Cookman University
Central State University
Clark College
Delaware State
Fisk University
Florida A&M
Grambling State University
Howard University
Jackson State University
Johnson C. Smith University
Kentucky State
Lincoln (PA) University
Livingstone College

Maryland State/UMES
Morehouse College
Morris Brown University
Norfolk State
North Carolina A&T
Oberlin College
Prairie View A&M
Shaw University
Southern University
Tuskegee Institute
University of New Orleans
West Virginia State University
Wilberforce University
Wiley College
Winston-Salem State University

## Personal Interviews

Willie Aikens *
George Altman
Dave Baker **
David Clark *
Andre Dawson *
William Downey
Marvin Freeman *
Ralph Garr
McVea Griffin
Al Holland
Condridge Holloway
Alvin Jackson
Roy Lee Jackson *
Fred Lewis
Gary Mays
Hal McRae *
Eddie Payton
Jacob Robinson
James Robinson
William Rutledge
Henry Triplett
Fred Valentine *
Rickie Weeks
 * Interviewed by Douglas Malan
** Interviewed by Dr. John Winters

# Index

www.ingramcontent.com/pod-product-compliance
Lightning Source LLC
Chambersburg PA
CBHW020442130626
46549CB00001B/263